What Real People Think Abc

"It's like the uncensored perils of dating in the 21st century. I have dated guys from different cultures before, but never really understood why they did some of the things that they did. This book finally answered all those questions and more. And 'The Pros' section, tales from a real cat house? That stuff was hilarious."

—Cindy

"*I Got the Fever* is a very fun book for anyone to read, but if you are an interracial dater it's not just a good read, it's your Bible!"

—Ming-Mei

"This book is a real page turner, enlightening and entertaining. As a white girl that has been in a few interracial relationships, I wish I had read this book five years ago; it probably would've saved me a lot of headaches. I know *all* my college friends would love it!"

—Charlotte

"I am married and white and I've never been in an interracial relationship, but this was the most interesting book I have read in a long time. I guess some stereotypes exist for a reason, but the good news is that J.C. uses them for good, not evil. If you want the straight dope about someone other than whitey, look here first."

—Bebe

"I don't agree with everything that J.C. says, but I am so glad that she said it! When you are in an interracial relationship you can't be walking around on pins and needles. You need to feel free to discuss everything, including race and culture. These cultures are our history and they are going on every single day. Why wouldn't you want to be a part of that?"

—Samantha

"As an Indian guy, I don't appreciate the small-dicks stuff, even though it's true. But I love that J.C. says that Indians are great lovers because we are, and we take a lot of pride in that. I also think the part about meeting an Indian family was really well covered. There are so many nuances there that it is easy to screw it up. J.C. really helps you through it."

—Ajay

What Real People Think About *I Got the Fever*

"Totally worth the read! As a Jew, I related a lot to the Jewish section, but since I've only dated white guys I really loved learning what it would be like to date guys from other cultures—living vicariously through other people, you know? It's *real* reading for pleasure."

—Beth

"J.C. tells the truth and even though some of it might be hard to hear, it's received well because it's told with humor. I am a black woman married to a white guy so I am on board with interracial dating. But a lot of women, especially black women, are waiting for permission to date outside of their race. J.C. gives the message that it is okay if you are attracted to white people, black people, Latinos, whoever. If you need permission, you've got it!"

—Danielle

"*I Got the Fever* is a fresh new look at dating in today's modern age. J.C. pulls you in with her clever descriptions and pithy interludes. Even if you've read every other dating and relationship book on the shelves, your eyes are not open until you've read *I Got the Fever*."

—Chloe

"I grew up biracial, so interracial dating was no big deal for me. But even so, I still learned a lot from this book. Which guys are more likely to: pick up the check, be cheating bastards, or be a freak in the sack. *I Got the Fever* gives you awesome, funny insights into what it's really like to date outside your race."

—Kayla

"As a married Indian woman I know most of the Curry Fever stuff, but I just never thought about it before. For an outsider it's a lot to know. And those comments from the prostitutes—wow, that was an eye opener."

—Lakshmi

"Thank you J.C.! After reading the book and following your blog I took the plunge. Best thing I ever did!"

—Bill

I GOT THE FEVER

Love, What's Race Gotta Do With It?

J.C. Davies

DOUBLEWIDE
PUBLICATIONS
NEW YORK, NEW YORK

Published by DoubleWide Publications
244 Fifth Avenue, Suite #264D
New York, New York 10001 USA
www.doublewidepublications.com

For product information or to inquire about quantity discounts for bulk purchases, contact us at (646) 470-2308 or info@doublewidepublications.com.

Project Editor Katherine Shoup

Development Editor Alyshia Davies

Photographer Bill Bernstein

Cover Designer Jeff Brandi

Layout/Interior Designer Shawn Morningstar

Proofreader Tonya Maddox Cupp

Publisher's Cataloging-in-Publication

Davies, J. C., 1968-

I got the fever : love, what's race gotta do with it? / J.C. Davies. — 1st ed.

p. cm.

Includes index.

LCCN: 2010926566

ISBN-13: 978-0-9827284-0-6

ISBN-10: 0-9827284-0-9

1. Dating (Social customs)--Cross-cultural studies.
2. Interracial dating. 3. Intercultural communication.
4. Man-woman relationships. I. Title.

HQ801.8.D38 2010 306.73
QBI10-600095

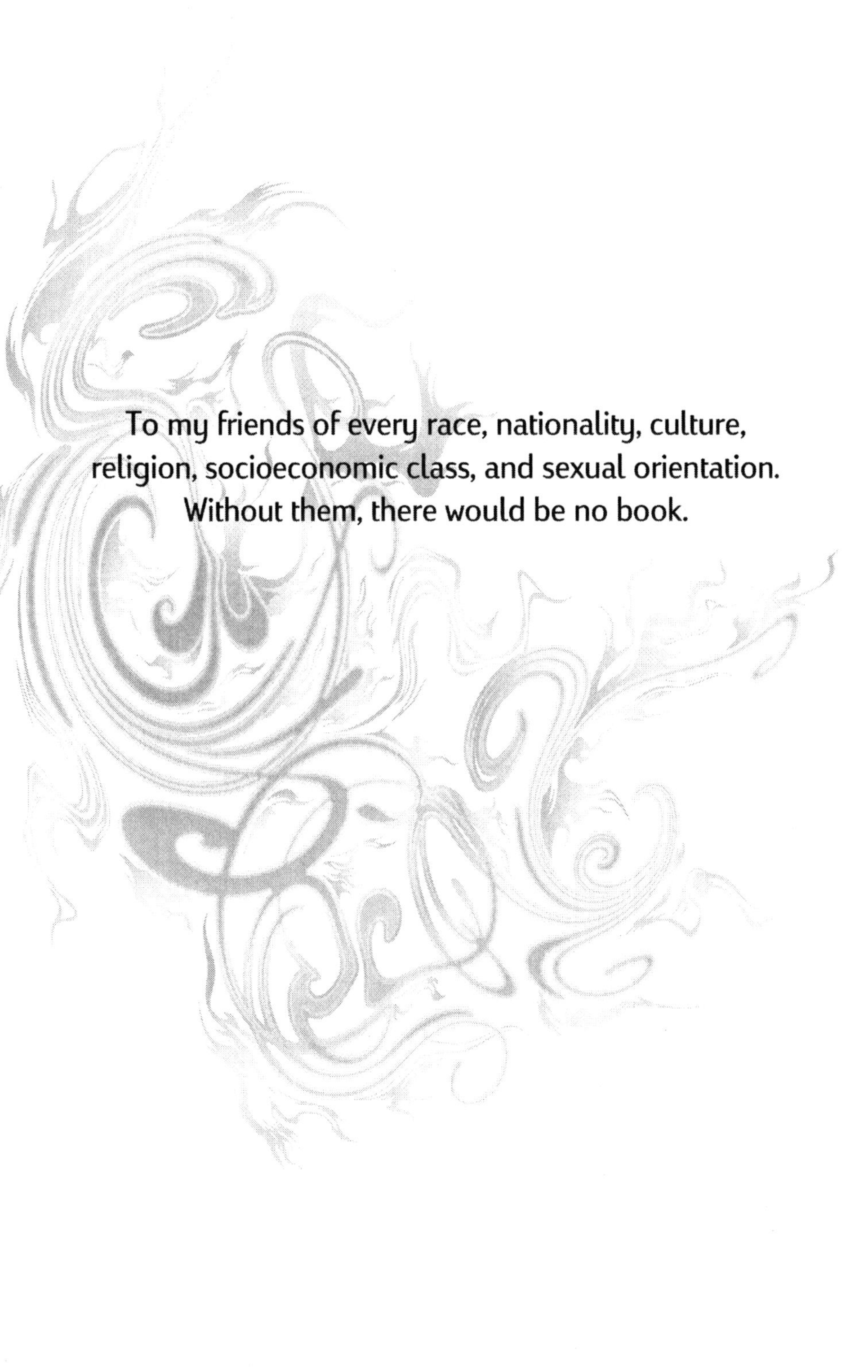

To my friends of every race, nationality, culture, religion, socioeconomic class, and sexual orientation. Without them, there would be no book.

"...Are racial reactions unpremeditated,
like our spontaneous reactions to different foods,
wines or works of art?

If so, is race the only sphere of life in which we are
not entitled to any personal preferences?"

—James Mellon, Bullwhip Days

Contents

You Got the Fever?

"Give me a man that regardless of the color of his skin who is nice to me who is sweet to me and who I strongly believe loves me."

—JUNGLE FEVER

Like a lot of people, by the night of the 2008 U.S. presidential election, I had begun to lose my faith in my country—a country I felt was sinking deeper into materialism, wallowing in apathy, and making little progress in fixing long-time problems, including sex and race discrimination.

Earlier that year, I had watched the movie *Bobby*, which revisits the pivotal year of 1968—incidentally, the year I was born. In this movie, newsclips showed Bobby Kennedy listing the country's problems: New York City was severely polluted and unhealthy, poor relations between black people and white people were leading to mindless violence, and we couldn't help our nation's poor because we were supporting a foreign war with no end in sight. All I could think was that in 40 years, my entire lifetime, *nothing* had changed.

Exhausted, I went to bed before the election results were in—but I didn't sleep well. (This was nothing new; I hadn't slept even a single night since being laid off from my job the week before.) Although Obama was favored to win, I questioned whether Americans could vote to put a black man in the country's highest office. Yet again, we'd be stuck with the status quo: another old white man in the White House. Finally, at 3 a.m., I gave up on sleep. I was nervous about turning on the TV; instead, I checked my phone. On the screen was a text from my friend Dominique: "Yes we can!" Obama had won.

To be honest, I was never a big Obama supporter. What I disliked most was his "hope" campaign. It just seemed so empty—something a politician would say to avoid making any real commitments. But that night, when I turned on my TV and watched the replay of Obama's powerful acceptance speech, I had to admit, I *was* hopeful. There was a brother in the White House. Now *that* was something different from 40 years ago! But it was more than that. I couldn't help thinking, If the country was ready for Obama, it might be ready for *me*.

Who the Hell Am I?

After working on Wall Street for more than a decade, I was considered an expert in my field, equity investing. But as I began to develop the idea for this book—a book that would serve as *the* definitive guide to interracial dating—I realized I had been dating outside of my race for almost twice as long. My first interracial relationship, which lasted eight years, was with a Latin man. In 1999, I moved to New York City and began dating black men; I did so exclusively for over a decade. In the last few years, I have opened myself up more, dating Asians, Jews, and Middle Eastern men, among others. So while there are no formal qualifications, tests, or certification programs for being an interracial dating "expert," I'm probably as close as you can get.

Of course, even I don't know everything. That's why, in researching this book, I interviewed a variety of men and women of different races and cultures to get their views on the matter. I have always valued friendships with people whose backgrounds were different from mine, whether that meant they were of another race, culture, socioeconomic status, or sexual orientation, so I already had a vast network of friends, colleagues, and acquaintances to get me started. My quest for personal stories wasn't global, but it did cover every inch of Manhattan, the Bronx, Brooklyn, Queens, Jersey baby, and Connecticut. (I didn't make it to Staten Island, though. A girl has to have her limits.) Some of the people I interviewed said they found talking with me cathartic, others said it was eye opening, but most just had fun.

That Was Then, This Is Now

At most, race has been a minor issue in my relationships, and certainly not the cause of any breakups. However, I did face criticism—from my own friends and family as well as from those of my mates. When I was dating my first black boyfriend, Phillip, his best friend—*having just met me*—had no qualms telling me to my face that I was just with Phillip because I was "color struck." My own friends weren't much better; my long-time friend Kim took my preference for black men as a sign of some type of mental problem on my part. (I always found this ironic because Kim is a lesbian, and it wasn't all that long ago that they put gay women in mental institutions in an effort to reprogram them. Somehow, she never made that connection.)

In fact, my strong preference for the brothers during that period of my life was not the result of any ulterior motive or mental instability; I just found them more attractive. Sadly, however, it seemed that this preference was simply not accepted in American culture. In America, you could like someone because he was blond, tall, short, blue-eyed, buff, fat, or skinny; race, however, was off limits. But what is race at its essence but a collection of features, both physical and cultural?

Fortunately, we are moving past old racist attitudes. As the number of intercultural relationships continues to increase, so will others' acceptance of them. So what does that mean for you? It means more options are open to you than to any generation before.

Women like to complain that all the good men are married or gay, but they rarely challenge themselves to look outside the box—outside their own race or culture. Scared by the media, concerned about what strangers might say, afraid of parental disapproval, and fooled by the age-old myth that "interracial relationships never work," women reject men of other cultures outright before even considering them. When I'm out with my white girlfriends, we might wind up somewhere that's brimming with cute young professionals who are Indian, Black, Asian, or whatever, but all the girls notice are the three grungy, hunchback-looking white guys in the corner. I say, don't limit yourself! The man of your dreams could come in any shape, size, color, or culture. Open your eyes and look around. You never know where your soulmate will come from!

Sexual Deviance, Cannibalism, Virgin Sacrifice?

If you've never done it before, you might think that the problems that arise with interracial dating are of the earth-shattering variety—sexual deviance, cannibalism, virgin sacrifice, etc. Well, they're not. The major issues that interracial couples face are pretty much the same as for anyone else: intellectual and sexual compatibility, money, family planning, in-laws, and putting the cap on the toothpaste. That said, people in interracial or intercultural relationships cite two unique difficulties:

- **Food.** Issues pertaining to food are the most commonly cited problem among intercultural couples. Me? I have found most of the food from my various guys' cultures to be fantastic. But let's face it, the food in some cultures is—how to say this delicately?—foul smelling, nasty tasting, unrecognizable, and yes, possibly even still alive. While there may be some dishes to which an American palate will never adjust, most people in these types of relationships have found that they could learn to appreciate—and possibly really enjoy—even some of the more challenging foods of their man's culture. Besides, if food is the main problem in interracial dating, it can hardly be a deal breaker.

- **Language.** Here in America, most of the people you date will speak English—but that doesn't mean their parents, grandparents, and cousins will. While this can be a barrier to becoming close with your guy's family, it is one that can be easily overcome using one of two methods: learning their language or getting over it. A lot of the time, you may feel insecure, worried that the family is talking about you. That's because *they are*. What does it matter if it is in front of your face in another language or behind your back? Besides, if they speak another language, you can always enlist some young cousin of his to spy for you. Again, not a big deal.

Culture Shock

So you've decided you're going to do it. You're going to try dating outside your culture. Great! Before you do, however, it's important that you understand one critical point: You can't separate the race or culture from the man. And why would you want to? I can't tell you how often I see women pay no regard to the culture of the man they are dating, either ignoring it altogether or treating it as if it were an inconvenience. Repeat after me: This. Makes. No. Sense. He's your man! Don't you want to get to know him? See what makes him tick? He is the way he is, partly because of his culture.

Besides, with interracial dating, you are given a front-row seat to a whole new culture—a unique opportunity to learn about it from the inside. Take it! Even if it pulls you out of your comfort zone, I implore you: Don't ignore his culture. Embrace it.

Yes, it's true that race is rarely what breaks couples up. But if you don't respect your man's culture, it will diminish your relationship. Welcome it; you'll be richer for the experience. Diversity surely is the spice of life.

What This Book Is Not

Let me stress that this book is not a scientific study of interracial dating. There are plenty of those books out there—most of which are a total snooze. Having said that, it was important that this book be genuine; as such, it is based completely on true stories. All the names have been changed to protect the innocent and to protect all involved from the guilty.

It's also not a traditional "relationship book." Trust me: If that is what you are looking for here, you will be disappointed. This book will not explore the depth of your psychosis or anyone else's. I only have an undergraduate degree in psychology, so you're on your own on that one.

One day I went to The Strand, a book store in Union Square, to check out the competition in my book's category. I ventured deep into the basement to the relationship section. Looking at the book covers (which were all pink), I quickly began to wish I had sought out the hard-core porn section instead. At least that would have been less embarrassing! The titles—all condescending—seemed to prey on women with less self-esteem than Britney Spears, post–MTV Music Awards comeback. Without exception, these books focused on:

- How to get a man to date you.
- How to trap a man into marriage.
- How to keep said trapped man in that marriage.
- How miserable marriage is.

To fix your relationship problems, you were supposed to:

- Be a bitch.
- Act like a lady.
- Follow the rules.
- Travel to Mars.
- Or just finally accept, you pathetic excuse for a woman, that for God's sake, *he is just not that into you*!

To help you, I guess, these books contained:

- Techniques.
- Principles.
- Tools.
- Goals.
- Rules.
- A whole lot of acronyms to help you remember all that shit.

And of course, they all assure you that, while there are a lot of relationship books out there, theirs is different.

What This Book Is

This book is a guidebook to teach you about dating within different races, to prepare you for some of the cultural differences, and to point out some of the pitfalls. It's not meant to provide an exhaustive list of every cultural nuance; rather, it's meant to give you a taste of what it is like to date men of various cultural backgrounds.

This book is divided into five parts or *Fevers*: Salsa Fever (Latinos), Yellow Fever (Asians), Jungle Fever (Blacks), Curry Fever (Indians), and Shiksa Fever (Jews). Each of the five fevers includes the following sections:

- **Things to Know:** This section contains general cultural norms you should be aware of.

- **So You Don't Fuck Up!** Here, you'll find some of the dos and don'ts when it comes to dealing with your guy's culture.

- **What the Hell Did I Get Myself Into?** This section warns you about cultural elements that you may find distasteful.

- **What Is Hot?** Here you'll find out what those in the know found appealing about dating men of a certain culture.

- **What's Not?** You guessed it: This section outlines what those in the know found *not* so appealing about dating men within that culture.

- **Between the Sheets:** Ah, the good stuff. Here, you'll learn about sexual differences within each culture: equipment size, oral proclivities, talent in the sack (or lack thereof), and more. This section also includes expert commentary from those who work in the oldest profession—or as I call them, "The Pros." These "working girls" had no problem sharing their salacious secrets from behind the bedroom door.

- **Our Stories:** Here you'll find real stories about interracial relationships. Some of these stories function as anecdotal evidence to demonstrate a point, while others are simply to entertain. None of these stories are meant to describe a "typical interracial relationship." There is no such thing. What these stories do provide are actual examples of how cultural issues can play out in *real* relationships.

Before You Call Me a Racist...

A label—race, culture, or otherwise—can never adequately describe any man. Every man is shaped not only by his culture, but also by his upbringing, life experiences, the extent to which he accepts or rejects cultural norms, whether he was raised in the U.S. or another country, if he has done a lot of interracial dating, and more.

If you talk to enough people, however, you start to notice some similarities or general trends among racial groups. This book discusses the racial and cultural characteristics that were noted most frequently in my interviews. This book does not attempt to promote stereotypes and often dispels them. It also sheds some light on why certain cultural norms exist.

And yes, there will be people who will object to the content—indeed, the intent—of this book. But the fact is, you can't have a conversation about race and culture that provides women with practical, real-world advice while tip-toeing around the edge of political correctness.

Also, you can't describe the real down-and-dirty truth about sex and relationships while being prissy, proper, or prudish. Anyone who knows me will tell you that I can swear like a sailor. Who has Tourette's Syndrome. Who just got a paper cut. So if you're offended by language that's on the salty side, let this serve as fair warning. But if you are ready to expand your dating horizons and move out of your comfort zone into interracial dating, believe me, putting up with my occasionally strong language will be one of the easier challenges you'll face.

Look, anyone reading this book who is reasonable and tolerant will see that this book and its author (i.e., me) have good intentions. And you can rest assured that when it comes to the good, the bad, and the ugly, all men were treated equally. I have always been a tell-it-like-it-is kind of person, and this book is no different. I didn't throw curve balls, play favorites, or pull any punches.

I expect this book will strike a chord with many people who have dated or are currently dating members of any of the five cultures discussed in this book. And for people who haven't, this book will give them the information they need to feel more comfortable pursuing relationships with men outside their race.

Salsa Fever

"Ser latino quiere decir que uno reconoce todas las culturas que viven en uno."

(Being Latino means that you recognize all the cultures that live in you.)

—ANONYMOUS

When I was 21, I started my first interracial relationship with my boyfriend Paul. After we had been dating for only a short time, I was invited to a traditional Mexican family dinner, with his parents, brother, sister, and cousins all in attendance. Needless to say, I was nervous. Knowing nothing of their culture, I had no idea what to expect.

While we were there, everyone made small talk in Spanish and English, but I stayed quiet, just trying to observe, to blend into the background. Suddenly, Paul's sister Dianne turned to me and as loud as her lungs would allow asked, "So what *are* you anyway?" What am I? I had never been asked such a question. I didn't know how to answer, so I said nothing at first. Her words just hung in the air. Finally, I squeaked, "What do you mean?"

"Well, we are 100-percent Mexican. And you are?" The whole family sat in silence, their eyes focused all on me. I scrambled for an answer. "Right. Okay. Um, my grandmother is from Yugoslavia and my mom...I think she's part German? And my last name, it's Welsh...."

"So you're basically just a white girl," Dianne said.

Basically.

The family laughed out loud, for a good 10 minutes. And as mortified as I was, I could see the humor in Dianne's response. White people don't usually think of themselves in terms of race. It's not until we date outside our race that we are asked to define ourselves in racial terms.

At that time, I had no one to help me understand the nuances of dating men in Latin cultures. But you, dear reader, are far luckier. You have this section, "Salsa Fever," to help you. At last count, there were more than half a billion Latinos—not only in Central and South America, but all over the world. Nueva York's Latin population consists primarily of Puerto Ricans (a.k.a. Nuyoricans), Dominicans, and Mexicans, so although this section deals with a variety of Latin cultures, it concentrates on these three segments. There are lots of titillating tidbits in this section, so let's not wait any longer. *Vamos al mondo Latino*!

Things to Know

When it comes to dating a Latin man, there are a few important things to know—the first being how to refer to him or his culture. The second being how in Latin culture variety is the spice of life. And then there is the big one—not sex, not politics, but you guessed it: religion. As in any relationship—but especially with Latinos—religion is an area where you need to tread lightly.

Latino, Not Spanish

In New York, people often use the word "Spanish" to denote any person whose culture speaks Spanish. But most Spanish-speaking New Yorkers are *not* from Spain—and they don't like it when you try to say they are. People of Latin American heritage are also not wild about the term "Hispanic." The best word to use when referring to someone with a Latin American background is "Latino." In most cases, it covers all your bases; you don't have to worry about saying the wrong thing.

Ciel, 27, Dominican, office assistant, says, "I remember I went to Brooklyn to meet my boyfriend's parents for the first time. I am Dominican and he was black. His mom said to me, 'So you're Spanish?' And I said, 'No, Latina.' And then she started arguing with me! 'No, you definitely are Spanish.'" She adds, "I think *I* should decide what I'm called, right? I'm a lot of things: Latina, Dominican, and American, but I am *not* Spanish."

"I don't know when Hispanic went out of style," says Celeste, 35, white girl, fitness trainer. "But I said it once in a salsa club, and a whole pack of hot Latin guys that seemed to be hanging on my every word wrinkled up their noses and wandered off. It took weeks of emphasizing the word 'Latino' to win them back. Not to mention a lighter shade of blond hair dye and an even shorter skirt."

"I think they say Spanish as a compliment," says Elena, 41, Puerto Rican, surgeon. "Mainstream American society has this impression that we are all uneducated gang members and drug addicts. If we are different from that, they think we must be Spanish. They mean it as an upgrade."

"For my Dominican husband, it all depends on his mood," says Vanessa, 30, white girl, fashion buyer. "Sometimes he doesn't care what someone calls him. But if he doesn't like you or just feels like being a jerk, he will say, 'It's not Spanish, it's Latino!'"

In Latin Cultures, Variety Is the Spice of Life

Although this book deals in broad brushstrokes across several Latin populations, there are certainly cultural variations. Actual Spaniards, from Spain, are generally conservative, old-fashioned, European. When you first meet a Puerto Rican, he might grab you hard and give you a kiss on one cheek. Brazilians generally kiss on both cheeks, starting with the left. In Venezuela, handkerchiefs are considered bad luck and therefore do not make good gifts. In Argentina, giving knives is a problem, as they denote a "severing" of your relationship. Cubans are often conservative, Republican, and in most cases prefer to be called "Cuban" rather than "Latino." Each Latin population has its own distinct characteristics, so it's important that you learn as much as you can about your boyfriend's specific Latin culture. If in doubt, always ask.

Religion Plays a Big Role in Latin Culture

While Latinos practice all types of religions, the overwhelming majority are Catholic. And they don't limit religion to church; it permeates the household. You're likely to see crucifixes over the beds and statues of the Virgin Mary, Jesus, or various saints throughout the house. Also, because the Catholic Conquistadors found it easier to encourage conversion in Latin America by allowing the local Indios (native Americans) to keep some of their own religious traditions, there are certain "Catholic" traditions among Latinos that are a bit different from what most Americans are used to. For example, some Latin homes include altars with candles and gifts for the dead, such as glasses of water, chocolate bars wrapped in gold foil, dried chili peppers, bingo cards, and bottles of tequila.

"I think a lot of the cultural differences are related to religion," says Maria, 25, Argentinean, real-estate agent. "My family was Catholic, but I was never religious. I didn't know how to do the sign of the cross, which hand over which hand." She continues, "Religion was the main conflict with my Latin boyfriends. Some Latinos are very devout and conservative."

"You can't extract religion from Latin families, even if they don't practice," says Ricardo, 45, Puerto Rican, tax assessor. "They might say they are not religious, but once you say something about Jesus they are like, wait a minute. They do grow up with the idea of Christ, the Holy Trinity, and the Virgin Mary—and that is a woman you can't fuck with. Literally."

So if you're a Hindu, Jew, Buddhist, or agnostic, if you have an aversion to Catholicism, or you just aren't a big fan of the crucifix for home décor, you may want to proceed with caution into any relationship with a Latin man. Even if he says he's not religious, someone in his family will be.

So You Don't Fuck Up!

When it comes to Latinos, it's easy to fuck up. And the problem is, they often don't tell you when you are doing something wrong! Modesty and humility are valued in Latin cultures, making them more likely to say nothing or take a passive-aggressive tack as opposed to just coming out and saying what is on their mind. But don't worry. Latinos may not come out and tell you their cultural norms, but I will.

Keep the Greetings Formal and the Dress Conservative

In a Latin household, elders garner the highest level of respect. When you meet your Latin boyfriend's family, his older relatives will expect to be called Mr. and Mrs. until you are told otherwise (and for eight years, my Mexican mother-in-law—yes, I married the aforementioned Paul—never told me otherwise).

Also acceptable are Sir and Ma'am, *Señor y Señora en Español.* And, expect to dress conservatively. Translation: no cleavage or short skirts, and cover your arms and shoulders. If you don't, it will be considered disrespectful—not to mention lend itself to extensive family gossip. And for Christ's sake, no cursing. (I guess that leaves me out.)

"Even if you think they don't speak English and you don't speak Spanish, still acknowledge them with a formal greeting," says Elena. "Most families know some English, even if they don't regularly converse in it."

"Compared to more Americanized parents, Latin parents are very old fashioned," says Maria. "Very traditional gender roles. They expect the man to pick you up at your door, even in the city. Who picks you up at your door in New York City?" She continues, "Parents don't get modern dating. And even if my father says you can call him by his first name, he doesn't mean it. He is never comfortable being called by his first name."

"It didn't happen to me, thank God, but my sister-in-law Rosalinda got it good. The day she met her boyfriend's father for the first time, she said 'Nice to meet you Jorge,' and he *flipped,*" says Vanessa. "'That is Mr. Jimenez to *you!*' he said. She was really insulted. I would have been too."

"My family appreciates Sir or Ma'am," says Julio, 32, Puerto Rican, technology salesman. "And when a girl meets a Latin man's family for the first time, it's important to dress conservatively—pants and a nice shirt. If she wears a short skirt or her chest is showing, the older women in the house will talk about it."

So around your Latin boyfriend's parents, you definitely want to stick to Sir and Ma'am and dress with the modesty of a nun—or at least a young June Cleaver.

Don't Let Them Tell You Otherwise: Gifts and Help Are Welcome

When you visit a Latin household, it is customary—especially when meeting the family for the first time—to bring some type of gift: a cake, flowers, something to show respect and demonstrate your good manners. That seems easy enough—bring a cake, check, flowers, check. But of course, there is more to it.

The Latin culture follows a rulebook that you, a non-Latina, do not have. Nothing is said; everything is just understood. If you ask whether you should bring something, the likely response will be no. But will you be judged as disrespectful, impolite, or a freeloader if you fail to arrive with gift in hand? To quote Sarah Palin, "You betcha."

"Latin American households can be very old-fashioned European," says Elena. "Bringing a gift to the house shows respect and manners. They will always say you shouldn't have, but trust me, you still have to bring something."

"It's true, they will specifically tell you no—and then bad-talk you for taking them seriously," says Celeste.

"It is customary to bring a gift, but mostly only traditional women still do that," says Julio. "My parents appreciate it. It's respectful, and with so many traditions being lost, it's a nice thing to do the first time you meet the parents."

Part of this comes from another unspoken Latin rule: You should not accept gifts freely, as doing so might make you look greedy. Chances are an offering of cake or flowers will be accepted without too much fuss, but if you come bearing a more substantial gift, you may have to try to give it to them at least three times before they'll accept it. ("No, you didn't have to." "You shouldn't have." "Oh, I couldn't." "Well, if you really want me to have it....") And, per that unwritten Latin rulebook, if you don't offer the gift at least three times, it will be assumed that you didn't mean it in the first place.

The same goes for help. When you offer to help, they will almost certainly say, "No, no I'm fine." But again, with Latinos, three *is* the magic number. Always offer to help at least three times. After that, sit back and relax—but make sure the hostess knows that you can jump up at a moment's notice to help out in the kitchen or aid with the dinner service. Yes, it's a convoluted way to get things done, but that's how it is. Just learn it and do it.

As Elena says, "Always offer at least three times. Don't rationalize it, don't take it personally, don't say anything. Just hand over the cake and sit your ass down."

What the Hell Did I Get Myself Into?

My mom—who, God love her, is very peace-love-and-tofu California—raised us to be color blind. I love my mother dearly, but only through my interracial dating experiences did I learn that color blind is *not* the way to go. You can't pretend like your man's culture doesn't exist; not only does it affect him, it also affects *you*. Surprise family guests, long-held grudges, and negative gossip are among the common Latin cultural characteristics that might make you ask yourself, "What the hell did I get myself into?"

Prepare Yourself for the "Pop In"

Latinos are not plagued with concerns around being a little, well, intrusive. You can expect Latin parents and especially Latin grandparents to show up at your house unannounced at any time. They have few boundaries and often push the dreaded pop in to its limits.

"I'm even half Puerto Rican, but I still think you shouldn't just drop by the house," says Elena. "I see friends—especially if they're married—their relatives just come over whenever they want." She continues, "They don't call. They just drop by. The idea of personal space is very different in Latin culture."

"They never call first." says Enrique, 27, Mexican, physical therapist. "Someone has a new baby; they come and check it out. You get a new car; they come to check it out. You get a new dog, everyone comes to see it. Anytime we get something new, relatives just pop in to see it."

"My Dominican husband's mother has already told me, 'When you have this baby, you will have to let us help you raise it. It takes a village!'" says Vanessa. "I am due in a month and am getting a little nervous about the pop in."

So if the pop in is out of the question, you need to make sure your Latin man sets strong boundaries with his family from the beginning. If not, there is one other option: You can always move to Outer Mongolia. But I'm not so sure his Latin family won't find you there.

V for Vendetta

Latinos often have close families, but they also can take even a small family disagreement very seriously. To say they "hold a grudge" is to put it nicely. One slip-up, and you could be the subject of a vendetta.

"My mom had a vendetta against her sister for 30 years. I couldn't speak to my aunt because they weren't talking," says Elena. "Did you see *Like Water for Chocolate*? It's like that. I made you so I can kill you." She continues, "Latin mothers are very domineering and expect loyalty from you above all others. You go against me, you are dead to me. I never saw my aunt or cousins until after my mother died. We have no idea what they were fighting about. I am pretty sure they didn't know either. All this *dramatica*, and for what?"

"It's a stupid thing, but it happens many, many times," says Julio. "I even know two brothers that live in the same house. They are 50 years old and haven't spoken to each other for 20 years. When you sit with them at dinner they will talk to you separately, but never to each other."

"Sometimes, my husband gets in fights with his father, and they just don't speak for months," says Vanessa. "His father didn't like the name we picked for our baby. Instead of just stating his opinion, he said, 'If you are going to name the baby that, then I don't want to have anything to do with my new grandchild!'"

The idea of the vendetta was so interesting, I began to dig deeper. Vendetta, at its essence, is an issue of pride—you know, one of the seven deadly sins. I mean, aren't these people supposed to be Catholic?

To an outsider, ending a vendetta may seem simple: just get them all together, hash things out, and poof, no more vendetta. *No, no, y no!* Leave it be. Don't get involved. You cannot rationalize in an irrational situation. The vendetta will work itself out (or not), but it's not your battle to fight. Besides, if you get involved, you might well become the focus of the *next* vendetta.

Beware the *Bochinche*

In the Latin culture, some people have a way of making everything their bid-ness. Puerto Ricans call it the *bochinche*, which is slang for gossip. Don't be surprised if every little thing you do becomes fodder for family gossip sessions. This can range from what you wore to dinner last week to the new house you and your Latin husband bought to how you are raising your kids. When it comes to the *bochinche*, it's all up for grabs.

"When you go to a Latin wedding, all the older women sit together. The whole time, all they do is criticize people. 'Did you see what she was wearing?'" says Vanessa. "Clothing is a big focus, but it doesn't matter what it is. It's all open for family gossip."

"I love to dance, so at my regular salsa place, I am often one of the last to leave," says Celeste. "So I usually ask one of the very polite Latin gentlemen to walk me to a cab. No big deal, right? I found out later I have a reputation for going home with every Tomas, Ricardo, or Hector."

"I think it comes from a jealous place," says Ricardo. "People trying to make themselves feel better by criticizing others. It's very negative and exists throughout the Latin American community. I don't mind participating in some funny gossip, but I draw the line when it gets hurtful."

"In Mexico, they call it the *chisme*, gossip. It causes a lot of friction in Latin families. You can feel it," says Hugo, 35, Ecuadorian, physician. "But it also shows that someone cares. With the *chisme*, good or bad, at least you know you are not dead. If you are dead, people don't talk about you."

Not to sound like a broken record, but the best way to handle the *bochinche* or the *chisme* is to not address it. Getting involved just adds more fuel to the fire. In this case, ignorance really is bliss.

What's Hot?

When it comes to Latin men it almost seems ridiculous to ask what's hot. I mean, what *isn't* hot about a Latin man? Chiseled good looks, sexy accent, beautiful golden tan—and on top of all that, they pick up the check, love to cut a rug, and have no problem showing you (or the rest of the world, for that matter) how they feel about you. *Muy caliente*!

A Benefit of Machismo: They Pick Up the Check

Latin men usually pay the bill. This isn't just out of an innate sense of generosity; in most cases, it's part of exerting their manhood. Ah, the machismo!

"In my experience, they always paid," says Maria. "Latin men only feel manly when they pay. Even if it's their birthday, they pay—but then, that comes with all that macho stuff."

"You see it all your life: Mom never pays, Dad always pays. It gets ingrained in you," says Enrique. "I don't mind paying. Even for friends, I will pay what I can. My wife is white, and she likes to pay half when we go out sometimes, but that really bugs me."

"Yes, that is correct," says Julio. "The guy always pays for dates. That is not changing. If you were to come out with me for the night, you wouldn't have to spend your money." He adds, "But that is with a purpose in mind, of course."

"I have a 25-year-old lover, a Spaniard from Madrid," says Elena. "I make a lot more money than he does, but he's the man. He likes to take care of his woman. He would never let me pay." She continues, "One time we were going on a picnic and I brought the wine. He was embarrassed. He didn't want me to pay for the smallest thing, even a bottle of wine."

They Can Dance

If you like to trip the light fantastic, a Latin man is hands-down your best choice. According to the women I interviewed, most Latinos are undeniably great dancers and truly love to dance. And when I say they can dance, I don't mean that side-to-side white-guy dance. I mean salsa, tango, cha cha, swing, merengue, hip hop, disco, the works. If there is music, most Latin men can dance to it—and sometimes, they don't even need music.

"My Latin lover is always dancing," says Alec, 25, white guy, art-gallery manager. "He even dances by himself. We'll be walking down the street and he will just break out. He dances in the shower, in the chicken joint—it's ridiculous. I've left him in clubs because he wants to keep dancing and I was just too tired."

"Latin men are such good dancers," says Carolyn, 36, Filipina, hairdresser. "They're so suave. And they make you feel so pretty, you know?"

"They take the lead and twirl you around," says Maria. "In that sense, dating Latin men is great. They always do make you feel feminine, like women. They never blur the roles."

"My Guatemalan boyfriend was such a good dancer," says Ranisha, 35, black, PhD candidate. "He could *move*. He was so into music. For him, intimacy was dancing."

"Latin men know how to dance," says Pablo, 25, Puerto Rican, concierge. "Young people, too. We all still salsa and merengue."

PDA Is A-OK

Most Latin men are not afraid to show affection at home or in public. In fact, unlike many Americans, Latinos expect to see affection in almost all settings.

"When I took one of my white boyfriends home, he didn't touch me at all. He was trying to be respectful to my parents," says Maria. "Then, the next day, when I talked to my mom, she said, 'He is cold with you! Why doesn't he hold and kiss you more? I don't think he likes you.'" She continues, "My parents are always touching and hugging. They don't see things like my boyfriend putting his hand on my knee as offensive. Of course, my parents would also never let us stay in the same room unless we were married."

"My family doesn't mind PDA," says Hugo. "They would probably be on the sidelines rooting for me." He continues, "But if I really like a girl, I tend to be more conservative, especially around my family. I know my mom is watching, and I don't want any *chisme*."

"I am all about making out in the street, kissing, holding hands," says Marisol, 33, Mexican, saleswoman. "Openly telling people you are having sex is not okay in our culture, but making out is okay." She adds, "My mom still believes that I am a virgin, at 33! But in front of her at Christmas dinner, I can sit on my boyfriend's lap the whole time."

"My Latin boyfriend was definitely okay with PDA," says Ranisha. "He was very affectionate, always held hands, kissed, and hugged."

"Only time they don't like PDA is if they're players," says Elena. "Probably because they want to keep their options open."

What's Not?

Even though this section may result in a few vendettas against yours truly, it does you no good if I tell you what women like about dating Latin men if I don't also share which aspects of dating a Latin man my girls could do without. I don't want to give too much away, I'll just say, I hope you know how to make a mean sandwich.

Instant Boyfriend

Take one Latin man, add water, stir, and...instant boyfriend! If you are dating a Latino, watch closely; things can get real serious, real fast. If you are the kind of person who likes to date casually, a Latino is probably not for you.

"I dated this Latin guy once. After the first date, he thought I was his girlfriend," says Hanna, 30, Chinese, hairdresser. "I liked him, but from the time I met him, he was calling me all the time, checking up on me. It was just too much."

"I am not like that, but some Latin guys definitely are," says Miguel, 35, Puerto Rican, doorman. "My nephew falls in love every week."

"I wouldn't go as far as to say 'instant boyfriend,'" says Enrique. "But I think Latin men are definitely drawn to a relationship more than men in some other cultures."

"They just get very territorial, especially the Brazilians. You have a couple dances with them, and they follow you around," says Maria. "If you go to the bathroom, they follow you and wait for you."

"Not just boyfriend, but a soulmate. 'Baby, I knew it was you that first time I ever saw you. You're the one, you know. I'm looking for someone for life, you know,'" says Celeste. "One guy even told me he had prayed to God and God had sent me to him—after I'd known him for *a week*." She continues, "Then one day, you kiss your Latin prince good night and wake up the next morning with a frog—and that's when you know 'forever' actually meant 'until next Tuesday.'"

For some women, this one's tough. I'll pass on the bathroom escort (thanks), but if you like the guy, at least you don't have to worry about him playing hard to get.

Macho and Possessive

All the women I interviewed mentioned that the stereotype of Latin men being jealous, hot-headed, macho, and possessive rang true. It all seems to stem from one of the roots of the Latin culture: passion. Of course, Latin men can be passionate about you in a very positive way, making you feel like the most beautiful, desirable woman in the world. But that passion also has a negative side, which shows itself as good, old-fashioned machismo.

"Dominican guys are very macho. Puerto Rican guys too. Stupid stuff like, 'Are you looking at my girl?' and getting in fights for nothing," says Ciel. "My Latin boyfriend saw my gym teacher helping me stretch and threatened to kill him. I told him, 'You don't pay my bills and you didn't give birth to me, so you have no right to get into my business.' I always tell Latin guys, 'I am a New York woman. I don't need you to protect me. I have mace in my purse.'"

"When I am with my husband, no matter where we are, he always has his hands on me—my shoulder, my arm," says Vanessa. "If I am sitting in a chair and he thinks I am too far away, with one arm he will pull the chair over to him, with me still in it! He definitely acts like he owns me."

"Come on, all men are macho," says Pablo. Okay Pablo, that may be true to some extent, but the women I interviewed emphasized being macho and possessive when talking about Latin men —and *only* Latin men. And anyway, Pablo, even other Latin men disagree with you.

"Here, Latin men are too possessive and loud-mouthed," says Julio.

"The majority of Latin men are macho and possessive," says Miguel. "I am not the jealous type, but if some guy was talking to my woman or a guy was calling my house? Well, that would be a different story."

Bitch, Make Me a Sandwich

As you might guess, this section discusses how Latin men are used to traditional gender roles. But the title of this section, "Bitch, Make Me a Sandwich," actually relates to the fact that in my interviews, several women specifically mentioned an instance when their Latin man's mother came unglued because of a sandwich. Like in Vanessa's situation, with her Dominican husband: "We were at my mother-in-law's house for a party. It was going to start soon, and I was hurrying to finish the setup when she yelled for me to come into the kitchen. I thought there was some emergency; but then she said, 'Oh my God, Christian is hungry! Vanessa, you have to make him a sandwich!' And Christian is sitting in the kitchen! All I could think was, 'Why doesn't he make *himself* a sandwich?'"

"Traditional gender roles are part of our culture," says Marisol. "If I bring a guy home, my mother will ask me, 'Did you serve him cake and coffee?' The woman is supposed to wait on the man." She adds, "My younger sister married a white guy. He likes to do the dishes. My mom gets so embarrassed when he does that."

"In our culture the woman is supposed to serve the man," says Miguel. "Isn't it like that everywhere? Isn't the woman always supposed to serve the man?"

"Latin men like to be taken care of, but I am fair about it," says Hugo. "If she takes care of me, I will treat her like a princess."

He explains, "In Latin families, the guy usually works and the woman stays home. But if she was the one working, I would have no problem being the slave in the kitchen and doing the laundry. I don't believe that just because I am the man, women need to do those things."

"To be fair, we love traditional gender roles, too," says Elena. "We love when Latin men open the door, push in our chair, or notice we are having a hard time in our heels and offer to get us a cab. White guys don't do that." She adds, "He enjoys his sandwich, and I enjoy when he opens the car door, bitch. You want your man to be a man."

So if you like a man's man and don't particularly mind making the occasional emergency sandwich, a Latin man could be perfect for you.

El Infiel (a.k.a. The Cheating)

Latin men are gentlemanly, pick up the check, *and* like to dance. You might be thinking, What's the catch? Well, here it is, and it ain't pretty: It's cheating. Yes, there are exceptions—like my ex, who was loyal to a fault. But this is definitely something you want to keep an eye out for when dating a Latin guy. And be warned: The women I interviewed noted that they will go to great lengths to maintain their cover.

"There is a big double standard in the Latin community. It is frowned upon for woman to stray, but for guys, they use the excuse that it's 'just part of their culture,'" says Maria. "They can go out and be a Casanova, but they must have a Virgin Mary at home." She adds, "I have never had a serious Latin boyfriend for that reason. My friend dated this guy from Mexico; she found out later that he had a girl in Monte Carlo, one in Brazil, and her in New York. And they all thought they were the only one."

When it comes to cheating Latin men, Elena is an expert. Starting with her great, great grandmother, four generations of Latin women in her family have kicked out their husbands for cheating. "If you have a good marriage, you can weather anything," says Elena. "We are losing this concept. Latin guys screw up when they are all about the instant gratification. They think short term. Short-term pussy versus long-term gratification."

"They cheat, it's 100-percent true," says Julio. "A man is not content with one woman. They need to see what else is out there. God made men with that defect. They are never satisfied. I am telling you, they all cheat. It's not 99-percent, it's 100-percent true."

Okay, well, not 100-percent true.

"It's not true for me," says Enrique. "I cheated maybe on a high-school girlfriend or something, but after I was married, no way. I would never do anything like that."

"I guess everybody does it at least once," says Miguel. "I did that when I was younger, but not anymore. It's not really right."

"Christian is a big flirt, but as far as I know there haven't been any transgressions," says Vanessa. "I do check his e-mail and phone every once in a while. There has been some flirtatious stuff, but it's minor." She adds, "You would think since his dad cheated so much and he saw how it hurt his mom, he wouldn't do it, but most guys with cheating fathers do cheat." One more thing: "Um, know this: If he does, I will kill him, and I wouldn't feel bad about it." Better watch your back Christian.

There are many Latin men in loving, loyal relationships. There are even some in this book. But keep a look out. If he seems more Don Juan than dependable, more Casanova than confidant, more Lothario than loyal, cut him loose.

Between the Sheets

"When love is not madness, it is not love."

—Pedro Calderon de la Barca

The words "Latin" and "lover" go together better than "peanut butter" and "banana." Simply put, they are known for their passion. In fact, the women I interviewed affirm that Latin lovers more than live up to their reputation—and that their bananas ain't half bad either.

Latin Lovers Live Up to Their Reputation... and Then Some

The expression "Latin lover" has always had a positive connotation: hot and spicy, passionate, sexy. And I'm happy to report that according to my ladies, Latin men live up to their reputation, *and then some*. In fact, they had nothing but good things to say on the topic.

For a Latin man, sex is *not* just about a release. It's *not* about getting off. It's about enjoying everything about a woman and her body. They take a lot of pride—and a lot of time—in pleasing their woman. Can't argue with that!

"It's true, it's really great," says Elena. "That's where the machismo works in your favor. They won't come if the woman doesn't come."

"I had to stop dating Latinos," says Monique, 50, Cuban, madam. "They were so sexual, so passionate, they became very addictive."

"Forget what they say about the French," says Celeste. "Your Latin man will take your breath away. Trust me, you won't have to fake it. And there will be no need for the question, 'Was it good for you?'"

"I would have to agree on that," says Hugo. "I have never had an unhappy customer."

"I was having sex with this white woman once and sucking her toes at the same time," says Julio. "She couldn't get over it. She just kept saying, 'That was so incredible!' She had never had anyone do that to her before."

So if you don't just want to "have sex," but have someone make mad, passionate, crazy love to you, Latino is the best way to go. Women were unanimous on that one.

Adequately Equipped

According to the women I spoke to, Latin men have ample equipment.

"Yes! They are well equipped, and know what to do with it," says Elena.

"That is true. But it is more than size," says Hugo. "When a Latin man makes love, you get the total package."

"For me, they have always been pretty average," says Maria. "No small ones."

The Pros

The pros were more complimentary. They say Latin men are average to large and—something that most women agree is important—more wide than long.

If you have concerns about whether that cute Latin guy at the office measures up, fret no more. It's probably all good.

Drama as Foreplay

As I mentioned, Latinos love their *dramatica*. In fact, they love it so much, they even take it into the bedroom.

"I would get home from work sometimes, and my Puerto Rican girlfriend would start right in on me. Yelling at me about some minor thing," says Ferrell, 44, black, business executive. "When I finally started to yell back to defend myself, she grabbed me hard and kissed me passionately. After a while, I realized she was doing it on purpose. She argues when she wants hot sex."

"Drama as foreplay, sure," says Ciel. "It is the best sex you will ever have. Works like a charm."

"They like to push your buttons, love when women get mad even though they say they don't. They definitely fight with you. That is why my relationships with Latin men never lasted," says Maria. "They only lasted as long as they did because of the Latin lover thing."

"I have definitely found that Latin men start arguments to get the make-up sex. They are very passionate—and that is good—but the fighting never stops," says Carolyn. "It becomes unhealthy. I don't want to have to be angry to have great sex!"

Drama as foreplay can be a perilous game—one not all Latin men are willing to play. "That's crazy to me," says Miguel. "I guess they do it for the make-up sex, but you are taking too big a risk. If you make her too mad, you won't get any."

"I have zero tolerance for drama," says Hugo. "Even if she was the most beautiful girl in the world, if she liked drama, I would say 'No.' I would rather take her to a romantic dinner than get in an argument."

Kim, a Latina who dates mostly other Latinas, had this to say on the subject: "Within the gay community, drama is *big*. So it's hard to tell if the drama is from being Latina or just from being gay."

Some Like It Rough

While it doesn't apply to everyone, many women I interviewed mentioned accounts of rough sex among Latinos. A guy known as Manfreak among my friends—half Mexican, half Dominican

—described sex within his community with one sentence: "We fuck like Klingons." For those non-Trekkies, Klingon sex is defined in the Urban Dictionary as "extremely rough, passionate, sweaty, primal sex, which can have an end result of broken bones, bruises...and in some cases a concussion, and maybe death." Of course, Manfreak was joking. I hope. But women did share many stories of hair pulling, ass slapping, and other forms of rough sex in the Latin community. It's important to note, however, that these women also said that Latin men are particularly adept at making things rough and passionate *without hurting you in any way*. As Elena said, "Don't try this at home."

"My first girlfriend was Puerto Rican," says Ferrell. "We were having sex, and she said to hit her. That is not really my thing so I just tapped her on the ass. And then she said, 'No hit me harder!' So I tapped her on the breast a little. And then she screamed, 'No hit me harder!' And at the same time, she slapped me across the face with all her strength. It really hurt! I would never hit a woman, but I guess it was just an automatic reflex. I smacked her back. She climaxed immediately." He adds, "Even though I was young then, I knew this was really specific to her. If I did that with a white girl, the next thing I know, the cops would be at my door."

"Yes, definitely one guy in particular. I had to remind him I didn't like that. Level eight is okay, but not twelve," says Maria. "The first time you are with someone, it should be exciting enough. You shouldn't need to get the equipment out."

"When people read this book, they'll think we're nuts or animals or something," says Elena. "It's not like that. I don't want people to get the wrong idea." She continues, "We always joke about how Latin guys can slap you on the ass in such a perfect way that it makes a noise, but never hurts. It's just playful. And if you don't like it, they would change it. Remember, it's about making you happy."

"I think that's really sexy, but no one I've dated has ever screwed it up, either," says Celeste. "It's not really rough; it's playing rough. My Mexican boyfriend said it was a matter of trust, just like dancing. I put myself in his hands, but I always knew he wasn't going to go too far and he always knew how far he could go without overstepping."

"You are going to think I am a boring Latino," says Hugo. "But when it comes to sex, I want to make sure I have conquered all of the basics, like I can make her speak Chinese when she is Latin, before I am more aggressive. It's important to establish yourself as a good lover with just the basics first."

"Me personally, I like it rough. Hair pulling, the works," says Ciel. "That's what is great about Latin guys. I once had sex with a Jewish guy. It was no good. Too soft."

Cunning Linguists

On the topic of licking pussy, young Pablo summed it up in two words: "Love it."

Hugo, a.k.a. Dr. Love, agreed. "I don't know any Latin men that have problems with licking pussy. It's important because that way, you know her anatomy, so you can really satisfy her."

"A Latin man will do anything to satisfy a woman," says Julio. "That is 100-percent true." (At least there is one good thing that is 100-percent true!)

"Yeah, it's like they were born to," says Celeste. "And with a certain level of pride and joy." She adds, "And they do not necessarily expect a return on their investment, aside from your delight."

"Yes, we always joke among my friends," says Elena. "We will ask 'Does he eat well?' 'Why yes, he does,' we say."

And they sure as hell aren't talking about a sandwich.

Given their great reputation in the sack, it's not surprising that they don't have any inhibitions. And everything is on the menu —including *you*.

Our Stories

You've got the basics down—some dos and don'ts, some things to look forward to when dating Latin guys, and some things to watch out for. But what is dating Latin really like? Of course, there's no way to tell exactly what *your* relationship with a Latin guy will be like because, like I've already said ad nauseum, everybody is different. What these stories will give you is a glimpse into how some of the various cultural issues have played out for real people in real-life situations.

A Marriage of Consequence

My sister and I were raised by my mom—a single parent in the '70s, when there were no single parents. Mom had a bachelor's degree, but what with being a woman and all, she could only get the most low-level clerical work. The money she earned doing that work, plus the $250 a month she got for child support, was all my mother had to raise her two girls. We moved almost every year, each time to a worse apartment. Candle-light card games were the norm when Mom couldn't pay the electric bill, which was fairly often. And then there was the period my mom called "the Campbell's soup years," where we could afford only Campbell's soup for dinner. My sister and I knew all the Campbell's flavors by heart (Sirloin Burger being our favorite).

I always thought we were poor—because, well, we *were*. But the first time my boyfriend Paul brought me home to meet his family, even *I* was shocked by how they lived. To say that Paul's parents' single-family, ranch-style house was "run down" is an understatement. The exterior paint, an eye-searing blue, was peeling in places. To fix it, someone had painted over the bare spots, but with a *different* shade of blue, magnifying the blight.

And the front lawn was littered with cars. They weren't on blocks or anything; rather, it was like they'd been parked by an insane valet, all criss-crossing each other. It just didn't make sense! We were in a run-of-the-mill suburb; there was plenty of parking on the street. (I found out later that this was done primarily for convenience. No one in the family wanted to walk farther than absolutely necessary to get to their car.)

As we entered the house, I heard the crunch of loose linoleum under my feet. The walls were a grungy white. Yellowed, thin drapes hung askew over the two living-room windows. The living-room furniture consisted of two dilapidated couches, both facing a '70s-style console television. This console television was no longer in use, but served as a stand for a newer TV. Paul's mom, gray-haired and wearing a gray sweat suit, sat on the tattered couch, her eyes fixed on the screen.

"This is my biology lab partner," Paul said.

"Uh," grunted his mom, her eyes still glued to the TV.

To the right was the kitchen—antiquated and stark, but very clean. The appliances showed their age, the ceramic on the white stove chipped and the handle of the refrigerator held in place by a liberal quantity of duct tape. A cold pot of refried beans appeared permanently affixed to the stove's back-right burner. Below the kitchen window was a table for six, white Formica with beveled metal trim. And beyond the kitchen was Paul's room, furnished with a small desk and the same twin bed he had slept in growing up, even though he was now six-feet tall and weighed around 200 pounds. I don't know why I was so astonished; I knew Paul's family was of modest means. Paul had already told me his mom was a teaching assistant and his dad picked lettuce in the fields. But...*damn*.

Paul was my first venture into interracial dating. He was Mexican, a self-proclaimed beaner. When we were first together, it made me feel so uncomfortable when he said those things—beaner, wetback, *vato*, *esse*. I had been taught by my mother to be very PC:

Chicano, not Mexican; Latino, not Hispanic; African American, not black; Native American, not Indian. I was raised color blind. But Paul invited me to join a club that could freely joke about taco jockeys and lettuce pickers. It was as exciting as it was terrifying.

By the time we graduated from junior college, only a few months after we started dating, I was deeply in love with Paul, that Latin instant boyfriend. Part of it was real love; truly, it was. But part of it was that insecurity shared by all 20-somethings about being alone. I believed I couldn't live without him. And with us going to different schools, a whole two hours apart, I was sure I would lose him. So I decided: I would ask Paul to marry me. I would have to buy a ring. Money was no object; I would put it on my Sears card. I bought a gold ring with five small diamonds on the top for $500.

A friend recommended a romantic restaurant in Berkeley where I could pop the question. It turned out, however, to be a glorified pizza joint, complete with fake grapevines cascading down from the ceiling. Obviously, I couldn't ask him there. So we left and drove closer to the Berkeley campus. For an hour, we peered into restaurant windows. "No that one is no good," I would say. At what seemed like restaurant number 501, Paul finally put his foot down. "We will be eating here," he said. I tried to play it cool, but my mind was still racing. I had gotten up the courage to do this. I had bought the ring. I had planned to do it tonight, and goddamn it, I was going to do it if it killed me—just not in the casual vegetarian Vietnamese restaurant that Paul had selected, which had (wait for it) communal seating. As we left the restaurant I wracked my brain for a plan B.

"Let's take a walk on campus," I suggested. Spotting a picturesque tree in the moonlight I suggested we sit for a while. As we sat under the tree and gazed up at the moon, I fumbled around in my purse to find the ring. "You know I really love you, Paul," I said.

"I really love you too," Paul said light-heartedly. He smiled and gave me a kiss.

Nervous, I dropped my gaze from his eyes to his shirt. "Uh, will you marry me?" I said my voice cracking a bit. Then I opened the ring box.

And what came next? Complete. Total. Utter. *Silence*. I heard no birds chirping, no people talking, no cars honking, nothing. My attention was 100-percent focused on Paul, who just stared at that ring and said...*nothing*. "Holy fuck," I thought frantically. "This was a huge mistake. What did I do? Is he going to say no?" I hadn't even thought about that possibility! But then Paul, God love him, lifted my chin until my eyes met his. "I will make you a very good husband," he said. Jesus, the *relief*! As Paul hugged and kissed me, I could feel the anxiety leave my body.

My poor mother, what she must have thought? Thanks to little fetus me, my mother had a shotgun wedding, and had taught my sister and me from birth how babies were made. I was the kid who told all the other kids on the playground, "You can't get pregnant from kissing. The penis has to go *into the vagina*." So although I wasn't getting married because of a surprise pregnancy (thanks to Mom, I *always* used protection), I *was* getting married awfully young. I'm sure it took everything she had to not grab me, shake me, and scream "No! You are only 21! You cannot get married!" (But, in my mother's defense, there really is no telling me "No.")

To be fair, although we became engaged when we were 21, we didn't get married until we turned 26. In addition to stressing the importance of controlling our reproduction, my mother also drilled into us how critical it was that we receive a college education. Likewise, Paul, having seen too many relatives and friends knocked up by high school, was determined to be the first in his entire extended family to graduate from college. So we planned from the beginning to wait until after graduation to get married.

Not being one of those dopey girls who starts planning her wedding when she is six, and seeing how Paul wasn't terribly particular about things, we had a pretty basic white-American ceremony. Because we were poor, however, we did observe one Mexican tradition: the money dance. During the money dance, relatives and friends pay for the privilege of dancing with the bride and groom. When people dance with the bride, they carefully pin money on her veil. When they dance with the groom, they pin the money on his tuxedo in as silly a way possible. When my uncle Joe danced with Paul, he pinned one leg of Paul's pants up to his knee.

Paul's mother, my *suegra*, or mother-in-law, was never particularly happy with his choice of bride (but then, my *suegra* was not particularly happy in general). I was spirited, opinionated, independent, and not afraid to tell people what I thought. At the time, I didn't understand her dislike; now I see that I broke almost every rule in the Latin cultural book. As a poor college student, I never thought to bring gifts. I was young and still exploring my sexuality, so my dress was rarely conservative and sometimes downright trashy. I didn't know about the three-times rule; when my *suegra* declined my first offer to help, I just sat my ass on the couch. Raised by my hippie-dippy, casual California mother, I never learned to call people Sir or Ma'am; I called everyone by their first name. And because my mother raised us as feminists, that "Bitch, make me a sandwich" stuff was never going to fly with me. In fact, Paul did most of the cooking, which must have driven my *suegra* wild.

But more importantly—and no doubt the main reason for her vendetta against me—was that she was used to having Paul completely under her thumb. But after we married, Paul's loyalty shifted. His mother was still very important to him, but I was his wife. That meant I was now *numero uno*. Unwilling or unable to articulate her feelings about this, she focused on the fact that I was white. It was bad enough that her oldest daughter had married a white man and her oldest son had been dating a

Filipina for more than eight years; now, because of me, Paul had extinguished her last hope for a pure Mexican grandchild.

But I loved Paul, and I was determined to show him and his family that I was not just any white girl. I believed then as I do now that you can't date a man without dating his culture, so I immersed myself in all things Mexican. I took Spanish and Chicano Studies classes at Berkeley. I studied Mexican and Mexican-American history, Benito Juarez to Cesar Chavez. Pretty soon, I knew more about being Mexican than maybe even Paul did.

Although Paul had a deep respect for his Mexican heritage, he really didn't possess any of the negative traits that the women I interviewed had observed in Latin men. He was not macho or possessive. He didn't like drama. He didn't demand that we observe traditional gender roles. He was loyal to a fault. He also didn't speak Spanish. See, Paul's mother didn't want him to learn Spanish; she wanted him to fit in with the white kids at school. As a result, Paul spoke what I would describe as Advanced Spanglish. One time, his mother said to him, *"Necesito la maleta,"* pointing toward the kitchen, where a suitcase rested next to the Formica table. Paul looked at her blankly. Having now studied up on Spanish, I knew what she wanted; but I didn't want to show up my new husband. Frustrated, his mother repeated, *"Necesito la maleta!"*

"Paul," I finally said quietly, "she wants you to bring her the suitcase." A mocking smile spread across my *suegra's* face. "The white girl knows more Spanish than you?" She giggled. Paul laughed, but he was clearly a little embarrassed.

I took part in all the family's events: his cousin's wedding, his nephew's christening, a friend's Quinceañera, and most importantly, the Mexican Christmas tradition of making tamales. The tamale-making process involves several steps: cooking the shredded meat (beef or chicken) with a variety of spices, spreading the cornmeal mush on the corn husks, spreading the meat on the corn meal, folding the corn husks into tamales, and then boiling them to cook the corn meal and seal in the juices.

Due to my whiteness, my *suegra* permitted me to participate in only one part of the process: spreading the corn meal on the corn husk. She figured it would be hard for me to screw that up—not that it stopped her from criticizing me frequently. "You are spreading it too thin," she said. Then, "No, no, now you are spreading it too thick." She huffed and puffed as she ripped the husk from my hand and scraped off the excess.

My *suegra* often sent Paul and me to pick up all manner of, er, *interesting* food items at the store. "*Cabeza de vaca*. Cow's head. Am I reading this right?" I said, reading off the grocery list. "That's right," replied my *suegra*, annoyed with my questions. "Paul knows where to get it." Another family favorite was menudo. Not just a boy band, menudo is also a Mexican soup—supposedly a delicacy, even if Mexicans are the only ones who think so. My first exposure to menudo occurred after Paul and I were married. During an overnight visit to his family's home, I was awakened at 5 a.m. from a deep sleep by a horrifying stench. Convinced my *suegra* had finally found a way to kill me, I started to cough uncontrollably. Gasping for breath, I clambered out of bed (where Paul continued to sleep soundly), threw on a t-shirt and jeans, rushed out of the room, past the kitchen—where my *suegra* was boiling *tripas* (a.k.a. intestines) for her menudo—and out the front door. Menudo brought me to my limits; I would partake in neither the music nor the soup.

In the end, Paul kept his promise: He was a good husband. As we grew into ourselves, though, we grew apart. Paul was happy living the role of suburban husband: watching football and barbecuing on the weekends, while I became more and more seduced by a fast-paced city life filled with fashion, celebrity parties, and Wall Street movers and shakers. After eight years together, we divorced. Paul eventually got his peaceful suburban life, and I claimed my life as a high-flying Wall Streeter. Lasting from the time we were 21 to the year we turned 30, our relationship spanned our formative years; really, we grew up together.

And I learned a lot from Paul. Not only did he provide me with an insider's view of Mexican culture, he kept me grounded. He kept things in perspective. I was always very ambitious, wanting to do more, to *have* more. But when I would get frustrated with things like our level of material success, Paul would always say, "At least we are not picking lettuce in the fields."

Latin Love with a Dash of La Diva Loca

One morning, Vanessa ventured into the dining hall for breakfast. While filling her bowl with a liberal portion of Froot Loops, she spotted a suave, sexy, and in all ways very cool guy checking her out. The two struck up a conversation over the sugary breakfast cereals, and Vanessa was instantly smitten. Christian was handsome—and given his confidence, he obviously knew it. He was also incredibly charming. Before Vanessa even realized it, Christian had become her instant boyfriend.

For the next two glorious weeks, Christian and Vanessa were inseparable—eating together, studying together, and making out together in her dorm room (nothing too scandalous; just heavy petting). Vanessa, a white girl, had never dated a Latin man before. Christian, half Dominican and half white, was unlike any man she had ever known. He was so romantic, so thoughtful, and so passionate—everything she imagined a Latin lover would be. He was always a gentleman, opening the door and pulling out her chair. And he was generous, never letting Vanessa pay for a thing, even though they were both poor college students.

At the end of their second week together, Christian kicked things up a notch, taking Vanessa out to dinner for her birthday at the fanciest restaurant in town: Olive Garden. He even bought her a birthday gift, a body pillow. Things seemed to be going swimmingly until, over dinner, somewhere between the salad and the pasta primavera, Christian noted one little wrinkle with the upcoming weekend. "Hey...um...I just want you to know my girlfriend will be coming in town this weekend." No big deal.

Just the smallest *problema*. Nothing more than a minor inconvenience. Really!

Vanessa's it's-the-fallin'-in-love-that's-makin'-me-high glow morphed instantly into an it's-the-bein'-in-love-that's-makin'-me-cry-cry-cry scowl. "You have a *girlfriend*?" She didn't even wait for his answer; snatching her body pillow, Vanessa rushed out of the restaurant.

Of course, Vanessa was done with him. She would wash that man right out of her hair and *move on*. She did the math: If it only takes half the length of the relationship to get over a man, she should be over Christian by the end of next week! She cried into her body pillow, did facials with her roommate, and ate a liberal quantity of both Ben & Jerry—anything to get her mind off him. Her healing process was rudely interrupted, however, by a threatening call from Christian's jealous main squeeze, who had found Vanessa's number in his phone. "Who do you think you are, messin' with my man? You fucking bitch!" screamed Christian's crazy girlfriend. Vanessa hung up and shut off the phone.

But Christian wouldn't go away. He wanted Vanessa back. He apologized for not coming clean with Vanessa, and even told her that he had finally broken up with his psycho-hose-beast of a girlfriend. Vanessa held steadfast. The required one-week mourning period had already passed, and she was *over him*. Christian's Dominican pride prevented him from chasing after her; he would have to admire Vanessa from afar.

Vanessa went on to date a few guys in college. By her senior year, things had gotten serious with a tall bo-hunking white dude on the football team. Vanessa, who had dated this guy exclusively for the last two years, believed he was *the one*, the man she would marry. That is, until Vanessa's new roommate divulged that her former roommate—not to mention a large percentage of the cheerleading squad and possibly various members of the teaching staff—had slept with Vanessa's boyfriend. Vanessa was devastated—and this time, she would need much more than a week get over it.

Although Christian and Vanessa hadn't been together since that disaster of a birthday dinner, he was always in the background. So when Vanessa's Prince Charming turned into a toad, Christian was there to pick up the pieces. "He knew I was vulnerable and swooped in," says Vanessa. "But it worked out. We have been together for over nine years now, married for the last three."

The two make a great match. They have a lot in common, and they enjoy each other's company. They lead a very active lifestyle, taking day trips to the Jersey Shore, walking on the beach, trying different restaurants in the city, and of course bowling. "He is obsessed with his Creamsicle bowling ball," says Vanessa. "We even have the shoes." That's not to say that Christian is always the easiest guy to get along with. The quintessential Latin man, Vanessa describes him as macho, argumentative, and feisty. (I'll take two!) Also, he always has to be right. But seeing as Vanessa is quite the catch herself—beautiful, thin, and plenty feisty too—she always calls him on his shit. Christian has a hard time saying he's sorry, but Vanessa makes sure the two never go to bed angry. So the two live in relative peace and happiness—most of the time.

But that doesn't mean there wasn't a lot about dealing with Christian's Latin family that took some getting used to. Like the fact that when you are with the Jimenez clan, you can never travel inconspicuously. Christian always rolls with an entourage—a large and often loud entourage. Case in point: the christening. "I am Catholic," says Vanessa. "And my dad said if he was going to pay for the wedding, we would have to get married in a Catholic church." It turned out, though, that despite his Latin roots, Christian *wasn't* Catholic. "His dad and mom had an ugly divorce," explains Vanessa. "He had cheated on her. There was a lot of bad blood. So out of spite"—a.k.a., vendetta—"his mom had the kids baptized Lutheran." Christian, however, was willing to convert. After a year of study, Christian was baptized in the presence of his entourage. "We were sitting in the church," recalls Vanessa. "It was so quiet, you could hear a pin drop. And then, all of a sudden, I hear his grandmother's cell phone go off with this loud salsa ring. Then his grandfather starts coughing uncontrollably. It was so embarrassing." She continues. "And then, from behind me I hear Christian's brother and father begin an argument about something that, no kidding, happened, like, 10 years ago." Vendetta anyone? "They argued all the way home." That was when Vanessa, typically quiet and low key, was forced to accept that blending into the background was going to be difficult if not impossible with her new in-laws.

Vanessa also had to get used to another kind of Thanksgiving holiday. Growing up on the east coast, Vanessa was used to cold, crisp, winter holidays, drinking hot cocoa and snuggling by the fire. Christian's family celebrates Thanksgiving in Miami. With 80-degree weather, there is no need for a fire, and a mojito, not cocoa, is usually the beverage of choice. And of course, "There was no turkey, no mashed potatoes, and no gravy," says Vanessa. "Just a lot of *concón*, Dominican burnt rice, and paella." They closed the evening with that "typical" Thanksgiving tradition: salsa dancing. Just like the pilgrims.

Vanessa plays the Latin woman role well. She always refers to elders in Christian's family as Sir or Ma'am. And she doesn't mind making Christian a plate at family gatherings. So her fitting in with his family should be easy sailing, right? Wrong. Why? One word: Mama. The 81-year-old Dominican family matriarch, Mama is an unadulterated diva who routinely dresses in black-leather pants, a cheetah top, and gold shoes, with a matching gold leather jacket. She is never seen without full makeup. And it's hard to believe, but she actually pulls it off. She attends all family functions, and is always the last one standing on the dance floor, scotch in hand. Mama requires the crowd's full attention and must be told she is beautiful 24/7/365. And if she is ever in a bad mood, Mama knows what to do: take it out on the wives of her two grandsons.

"Mama was someone I was just not prepared for," says Vanessa. "Even though Mama seems to like me, she still says the rudest things to me without giving it a thought. My sister-in-law, Rosalinda, gets it even worse. I don't mind making a plate for my husband, but Rosalinda is very independent ["independent" presumably being code for "not a submissive doormat"]. That could be what sets Mama off. Mama can be sweet as pie, and then *so* rude. And it comes out of nowhere." Like the family barbeque, during which Mama insulted both Vanessa and Rosalinda in succession. "I really don't like your shirt," Mama said to Vanessa. Then turning to Rosalinda, she fired an even more powerful blow: "Rosalinda, you know you really shouldn't advertise your ass as a married woman." And when both of Mama's granddaughters-in-law wound up pregnant at the same time, Mama had something to say about that, too. "Vanessa, you look so skinny even though you are obviously pregnant. And Rosalinda," Mama said, looking Rosalinda up and down. "Rosalinda, you look *so* pregnant. You must be so glad the pregnancy is almost over so you can finally lose *all* that weight!" Ouch. Really feelin' the love, Mama.

As of this writing, Vanessa is due to give birth to her and Christian's first baby, a girl, in less than a month. Although Vanessa and Christian are very happy—they feel truly blessed—Fetus Jiminez has already caused a few conflicts between them. First, there is the issue of who will be "in charge." Christian wants a 60/40 split, with the larger share going to him. Vanessa has countered with 51/49. Christian is fine with that, as long as it means Daddy has "the final word." Then there's what to name the baby. Christian has lobbied for Juanita Conchita Jimenez, but Vanessa isn't having it. The baby will only be one-quarter Dominican; Vanessa doesn't want to saddle her with something "super ethnic." She prefers Hannah. Mama's response: "I hate that name."

Vanessa is now well versed in Latin culture. And as it gets closer to the birth, Vanessa has grown more apprehensive about one Latin custom in particular, the pop in. "I am really starting to get worried about his family's expectations concerning our baby," says Vanessa. "Christian's mother keeps saying that we have to 'Let them help raise the baby.' And Mama talks about how important it is to have the grandparents around as much as possible in the baby's first few months." She continues, "I think once the baby is born, they will think they can pop in whenever they want." Or maybe they will just never leave.

Vanessa also has a few issues with her husband's ideas about gender roles. "He has these passive-aggressive ways of getting out of anything he might consider 'women's work,'" says Vanessa. "Like the other day, he washed his dirty sweat socks in with my fancy cashmere sweater." She continues, shaking her head, "I said, 'If you are going to do laundry, do it right!' To which he said something like, 'Okay, I won't do the laundry then!' I am a little concerned about how much he will help with the baby."

Vanessa hadn't expected Christian to be so excited about having a girl. But, she says, "He loves his nieces and always spends time with them, even more now that he knows he is having a girl." What she didn't understand—until recently—was *why* Christian was so excited. "The other day, he rubbed my belly and said, 'I can't wait until she gets here. Then I will have two slaves!'"

Little bitch, make me a sandwich!

Speaking Japlishguese

"The first thing I noticed about Valentina was her punctuality," says Akira. "Japanese men, punctual; Latin women, not so punctual." And when Akira says "not punctual," it is in his usual, ultra-polite, Japanese way. The truth is, Valentina was more than an hour late to their first date. Indeed, if not for that nifty modern invention called the "cell phone," the two might have never met. Fortunately, however, when Valentina finally arrived, she did not disappoint. For Akira, Valentina's petite, five-foot, two-inch frame and a beautiful, feminine quality brought to mind Latin rhythms *à la* "The Girl from Ipanema." And after they got to talking, Akira found there was much more to Valentina than her looks. She was intellectually exciting and extremely well read. From the start, they had great chemistry. It seemed Valentina was everything Akira had been looking for.

Not that everything was smooth sailing. In the beginning, language was a bit of an issue. Being Brazilian, Valentina of course spoke Portuguese—although having studied in Japan for several years, she also spoke sufficient Japanese. For his part, Akira spoke Japanese but no Portuguese. And both spoke decent English. It wasn't always easy; sometimes they needed to use words from more than one language. But they could communicate fairly effortlessly.

Another barrier was Valentina's, um, er, uh, *overzealousness*. "What they say about Latins being jealous? It's *true,*" says Akira. "Whenever I talk to other women, she gets so upset. It's a typical male reaction to turn your head when you see a hot woman, but she doesn't like that."

"It was really bad at the beginning," Akira recalls. "The worst was when I was at a dance club. Valentina went to the restroom, and while she was gone, I noticed Monica, a good friend of Valentina's. I went over just to give Monica a friendly hello." Akira shakes his head, "Boy did she punish me for that. 'I didn't like the way you looked at her,' she said." He continues, "It was *her* friend. *She* had introduced us." Male or female, it don't matter. Latin jealousy, Latin possessiveness—these are almost always a top concern for people dating within the Latin community. And in this case, given the Japanese propensity to be *über* polite, it was even more difficult to deal with. "I guess what you have to realize," says Akira, "is that Brazilians are a passionate people. That passion displays itself in different ways; you have to take the good with the bad."

This early in the relationship, that would have been it for me. Call me Snagglepuss. Exit stage left! "Did it get better as the relationship progressed?" I ask.

"Not really," says Akira. "I had to try to educate myself not to turn my head."

That's like trying to educate yourself not to fart.

Although the jealousy remained an issue, there was so much more to their relationship. "Valentina was the first person I really felt I could be myself around," says Akira. "In other relationships, I always felt that I had to act a certain way, to dress a certain way. Plus," Akira says, lowering his voice as if to soften the blow, "I found that American women are lacking in their feminine side."

What I want to say is, "Not feminine my ass! Do you know how many pairs of five-inch Louboutins I own? We American women are feminine and fucking charming too, you sexist Japanese asshole!" What I *actually* say is, "Hold on there, Akira. I think there are plenty of American woman who are feminine." (Finally, I earned my Girl Scout badge for self control!) It turns out what Akira means is that American women don't like old-fashioned gender roles; I'll concede that point. Akira was raised in a traditional Japanese household, his mother submitting to his father's every whim. Although that wasn't what he was looking for—"I didn't want a Japanese woman," Akira explains, "submissive and completely reliant on a man either. I wanted a balance"—he couldn't quite grasp the idea of his wife as head of household, or even co-manager.

"In other words you didn't want someone to be submissive," I say, "but you wanted to wear the pants in the family?"

"Exactly," says Akira. Someone, it so happens, like the Brazilian Valentina. "Feminism may be Greek to most Asians," but their views on the matter blend nicely with the "Bitch, make me a sandwich" attitude that pervades Latin culture.

Within three months of their first date, Akira and Valentina moved in together. (Take one Latina, add water, and stir—instant girlfriend!) "She was finishing up an exchange-student program and was going to have to move in a couple months anyway," explains Akira. "I had a nice apartment, so I asked her to move in with me." Those were just the circumstances, however. The *real* reason Akira wanted Valentina to move in, the clincher—and listen up ladies, because this comes up more than once—was that she took care of him when he was sick. "Whatever our other issues were," says Akira, "it was the care and tenderness that she took when I was ill that made the difference."

Akira was 41. He had never been married, had never lived with anyone—had never even had a serious relationship. Unsure how well Akira would share his personal space, Valentina kept her apartment for a few extra weeks after moving in with Akira, just in case. Indeed, living together was a real adjustment. "It is not that I am super clean, but she doesn't do things my way," says Akira. "Like, she doesn't put the cap on the toothpaste. That really bothers me." Even so, he fell for her. "There was just such a warm feeling I got from her. That's what made me fall in love with her."

Akira's parents didn't mind that Valentina wasn't Japanese. They welcomed her warmly into the family, in their reserved, Japanese way. Frankly, they were just happy to see Akira settle down, given that he was, as they put it, "relatively old." Because Valentina had lived in Japan, meeting Akira's parents didn't cause her any culture shock. But when the tables were turned, and Akira traveled to Brazil to meet Valentina's family, he was not so lucky. As the quiet and reserved Akira entered the Barbosa family home, he was immediately surrounded by Samba music, caipirinhas, and more Latinos than he had seen in his life. He was shocked to learn that this was not the whole town out to greet them, or even the neighborhood—these were just Valentina's relatives!

Still reeling from the sheer size of her family, Akira next had to contend with the PDA. PDA may be a no-no in Japanese culture, but with Latinos, it's not just welcome, it's expected. As he walked through the family's home, he was stunned by the whirlwind of kissing, hugging, and dancing. Valentina's mother strode up to Akira and, saying nothing, wrapped him in a huge hug. Akira's eyes grew wide and his body stiffened, but Mrs. Barbosa just kept on hugging. "This," he thought, "would *never* happen in Japan!"

Akira and Valentina are now married and trying to start a family. "Well, I am not getting any younger," says Akira, with his palms in the air. (No doubt, his parents frequently inform him of that fact.) "We are doing well, very happy." He adds, "The toothpaste is still an issue. After three years of marriage, we are still fighting about that one." But even with their differences, the couple has no problem communicating—in three languages, no less. "We both speak Japanese and English; she speaks Portuguese, and I am starting to get better at it," says Akira. "We have even created our own language using all three, a language only we understand."

The way I see it, all we can ask for during our short time on this Earth is to learn from others. And it seems to me that Akira and Valentina have done that and more. They have created something —a closeness, a bond, even their own language. I don't think you can ask for more than that. Or, as they say in Japlishguese, *"Tu can't pede taishite mais yori that."*

Yellow Fever

"By nature, men are nearly alike; by practice, they get to be wide apart."

—CONFUCIUS

The year I started undergrad at the University of California at Berkeley was the first year Asians overtook whites as the student majority. During my time there, I learned a lot from my brothers and sisters of the Far East, including how to use chopsticks to eat sushi, how to order dim sum, and how to say "Please" (*m goi*), "Thank you" (*dòh jé*), and "Fuck you and all of your ancestors" (*diu lei hm ga tsan*) in Cantonese.

But what really sticks in my mind was the time one of my fellow white people, Jim Bob, made the *faux pas* of the century. I was sitting with Jim Bob and some of our Asian friends at a large, round dim sum table. When Jim Bob got up to use the restroom, he thoughtlessly stuck his chopsticks into the rice. "Argh! No! Don't!" My Asian friends screeched, as if trying to prevent a car accident. "What? What?" cried Jim Bob. Finally, our friend Susan snatched Jim Bob's chopsticks from the rice and laid them next to his bowl. Turns out, leaving your chopsticks in the rice is taboo. A friend later clued me in as to why. "In China, people often leave out a bowl of rice with the chopsticks sticking out as a tribute to the dead," says Hanna, 30, Chinese, hairdresser.

Yellow Fever, which describes an attraction to Asians, is one of the most common of the Five Fevers. Obviously, the term "Asian" spans a large continent containing a huge range of cultures and attitudes. This book focuses on some of the largest Asian groups in the U.S.—Chinese, Koreans, Japanese, and Filipinos.

It should go without saying that these four groups can all be very different, sometimes as much as the English are different from the Turks. There are also cultural differences between the generations; between Asians raised here and those raised in their home country; and between those raised traditionally and those who were not. Nonetheless, in the course of my interviews, I detected various traits that people of these cultures have in common—traits that are generally very different from those found in Western cultures. Hopefully, this section will help you both appreciate and understand these differences. The goal in this section is not to stereotype Asians, but to make you aware of some ways that dating within the Asian culture can be very different, and to help you navigate some potential problems.

Things to Know

What are some things you need to know if you have your eye on that hot Asian guy three cubicles down? First, most of the Asians I talked to said their culture places the highest value on how you make a living—i.e., your job. Second, they are all about food. In America—home of fast food, instant food, ready-made food, microwaved food, and my favorite, cheese food—food seems to be something you just "get over with" to get on with the other things. In contrast, Asians prepare food with great care.

For Asians, food is a social lubricant—the grease that makes social interaction possible and an expression of how they feel about you. Finally, as it concerns your acceptance by your Asian man's family, I have some good news for you: It may be easier than you think.

You Are What You Do

Nearly everyone I interviewed noted that for Asians, your career and your education are not just important; they define you as a person. In fact, when introducing you to others, many Asians will even include your occupation and education.

"You mean, if I met your family, you would say, 'This is J.C. Davies, an author and Harvard graduate?'" I ask my friend Alicia, 42, Filipina, hospital administrator.

"The first thing I thought of when you said that was what my parents would say: 'Author—is that a real job?'" says Alicia. "Doctors, lawyers, and investment bankers—those are the acceptable occupations in Asian cultures. You did go to Harvard, so that would give you some points. But you still need a real job."

Hanna, a smart, beautiful, and good-humored Chinese hairdresser, has no problem meeting white guys who want to date her, but Chinese guys are often put off by her choice in careers or by the fact that she is a college dropout. "All Asian guys care about is if you look good on paper," Hanna says. "And all your parents want is for you to get married. They don't understand things like chemistry. He has a good job? That should be good enough."

"With my Filipino boyfriend, his job always came first. He would drop everything if his boss called, even on the weekends," says Alec, 25, white guy, art-gallery manager. "I was working as a handyman in the gallery then, which was an issue, but deep down I think the fact that I was a 'blue collar worker' turned him on. He loved when I wore my hard hat." (It's fun to stay at the Y-M-C-A!)

"That is definitely part of Asian cultures," says Bernie, 46, Filipino, marketing executive. "But I don't think that way anymore." He continues, "Divorce changes you. Before, my job title was really important to me. Now I just care about spending more time with my son."

Ellen, 37, white girl, consultant, lived in Japan, so she knows how important a person's occupation is to Asians. She recalls, "In Japan, I forgot my business cards once. It's a *grave* mistake to forget your business cards. You can't even speak to anyone before you look at their card because you have to know what their ranking is first."

So those of you who are struggling artists, entrepreneurs, or anything else a little outside the mainstream, prepare yourself. Becoming accepted by your Asian man's family will be a bit of a challenge.

Food Is Bigger Than God

One thing Asians share is a love of food. It's not revered just for sustenance, but for the cultural interaction that takes place during meals. Food is so important, it's the main reason Asians often live in close proximity to each other and to the Asian market. Families and friends come together to eat, drink, and get caught up on family events. Whether it's hanging out at the sushi bar for hours or spending half the day at dim sum, food is where the family is.

"Food is huge," says Hanna. "The Chinese have an expression: 'Food is bigger than God.' It's all about survival. You have to realize that this has been ingrained in people for thousands of years."

Also, the food itself can have great meaning. "Food is so important in Korean families," says Hyo-Sonn, 29, Korean, analyst. "When my fiancé and I went to my parents' house for dinner for the first time, my mom agonized for a whole week about what dishes she would prepare." She adds, "Food communicates a lot about how people feel about you."

"The Chinese are so into food. My boyfriend's family would always have multiple dishes at once," says Becky, 25, white girl, graphic designer. "It's how they express how they feel about you. Everything they did was around food. I used to call them 'the feedings.'"

"When my Chinese boyfriend found out I could cook, he was so excited," says Ranisha, 35, black, PhD candidate. "And it didn't matter what I cooked: beef and broccoli or my mama's recipe for catfish and cornbread, he would eat the whole thing. There were never any leftovers, and I like leftovers."

"My wife says it all the time: You put your love in your food," says Ferrell, 44, black, business executive. "In Japan they have a rule that a child must have at least five different-colored dishes in their lunch. If you don't do that, people will say that you are not a good mother."

"My father was the head of the family and high earner," says Mark, 35, Korean, analyst. "But it was my mom and her cooking that made it a home. My family pushed me to be successful academically and in my career, but food established the security."

"The first question Filipinos ask about the party last night is not 'What was it like? Was it fun? Who was there?' but 'What did they serve?'" says Alicia.

More Accepting of Interracial Relationships

Generally speaking, most Asian parents would prefer their children marry within their heritage—Korean with Korean, Chinese with Chinese, etc. As early as 1945, however, American men were permitted to marry Asian woman as part of the War Brides Act (although the last laws banning interracial marriage weren't overturned until 1967). This gave Asians at least a 20-year head start on other interracial relationships. As such, these relationships have gained some acceptance within Asian communities.

"I never really have any problems with other people when dating white guys," says Hanna. "Maybe I got some stares when I was in Chinatown, but not much."

"Unlike with my black and Latin boyfriends, when I went out with my Filipino boyfriend, I never felt judged," says Alec. "I even met his parents. They were fine with it."

"My parents didn't care that my wife wasn't Filipino," says Bernie. "They were more worried that her Italian family might not accept me."

Sometimes, Asian parents even prefer mixed children, especially white/Asian. When Aaron, who is Jewish, and Brenda, who is of Chinese heritage, had their first child, Aaron was a little surprised at his in-laws' excitement. "They said they couldn't wait to show off their 'whitened-up' grandchild to their friends in Hong Kong," says Aaron, 48, Jew, entrepreneur.

"Asians can be accepting of interracial relationships, but it depends on the race," says Piao, 32, Chinese, marketing executive. "White people, yes. I have an aunt in China who wants me to marry a white girl because she thinks we will make a 'pretty baby.' But if I brought one of my black girlfriends home, it would be a problem. My mom would be good, but my relatives in China would freak out."

"I never heard from my parents, 'Oh my god she's dating a white guy,'" says Alicia. "But I would hear things like, 'Oh my god, we are going to have great-looking grandchildren.' At which point I would have to say, 'Slow down! We have only been dating a week!'"

So You Don't Fuck Up!

This section does its best to give you some tips to keep you from stepping in it, but in Asian cultures, stepping in it seems almost inevitable. First, unlike in the U.S., everything among Asians is handled using a strict hierarchy—which may be difficult for you to ever truly understand. And then there are the food rules!

As Hanna says, "Food is *huge*." Not only is it important *that* you eat it, but *how* you eat it (which can vary widely depending on which Asian culture you are dealing with). After you get a handle on all that, remembering to take your shoes off won't seem like such a big deal.

Respect for Elders and Acting Within a Strict Hierarchy

In most Asian cultures, there is a fairly rigid social hierarchy. When you greet people, you must use the appropriate honorific title as well as their surname. When elders speak, you cannot interrupt or speak over them. Nor, when it is your time to talk, can you disagree with them. (Well, not technically anyway.)

"My father and I have a lot of disagreements. I hate being told what to do," says Mark. (He is Korean, after all.) "I think that happens a lot with first-generation Asian Americans and our parents."

"Talking back to your parents—you would *never* do that. And there is definitely a hierarchy," says Bernie. "I am the oldest son in my generation, so all my cousins and my sister call me 'Kuya,' which sort of means 'Big Brother.' It's an important term of respect. They look up to you, so that puts you under a lot of pressure. Believe me, when I got divorced, that was a *big* deal."

"Among Koreans, women are not supposed to talk much at all in general," says Hyo-Sonn. "Men don't want you to talk about any unnecessary things." Ouch! (That was me, biting my tongue.)

Even funerals are managed by age and ranking. "It seemed so strange to me that I was given so much prominence at my wife's grandmother's funeral," says Carter, 33, white guy, telecom engineer. "My wife is Chinese, and she's the oldest daughter of the oldest son. So as her husband—even though I am just some white guy who married into the family—that put me above her grandmother's other children in the funeral procession. It was quite bizarre."

Food and Beverage Decorum

Seeing as how they take dining so seriously, you can imagine there are a lot of rules around eating and drinking (aside from the aforementioned chopsticks disaster). As can be expected, eating begins in order of seniority. And all Asians believe that finishing your meal—especially your rice—is a must; it shows your respect. It's after that that things get tricky. For example, in China, you can eat directly from the communal plates, and reaching across the table is not considered rude. The Chinese and Japanese raise their bowl to their mouth to eat, but Koreans find that terribly gauche. The Japanese don't find it offensive if you loudly slurp your soup; they encourage it. It's considered the highest compliment to the chef. But don't do that with Chinese or Koreans; to them, it's uncouth.

Tea also plays an essential role in Asian societies. And when you pour tea, a hierarchy is strictly followed in *all* situations. "I remember in college, even the sophomores had to pour tea for the juniors," says Hyo-Sonn. "And also important among Asians: Women *can't* pour liquor. If you do, you are considered a woman of, uh, low morals." Also important to note is that in China, you must always thank whoever pours your tea. (Don't worry if someone is talking while the tea is being poured; it is perfectly acceptable to tap on the table with your knuckles to signal your thanks.)

"I am not the best person to give tips on food decorum, but I can tell you that it's very important to Asians," says Piao. "I have been told that I can't hold my chopsticks right. My family always says they can't bring me anywhere because they will be shamed by how I eat."

The etiquette involved with Asian eating and drinking is a book in itself, and customs can vary. It's always safest to ask your man ahead of time instead of just guessing.

No Shoes, Please!

In most Asian homes, it is customary to remove your shoes before entering. "It just extends from hygiene," says Akira, 44, Japanese, equity salesman. "You don't have to vacuum the carpets as much. The whole house is just a lot cleaner."

"Oh Lord, yeah. I lived with this Japanese family for a while. Not only no outside shoes in the house, but when you went to the bathroom, you were supposed to use special bathroom slippers," says Ellen. "Once, I forgot, and walked around the house with bathroom slippers on. When they saw me, they flipped out." Due to Ellen's flagrant misuse of the bathroom slippers, her hosts were forced to clean the whole house.

"My Chinese boyfriend's family took that very seriously," says Becky. "They actually didn't even let shoes inside the house at all. Your shoes had to be placed in plastic bags outside of the house."

Some of the Asians I interviewed mentioned that Becky's boyfriend's family seemed a little extreme. Can you imagine? Prada left outside the house? Say it ain't so! But don't worry, in most houses, it is customary to leave shoes in the entry way.

What the Hell Did I Get Myself Into?

As Americans, we are taught to be individuals, to stand out, to make a mark for ourselves. Asians, on the other hand, are supposed to be successful—but to blend in with the crowd at the same time. I mean, how the hell is that even *possible*? This all relates to the Asian concept of saving face, which was, for me, one of the hardest parts about dating Asian. The good news is that if you can master saving face, living with your in-laws will seem like a breeze.

Face Is Everything

Saving face—ensuring that you maintain the highest level of honor, respect, and reputation—is *the* most important thing to understand about Asian cultures. It permeates everything in Asian life, including career, family, food, and even sex. Everything is done to please the collective. (*Star Trek* fans, does this remind you of anyone? Like, maybe, the Borg?)

"Asians are a collective culture," says Hanna. "It's important not to stand out."

Saving face includes acting within social norms at all times, doing nothing that could cause public embarrassment, and suppressing one's own feelings for the good of the group. Often, this results in lots of silence. Instead of disagreeing with a member of the group, either personally or professionally, Asians stay mum. They must also be stoic, as even a disapproving facial expression can cause you and others to lose face.

"It's very opposite of the American ideology of individualism," says Piao. "It doesn't matter what you want; it's all about what *other* people want." He adds, "I can't understand that. I do what I want and say screw everything else." Piao continues, "It's very uncomfortable dating an Asian from that background, because it's like they have multiple personality disorder. They are one person with me and a whole different person with their family. I want to say, 'Who are you, really?'"

"Most Koreans put up a facade in order to be accepted," says Hyo-Sonn. "They have to have nice cars, expensive shoes and handbags. And they *must* send their children to the best schools."

"When my sister had to cancel her wedding," says Bernie, "my parents' first thought was not about my sister, not even about the money really, but what would other people think?"

"That is why I married a Latin woman," says Akira. "I could be myself. I didn't have to worry about saving face."

Saving face elevates what "other people" think to the highest priority, and can limit Asians' choices in many facets of life. "You have to be successful, but the *right kind* of successful," says Mark. "The guy who created *Girls Gone Wild* is a multi-millionaire, but an Asian family would never tolerate that. Loss of face." He adds, "I was a music major. I didn't have to go into finance. I could have been a classical violinist, something high culture, but not counter culture or pop culture."

Being a tell-it-like-it-is person, I guess that neither I nor any Asian within a five-mile radius of me likely has or ever will have any face. And yet, Asians still hang out with me. Clearly, this is one of the more complicated issues for those with Yellow Fever. Like the whole food-and-beverage decorum thing, it's probably best if you have your Asian main squeeze help you get a handle on this issue. But of course, seeing as how Asian culture is so different from American culture on this topic, don't be surprised if it still involves a painful process of trial and error.

Mom and Dad Are Movin' In

In most Asian cultures, it's customary for the parents to live with the oldest son when they become elderly. This is considered the son's responsibility because when a daughter marries, she becomes part of her husband's family. What this means for any woman dating an Asian guy is that if things get serious and he is the oldest or only son, *you* will be the one taking care of Mom and Dad. And you won't just be taking care of them, you will be sharing the same roof.

"That was one of my biggest concerns when things got serious with my Chinese boyfriend," says Becky. "His grandparents lived with his parents, and I knew if we got married, his parents would expect to live with us."

"My mom raised me herself, a single parent. She doesn't expect to move in with me, but I do feel responsible for her," says Piao.

"The best-case scenario is that I have a really big house with a separate guest house *way* in the back and she could live there. But it would be separate from my house, you understand. Separate."

"I'm in arrested development; that's no secret. But if I ever become mature enough to have my own family for my parents to move in with, that would be a possibility," says Mark. "But my younger brother feels equally responsible for our parents." He adds, "As it concerns Asian in-laws, people need to know they will be very *involved*. That is the best euphemism I can think of."

So watch out: Grandma might be movin' in. On the plus side, she is probably a great cook.

What's Hot?

While it may seem like there is a lot about dating an Asian man that is different from dating within the broader American culture, sometimes different ain't half bad. In fact, as Martha Stewart would say, "It's a good thing." An old-fashioned courting process and your hard-workin' man generously picking up the tab are just a few things to look forward to when dating Asians.

They Like to Get to Know You

New York City's fast-paced, dog-eat-dog lifestyle extends even to romance—men and women dating, dining, and screwing at a breakneck pace. But Asian men like to take their time. Dating an Asian man starts with a "hanging out" period, during which you get to know each other. And there is usually no pressure to have sex right away.

"In my case, that really applies," says Akira. "But guys are guys so it's probably not like that with everyone."

"Asian guys do take time to get to know you. I am like that in general. Uh, unless I am drunk," says Bernie with a laugh.

"I think Asian guys are just more realistic," says Piao. "It's not that we don't want sex, but we just don't expect it. If it happens, that's great. But just going out with a girl is already great."

"Asian guys take it slow," says Hanna. "You know a Chinese guy really likes you when he holds your hand."

Aw, how sweet. Sex after the third date with a virtual stranger is the norm where I live. But I—and most of the women I spoke with—really appreciate a longer courting process. Score one for Asian guys!

Picking Up the Tab Is Never a Question

With most men, your experiences with the check can vary widely. Guys might a) split the check, b) pay (but do so begrudgingly), c) expect some reciprocal "payment," or my personal favorite, d) "accidentally" forget their wallet. That would never happen with an Asian man. With them, you don't have to give it a second thought; it is simply understood that he will pay, and there is no *quid pro quo* required. And it's not just dinner, by the way. In general, Asian men and their families are very generous with their money.

"I remember when I went out with my first white boyfriend," says Hanna. "I ordered the lobster, the most expensive thing on the menu." She continues, "He told me later that he almost didn't ask me out again because of it. I didn't even think about that. Asian guys always order the most expensive thing! I didn't know that you weren't supposed to do that."

"I would agree," says Bernie. "Never Dutch. I always pay for dates."

"Asian women have trained Asian guys well," says Piao. "American girls will offer to split it sometimes, but never Asian girls. And if you even *mention* splitting the check with an Asian girl, you are an automatic douche. It's unthinkable. You are done."

"With Asian men, they get insulted if you even offer to pay, no matter how much," says Ranisha. "I am a very independent woman, so I am used to paying my own way—but not with my Chinese boyfriend. One time, we were in the grocery store and he got really mad at me because I wouldn't let him pay for my tampons. My tampons! That was just too much."

Takin' What I'm Given Cause I'm Workin' for a Livin'

Probably in part because of the whole saving face thing, Asian men have a well-earned reputation for being hard working. Indeed, Asian men are very dedicated to establishing a solid career and having the means to care for their families.

"I think in general Japanese do work harder than most other people," says Akira. "But that is not really true in my business. In finance, everybody has to work their butt off just to survive."

"Yeah, my boyfriend's family was very hard working. They didn't do anything half-assed," says Becky. "My boyfriend would always say to me, 'If you are going to do something, do it right. You don't want to have to do it over again.'"

"It comes from all that 'your job is your identity' stuff," says Piao. "You have to have a good job, so you have to work hard. By the American definition, all Asians are probably workaholics."

"In the Japanese culture, work is very highly valued, sometimes above all other things—even life itself," says Ellen. "They even have a word for it: *karoshi*, or death from overwork."

Most women agree: Being career oriented is definitely hot—within reasonable limits, of course.

What's Not?

What's the good without the bad, right? People talk about Latinos being macho, but they're not the only ones; the truth is, Asian men display their fair share of that trait. Picking up the check, macho good; an expectation of traditional gender roles, macho not so good. And don't think that our old friend saving face doesn't rear its ugly head here in the form of a smidge of keeping up with the Joneses, followed by a dash of passive-aggressive behavior, and dollop of intimacy issues.

Keeping Up with the Changs

In Asian cultures, it is important to keep up with the Joneses—or, in this case, the Changs. As such, most Asians are very label and brand conscious. Some Asians insist that buying nice things is considered an "investment," but most admit it's more for bragging rights or status.

"*So* materialistic. Men and women," says Hyo-Sonn. "And Koreans make the best shit. Only Koreans care so much about material things that they have a whole industry dedicated to high-quality knock offs." She adds, "And if you have a Ferragamo purse, you *have* to have the matching shoes or you can't go out for coffee with your friends. You can't get respect at coffee if you don't have the matching shoes!"

"That has been very true in the past, but I think the collapse of the economy in Japan and in the U.S. is changing people's behavior," says Akira. "It's still a problem, but less than it used to be."

"I am more about what looks good than the brand," says Piao. "But most Asians are very materialistic. My cousin in China bought this platinum cell phone for $6,000. It's expensive—not because of the phone, but the special services that come with it. I told my cousin, 'Why did you spend all that money when you can't even get the services in China?' He said he *had to* because it was such a status symbol."

So if you're a hippie-dippy granola who's more worried about your carbon footprint than your dress designer, if you can't tell the difference between Crocs and Christian Louboutin, or if you think Jimmy Choo is a Chinese dignitary, dating an Asian man may not be for you.

Feminism Is Greek to Most Asians

The stereotype is that Asian women are submissive, and that Asian men like submissive women. I guess one out of two ain't bad. The fact is, Asian women—especially where I live—tend not to fit into this stereotype. And while Asian men may understand that Westernized women are less likely to be submissive, they may still experience a steep learning curve when dating one.

"I dated Asian men, and I also lived in Japan for several years," says Ellen. "When I was over there I noticed that I was becoming a militant feminist. That is not me *at all*, but I was just reacting to them. They have *no* respect for women. It's all about the man."

"Japanese men are predominately known for being assholes," says Akira. "There is a saying in Japan that a man only wants three things when he gets home: one, a bath" (and no, he doesn't mean a romantic candle-lit bath together), "two, a meal" (which you, the wife, cook), "and three, bed" (and no, he doesn't mean sex; he means sleep). He continues, "I am very liberal; I do the laundry. My wife says I am better than most Brazilian men." Congrats, Akira—but that is a pretty low bar.

"That is one of the benefits of Communism. All our mothers worked, so Chinese men are not put off by girls who work," says Piao. "They are not like Korean and Japanese, afraid of strong women. Personally, I think men and women are equal. A girl can do anything I can do. That is my philosophy."

"In general, my wife thought I was fair with gender roles," says Bernie. "But every once in a while I would sort of take charge, strictly for the sake of being expeditious. And my wife would say, 'Excuse me I am not Asian. I am not walking 20 paces behind you. You are in America!'"

"I think it's generally true, but obviously not 100 percent," says Mark. Of course not, Mark. You would never!

For most women, this may be a big problem. But if your Asian man is a second- or third-generation American, has done a lot of dating in the U.S., or has done a lot of interracial dating, don't count him out. It could be less of an issue.

Passive Aggressive

Often, Asians will not confront issues head on. Instead, they will be very passive aggressive.

Tim, 51, white guy, hedge fund manager, spent 20 years and two marriages in Japan. "Often, if the Japanese don't feel comfortable talking to you directly, they will go around you and talk to your friends instead."

"Yes, that's a problem," admits Hanna. "We all do it. Asian women do it too. We all try to avoid confrontation."

"They are non-confrontational," says Piao. "When they are not in a position of power, they feel uncomfortable." He adds, "We are in our 30s and my friends still ask me, 'Can you go tell that girl that I like her?' My standard answer is, 'If I go talk to that girl, she will like me instead.' To which they usually say, 'Okay, I'll ask someone else' instead of the obvious, 'Maybe I will just go talk to her myself.'"

Dealing with a passive-aggressive man can be extremely aggravating—something to which Ranisha can attest. "He was not good at communicating," says Ranisha of her Chinese boyfriend. "If something was wrong, instead of just telling me, he would huff and puff and slam dishes around. Finally, I just had to curse him out. If there is something wrong, you need to say it. 'Stop acting like a little bitch!'"

"My wife says I am passive aggressive, and all my ex-girlfriends say I am, so I guess I am," says Akira. "My wife recently reminded me of this time when she lost a watch. For years after that, when I would buy something for her, I would say, 'Remember the watch? Maybe I should buy two just in case....'"

Honest communication in relationships is difficult under the best of circumstances, and having unresolved issues can be a serious source of tension. I don't have to tell you that how you handle conflict has to be compatible; otherwise, that relationship is likely to be short lived. So if you like to huff and puff to answer "Nothing" when asked "What's wrong?" then an Asian man may be great for you. If not, keep it movin'.

Intimacy Can Take Longer to Build Than the Great Wall

Building intimacy with an Asian man can be difficult. Of course, you're probably thinking, "Building intimacy with *any* man is difficult." Touché. But with Asian men, the women I interviewed said it can be even harder. It seems that these intimacy issues go to the very core of how many Asian men are raised.

"We are educated not to show emotion, not to cry," says Akira. "In Japan, if you cry, they say you are a woman." (Just to be clear: In Japan, that is an insult.) Akira continues, "I think my wife and I are close, but she says sometimes yes and sometimes no." He adds, "It's true I don't express myself. I keep my feelings in. It's an Asian tendency."

"I dated this Asian businessman. You know the kind: right off the boat," says Alicia. "I think he really liked me, but there was such an emotional barrier between us. We dated several months, and all I kept thinking was, 'Is this it? Is this as far as we could go?'" She adds, "Actually, I had found the same problem even with Americanized Asian guys. Even if they are second generation, if their father was cold and closed off, they usually are too."

"I look at my parents; they were not intimate," says Piao. "When my friends talk to their wives, there is no tenderness. It's more like they are talking to a subordinate." He continues, "For me, I think it's just that I have commitment issues. I *can* be intimate, but then you get attached, and then I feel trapped."

"When you open up, you invariably show vulnerabilities. If you are worried about loss of face it's really hard," says Mark. "It's tough to build up intimacy with me. I am a bit reserved in terms of my nature. That has been my downfall with women in the past. But I am trying to be warmer and open up."

But of course, it's not true for everyone. "I never got that one before," says Bernie.

Between the Sheets

"I think men are universally perverted; it's just that in Japan, we do something about it."

—JOAN SINCLAIR, *PINK BOX*

It's no secret: Asian guys don't have the greatest reputation in the sack. I would like to say my research busted that old stereotype, but if anything, it reinforced it. But not all Asian guys should get a bad rap; I interviewed many Asian men who were very focused on meeting their woman's needs in the bedroom. But those same men were also the first to criticize other Asian men for failing to perform up to par. This section flags lots of things about Asian men that you might expect, but it also highlights a lot—like their issues with Brazilians—that even I found surprising.

Asian Average

Look, I will say it: The prevailing stereotype is that Asian men have small dicks. And people always make it sound so extreme, like they are packing a Vienna sausage or something. But Hanna describes Asian men as "average."

Of course, I have to dig deeper. "So, like, six inches?" I say.

"No, Asian average," says Hanna. "More like five."

The Pros

The professionals say that in general, Asian men are built small, but that in their experience, Japanese and Filipinos are the largest and Chinese and Koreans the smallest. Monique, 50, Cuban, madam, did share a story of an Asian guy that one of her girls encountered, a real outlier: "This Chinese guy was so small, it was crazy. His pubic hair was longer than his dick. I'm serious."

Asian men were surprisingly candid, agreeing that they were on the lower end to slightly below the U.S. average of five to six inches. "Probably true," says Mark. "More likely on the smaller side than larger." He adds, "I know I'm not going to have a career in the adult-film industry, but I also won't be a forward for the Knicks. I wasn't given those genes either."

"I have been in the locker room, I have an idea of where I stack up," says Bernie. "I know I'm slightly below average. I guess like most Asians." He continues, "One time, I was having sex with this white woman, and she kept saying 'Oh you are so big!' And I just kept thinking to myself, 'Why is she saying that?'"

"Personally, I stack up fine," says Piao. "But I have heard many horror stories from my female friends who date Asian guys." He explains, "One of my white friends was dating this Asian guy who she said had a penis the size of a big toe. We used to make fun of her all the time, saying things like 'How's Big Toe doing?' As an Asian man, I think I am allowed to make fun of that."

On the whole, people said Asians were average to slightly-below average.

PDA Is Not OK

Okay, I admit: On more than one occasion, I have been urged by passersby to "get a room." So it could fairly be said that I am certainly not against a little PDA. But among Asians, PDA—that is, public displays of affection—is a big no no.

"At most, my Chinese boyfriend might hold my hand—but usually not," says Ranisha. "Mostly, he would just walk near me and occasionally touch the small of my back to make sure I was still there. People couldn't even tell that we were together."

"My Filipino boyfriend was not into PDA," says Alec. "We couldn't touch or hold hands on the subway." He adds, "We would have to hide behind something to kiss, but I thought that made it kind of exciting."

"In Japan, you rarely ever see someone kiss in public. They hold hands or maybe have their hands on your shoulder, but that is it," says Akira. "Korea is even worse. You aren't supposed to show affection of any kind."

"My Chinese boyfriend wasn't traditional," says Becky. "But when it came to PDA, he would hold hands maybe, but that was it."

Of course, as with everything, there are exceptions. "PDA is okay with me," says Bernie, "but I am a coconut, there is no denying that. If someone grew up with strict Asian parents, I could see PDA being a problem. But once you assimilate, you just don't look at it through that filter anymore."

Brazilians Are Out of the Question

Most Asian guys think your hair "down there" should be one style and one style only: *au natural.*

"I usually have a Brazilian. So when I go to an Asian spa, I make sure to book my appointment far enough in advance so I can make sure to grow it out in time," says Hanna. "If I don't, I will get scathing looks from the other women. For some reason, it freaks them out."

"In China, having sex with a woman with no pubic hair is supposed to give the guy bad luck," says Piao. "Not me, though. I love Brazilians, and nothing bad has happened to me yet."

"When I go to the hot springs in Japan, they stare at me," says Valentina, 30, Brazilian, homemaker. "Even in my gym in the States, Asian women stare." She adds, "Some Asian woman have a lot of hair down there; it's so much, it could be on your head. I'm serious. But I can't do that. It's part of my Brazilian heritage: I need to wax."

"Yes! I usually have a Brazilian, but my Chinese boyfriend asked me to grow it out," says Ranisha. "I tried to accommodate him, but after a while I was just like, look, you are going to have to deal with it."

Some people say it's considered bad luck to shave; others say it's just "not done." One thing is for sure: For most Asians, hair is in, and hairless is out.

Domo Arigato Mr. Roboto

Although Asians score big points for their courting ways, they seem to lose them all and more in the lovemaking arena. This seems counterintuitive; after all, when a man spends time to get to know you, there is usually a greater connection—and a greater connection usually leads to a higher level of intimacy and thus, a better lay. Asian men seem to defy this logic, however. In fact, they have a reputation for being selfish lovers. For Asian guys, "the act" is about them, not about you. The proof is in the pudding—and by "pudding" I mean "orgasms." According to a recent article in *The Guardian*, "In the West, about 90 percent of women have experienced orgasm, but in China the number is only 28 percent."

"If you didn't get yours before it was over, then, well, maybe next time," says Ranisha.

"For Asian men, sex is all about them," says Hanna. "One round doggy style, and he's done. By the time I am getting started, it's over." She adds, "And if you're looking for foreplay, well, all I can say is, it's a good thing Asian men always pick up the tab."

The Pros

The professionals concur. "Most of our clients like warmth, and often get very attached to the girls," says Monique, who runs a particular type of cathouse called a "girlfriend shop," with mostly regulars. "Asian men, unlike other men, never get emotionally attached to the women and are often very cold and robotic. For them, it's just about the release."

Some men disagreed—well, sort of. "It depends on the person," says Akira. "I have an Asian friend that is really into satisfying women." He adds, "I am kind of both. If I am tired, it's about me. Otherwise, it's about her."

"I am a giver," says Piao. "I wouldn't say I succeed all the time, but I will give her a good time. A lot of other Asian guys are not good in the sack, which gives me the advantage."

And then there's our buddy Mark: "Not me. I want to make sure she has a good 'O' one way or another."

Not Cunning Linguists

This brings us to one of the most—if not *the* most—important point: Most Asian men do not lick pussy! Among Asians, the female genitalia is often looked upon as dirty. That means when it comes to oral sex, you can expect to give, but not to receive.

"My friend's husband is traditional Chinese, and she's not even allowed to wash her underwear with her husband's clothes because women are considered unclean," says Hanna. "Trust me: Asian men are *not* licking pussy."

"That is true for a lot of Asian guys. They talk about how they like blow jobs, but they would never lick pussy," says Piao. "I have a friend that only watches old Japanese porn because they edit out the pubic hair. He says he can't look at vaginas because he thinks they are disgusting. It makes no sense to me, but that is how some Asian guys are." (Hey Piao, isn't being disgusted by vaginas pretty much the definition of being gay? Your buddy might want to consider switching teams. I'm just sayin'....)

The Pros

Our professionals agreed. "White men will pay to lick pussy all the time, but Asian men never request it," says Monique. "But of course they like having it done to them."

As always, the more Americanized Asians can be the exception.

"That is not true for me," says Bernie. "My wife and I had a good sex life, and that was part of it."

"I don't know if I am any good at it," says Mark. "You know it makes women happy, so if you get positive feedback, you're more into it. If you get 'the tap' and the manager pulls you out of the game, less so." He adds, "Not really the Asian guy's thing, but I will certainly do it if it pleases my partner." Such a good boy, that Mark.

For many women, this is too tough a pill to swallow (pun intended). So you may choose to take a pass on our brothers from the Far East. Alternatively, you can always adopt Ranisha's approach: "I was going to try to train him."

Our Stories

Having read thus far, you've armed yourself for dating within the Asian community. But what can you expect when you're actually in the trenches? These stories about real-life interracial relationships will show you how the various cultural differences have come into play for actual couples.

They All Look Alike

Becky, a straight-up white girl who was born and raised in Virginia, yearned for a life in the Big City. Although her parents were a bit leery, Becky was determined; the day after graduation, she set out for a new life in New York City. It was there that Becky, while in her second year of undergrad at Columbia, met Grant. At 27, already boasting a full-time career with the EPA, Grant was Becky's "older man." After a series of childish high-school boyfriends, Becky was thrilled to finally be dating someone "mature."

Grant was a contradiction wrapped up in an enigma and served with a side of red-hot chili sauce. He was of Chinese heritage, but he was born and bred in Brooklyn's Bensonhurst neighborhood, known for its Italian roots. Although Grant was brought up in a conventional Chinese family that practiced traditional Chinese customs, all of his friends were guidos from the block (also acceptable: guineas, goombahs, and mooks). Not surprisingly, it was these guys, not his parents, that Grant emulated. The rare Chinese guido—yes, they do exist. While Grant's parents were very accepting, swallowing with a spoon full of sugar every strange American custom their only son dragged home, some of his friends' ideas still had to stick in their craw. Like Grant's incessant tanning. In China, lighter skin is considered better, more attractive, and more prominent, so Grant's constant visits to the tanning booth with his buds gave his mother heart palpitations. His mom also could not understand his need to shave himself from head to toe in the summer time. Neither did Becky, but she surmised it had something to do with the tanning—or maybe the "gun show," to which Becky was regularly treated following Grant's workouts at the gym.

Becky always felt safe with Grant. The courting period was long; it was several dates before he even held her hand. She never felt rushed about getting physical. And when they did have sex, Grant was a selfless and attentive lover—although oddly, he did require Becky to be fresh out of the shower if she was angling to be on the receiving end for oral sex.

Grant was also always very generous with his time and money; picking up the tab was never a question. Grant represented a welcome change from Becky's first Chinese boyfriend, Lee, who she had met during her senior year of high school. Lee was selfish in bed, packing a thumb, and controlling to such a degree that his behavior bordered on stalking.

For Becky, the fact that Grant was Asian was no big deal. She knew her family—which had always prided itself on being color blind—would be fine with it. But she wasn't sure his traditional Chinese family would be so accepting of her. She was Grant's *first* white girlfriend, after all. Her fears were in no way assuaged the first time she entered Grant's family's home. "We walked into his mother's house, and I had to force myself not to grab my ears to muffle the loud screaming," says Becky. "When we turned the corner, I could see his mother and grandmother. They were yelling so loudly, and talking feverishly with their hands." Where Grant was completely calm, totally unaffected, Becky felt like a lobster near a boiling pot of water. The conversation seemed so angry! She wanted to high-tail it out of there. But when Grant's mother finally noticed Grant and Becky standing there, she switched on a super-friendly Hello Kitty look (yes, I know Hello Kitty is Japanese, not Chinese), nodding her head at Becky as Grant introduced them. Becky found Grant's mother nice enough, even though at times she was hard to understand due to her harsh Mandarin accent. As for Grandma, Becky wasn't so sure. She was a bit more reserved, hanging back in the corner and waving a weak hello.

As Mrs. Chang prepared dinner, Grant and Becky watched TV in the living room. Shaken up by the heated argument she'd witnessed, Becky turned to Grant and whispered, "Is everything okay?"

"What do you mean?" Grant said. "Everything is fine. My mother seemed to really like you!"

Becky was confused. "When we came in, they seemed so angry. I don't mean to pry; I assumed it must be some big family fight."

Becky placed her hand on his shoulder to console him.

"No," Grant laughed. "They were just talking about what we were going to have for dinner." To Becky's Western ear, even planning the evening's menu in Mandarin sounded like World War III.

Becky quickly learned that her fears about not being accepted by Grant's family were unfounded. Grant's parent's had no issue with Becky's race, and welcomed her into their family from the beginning. In fact, they treated her like a queen, always making special Chinese dishes for her when she came to visit. Even after she had been dating Grant for some time, they never let Becky eat leftovers, insisting she always have something freshly cooked. Grant's sister also loved Becky; they often had long talks on subjects ranging from recent news events to Becky's studies in green engineering. Really, the only family member who seemed weird around Becky was Grant's grandmother. In fact, Grandma seemed to have a perma-scowl on her face. Grant assured Becky that the scowl wasn't directed at her; it was just Grandma's general constitution. But it was hard to know for sure; Grandma didn't say much, and when she did, she said it in Mandarin.

The language difference was a big problem all around. Although the Changs had been in the U.S. for more than 30 years, they still knew very little English. "It was just a real barrier to me being able to build a relationship with his family," says Becky, sipping on her Starbucks triple shot, no foam, vanilla, non-fat latte with extra whipped cream. "It was so frustrating sometimes. There was a point when I considered learning Mandarin."

There were a few other things about the Chinese culture that made Becky wake up in a cold sweat. While she liked the fact that Grant was so family oriented—after all, she was too—she felt his family was a bit too close for comfort. For one thing, his whole family—brothers, sisters, aunts, uncles, and cousins—lived within a one-block radius of each other. *One block*. More troubling was the fact that Grant was the oldest son—indeed, the *only* son—meaning that according to Chinese tradition, it was his responsibility to care for his parents as they aged. In fact, his parents would expect to *live* with Grant. As you can imagine, Becky was none too thrilled by the prospect of wiping drool from the chins of both her future children and her future in-laws.

But race or culture was never a big problem for the couple. By far the biggest problem was that Grant was a real man-child. Yes, he *appeared* to be a grown up, with a full-time job and other responsibilities. But at 27, he was still—are you sitting down?—*living with his parents*. To this day, Becky remembers the shock of that discovery. Upon meeting Grant for lunch at Columbia, she had been terribly impressed by the food he pulled out of his sack lunch. "You must be a great cook!" said naïve little Becky. Sadly, she quickly learned that it was not Grant who was the good cook. No, it was Grant's mom, who still packed his lunches for him.

Becky's hopes for a mature, adult relationship with Grant were forever dashed when Grant demonstrated loud and clear his total inability to handle conflict in a relationship. Case in point: the time Grant forgot their anniversary. That day, Grant went out with friends and got totally wasted. He then arrived at Becky's apartment hammered and proceeded to pass out on her bed. Then, when Grant sobered up, he blamed Becky for his lapse, claiming she should have reminded him about their important milestone. Naturally, Becky was *super* pissed. She became even more so when Grant said, "I don't know why you're getting so upset. Is it that time of the month?" And when Grant commenced sulking, Becky became borderline enraged. Realizing there would be no quick ending to this argument, Grant's solution was to call Daddy for a ride home—something Becky could tell he had clearly done before. Talk about passive aggressive!

Although their relationship definitely had its rough patches, most of the time Becky enjoyed being with Grant and his family. And there were a lot of aspects of Grant's culture she really enjoyed. Like Chinese New Year, for instance. For the Chinese, New Year isn't just a few bottles of Champagne, some streamers, and the lowering of a disco ball at midnight. No, the New Year is the biggest celebration of the year—and the celebration often lasts for a week. During this period, Chinese families are very generous, lavishing red envelopes of money on everyone they meet. "That's when I knew I was 'in,' part of the family: when I got the red bags of money at Chinese New Year," says Becky. "His family just makes everything so fun. Big parties, great food, and they are so friendly and generous with everyone."

The Changs' munificence wasn't limited to Chinese New Year. After emigrating from China with a mere $25 between them, the Changs spent 30 years working tirelessly running a dry cleaner and became wealthy as a result. They were always very generous with their money, treating Grant and his friends to lavish dinners and gifts. And of course, they bought the best of everything—they always drove fancy cars like Mercedes, BMWs, and Range Rovers—viewing material items as investments.

One summer, Grant's parents took the whole family—including honorary member Becky—to upstate New York for a real family vacation. After settling into their accommodations, the family met for dinner in the inn's restaurant. It might have looked odd: a huge party of Chinese, plus one little white girl. But to the Changs, Becky's presence had become the norm. Even though Becky was the first white girl their son had brought home, she was treated no differently from any other member of the family—or so she thought. As always at dinner, Becky sat down next to Grant and Grant next to his grandmother. Suddenly, in the middle of dinner, Grant started to laugh. Then he laughed some more. He laughed so hard, he could barely breathe. "What is it?" Becky asked over and over, but Grant was too incapacitated to answer. "Grant!" hissed Becky, growing impatient. "What is it?" Finally, Grant paused to catch his breath. "Grandma just said that you are so much nicer than the other white girl I used to bring around."

Well, I guess all us white people probably do look alike....

As time went on, things between Grant and Becky got very serious. They even considered marriage. But as with most interracial couples, race wasn't the pivotal factor in their final decision to stay together or break apart. "It didn't end up working out in the end," says Becky. "It was really the mama's-boy stuff I couldn't deal with." She explains, "He finally moved out of his parents' house, at almost 30. He thought it would be good for me to stay with him over my summer break so I could save on rent. I think we both also thought of it as a trial marriage of sorts." She continues, "But after two weeks, I was done. He expected me to do all the laundry, make his lunches, make dinner—all the things his mom used to do."

"And you wouldn't do it?" I ask.

"No, worse. I *did*. For two weeks, I was a doting housewife. I was working my ass off to do everything he thought he was *entitled* to. And then one day, I thought to myself, 'Why the hell am I doing this?' I moved out shortly after, and that was the end of that."

Middle East, Far East, Midtown East

Aaron, a Jew, immigrated to New York City as teenager, seeking political asylum from Afghanistan. For the next 20 years, he tried to make his parents happy—especially when it came to dating. Proud of their heritage, Aaron's parents pushed him to marry an Afghan Jewish woman.

When it comes to Afghan Jews in the greater New York City area, the pickings are slim. They comprise less than 0.0001 percent of the population—and most of them are in Queens. But Aaron didn't live out in Queens; he lived right in the heart of the city—midtown, the east 40s. And even when he found the occasional needle in the haystack, the elusive Afghan Jewish woman, things didn't go well. Aaron tells nightmarish tales of being met at the door by Nuremberg-style panels consisting of various members of his potential date's family. There were no warm greetings, no polite small talk—just Aaron on the defensive as he was grilled about his education, career, and finances. Not surprisingly, most of these encounters ended in Aaron making a beeline for the door, often without even meeting the woman in question.

And even when Aaron managed to make it past the panel, he found his prospective partners to be a poor match. Aaron says, "Most Afghan women just want to be housewives." That's a problem given Aaron's position as a work-from-home entrepreneur, less likely to *support* a housewife than to *be* one.

By his late 30s, with nothing happening on the relationship front, Aaron decided to lay down his parents' burden and just look for someone to love. "I think I just grew up," says Aaron. "I stopped trying to please my parents, but also began to understand that I am not going to find that perfect person. There is no such thing. People have their pluses and minuses. You have to decide what's going to be important in the long run, and when you find someone who has those qualities, you just do it." He had mixed results with Internet dating but eventually met a traditional Chinese woman, Brenda, on eHarmony who he thought might be a good fit.

Aaron knew that Brenda was very traditional. And even though he'd never dated a traditional Chinese woman, he had dated a few traditional Afghan women, so he knew enough to know he shouldn't push the sex stuff right away. Aaron's old-fashioned courting style quickly put Brenda at ease. Aaron seemed genuinely interested in getting to know her. Two months into the relationship, when Aaron and Brenda took their first weekend trip together, Aaron even paid for two rooms so Brenda would feel more comfortable. Most guys would expect to be officially sainted for such patience.

But after their trip, the relationship floundered. Aaron began to worry it might not work out. The problem, he later discovered, was he was taking things too slow. They had been dating for nearly three months—*three months*—and he'd made *no* sexual advances. Torture! Of course, part of it was that Aaron had tried to be respectful of Brenda's traditional values. But the main problem was due simply to cultural differences. Aaron just didn't know how to communicate his interest in Brenda in such a way that she would understand. For example, he had kissed Brenda after about a month of dating, but Brenda interpreted that as mild interest at best. For her it came down to one main sticking point. "The kissing was okay," Brenda says, "but it didn't seem like Aaron really liked me because he never held my hand!" For the Chinese, who typically don't engage in PDA, public hand-holding represents a very significant demonstration of interest in Chinese culture.

Although there were some misunderstandings early on, Brenda certainly viewed Aaron as a step up from the Chinese guys she had dated. In fact, Brenda's experiences with her "own kind" were not too different from Aaron's. On one occasion, Brenda's Chinese date brought his sister along (which—watch out, ladies—is not uncommon in Asian communities). Although Brenda's date was quiet, almost mute, his sister didn't hesitate to launch an onslaught of detailed questions—part Maoist inquisition, part *Housewife Jeopardy* ("I'll take 'Cleaning the Oven' for $500, Alex.")—about Brenda's domestic capabilities. "Can you cook?" "What dishes and how well?" "When you clean, do you get on your hands and knees in the kitchen, or just mop?" "For hardwood floors: Pine Sol or Murphy's Oil Soap?" And finally, lowering her voice and giving Brenda a conspiratorial wink, as if sharing the secret to winning her brother's heart, she declared, "Just so you know, my brother doesn't like too much starch in his collars." She then shifted her gaze downward to ensure that Brenda had the requisite child-bearing hips. What made this all the more ridiculous was that Brenda is a highly educated career woman who makes some serious coin as a surgeon in a top medical center in the city. She is the consummate hard-working Asian, often working more than twelve hours a day. In a city recognized for its culinary offerings and excellent maid services, Brenda's cooking and cleaning skills are about as relevant to her ability to be a good wife as her aptitude for mahjong.

In keeping with Chinese tradition, Brenda had had only a few lovers before Aaron, all of whom were Chinese. None of them were particularly loving or affectionate—more like cold and selfish.

Brenda, naturally, had found sex with these men to be quite unsatisfying—but because Chinese culture does not permit women to talk about sex, make sexual requests, or initiate sex, there wasn't much Brenda could really do about it. So when Brenda and Aaron finally slept together, Brenda was pleasantly surprised that what they say about Jewish men being good, attentive lovers was true. But there was one surprise that was even more pleasant than the others: Aaron's willingness to "go downtown"—something none of her traditional Chinese lovers were willing to do. In fact, she liked it so much she gathered up the courage to discuss it with Aaron.

"So," said Brenda. "You know that thing that you did last night?"

"What thing?" said Aaron, feigning cluelessness.

"You know...." Brenda waved her hand below her waist.

"Yeah, I know," Aaron smiled.

"Well I was thinking..." Brenda paused, nervous about discussing such a taboo subject. "I think we should do that every day."

Aaron laughed, choking on his morning coffee. "I don't know about *every* day."

Brenda paused again before commencing with the negotiation. "What about every *other* day? I think we could do that *at least* every other day."

"Why don't we just see how it goes?" said Aaron pulling her toward him and giving her a big kiss.

Brenda and Aaron's relationship was a bit of a perfect storm. Brenda found Aaron to be delightfully different from the men she had dated in the past: independent, thoughtful, and affectionate. And unlike most of the Afghan women Aaron had dated, Brenda didn't mind the fact that he didn't have a "real job." And she was in no way interested in becoming a full-time housewife. Not that they didn't have differences, too—there were many. Brenda ate meat; Aaron was a vegetarian. Aaron ate all types of food—Mexican, Italian, Afghan—Brenda ate only Chinese.

Aaron loved cats (particularly *his* cat, Cuddles); Brenda was afraid of animals. But they found that what they lacked due to their differences, they made up for in chemistry. With both Brenda and Aaron staring down 40 and ready to settle down, things just began to fall into place.

For Aaron and Brenda, the family stuff also worked out much better than expected. When Aaron, then age 40, brought Brenda home to meet his parents, they didn't voice a single objection—even though Brenda was clearly neither Afghan nor Jewish. "I think they were just so happy that I was getting married at 40," says Aaron, scratching the modest remains of what was once a great head of hair. "They genuinely didn't care anymore."

Six months into their relationship, Aaron traveled with Brenda to Hong Kong to formally ask for her hand in marriage. Brenda's parents welcomed Aaron from the start; his race was never an issue. They did have significant concerns about Aaron's lack of a "real job," but with Brenda well past 30—the age at which most unmarried Chinese women are officially declared old maids—Brenda's parents felt it was prudent to overlook them.

The trip seemed to be going perfectly—well, until the Extra Pillows incident. See, in China, even in the finest hotels, prostitutes are readily available—a sort of turn-down service, but instead of a mint on your pillow, you get a hooker. (Sweet!) One evening, Brenda left their hotel room to run an errand and in her haste forgot to give Aaron these oh-so-important instructions: "If they ask you if you want extra pillows, say no!" Fortunately, Brenda returned before the unintentionally ordered "entertainment" arrived. She wasn't angry, of course; she just laughed. You have to watch your *gwai lo*—the Cantonese equivalent of *gringo*—closely when you are in your homeland!

Brenda and Aaron married shortly after their return from China, and Brenda soon became pregnant. And that is when their trouble began. Although Brenda was not a cat person, she had tolerated Aaron's cat Cuddles when they moved in together. But now, all Brenda could think about was the old Chinese superstition that cats can suck out a baby's breath, killing it in its sleep. That naturally meant Cuddles had to go. "Of *course* you have to get rid of it!" she cried, her voice rising an octave. "We are having a baby!" The problem was, Aaron loved—nay, *worshiped*—Cuddles as though he himself were born Egyptian, not Afghan, and Cuddles was the Egyptian cat goddess Bastet. Chinese superstition or no, he couldn't possibly give Cuddles up. As Brenda's due date drew near, Aaron's anxiety spiked. He wasn't really worried about becoming a new father or even particularly apprehensive about the fact that, according to Chinese tradition, Brenda's parents' would be staying in the newlyweds' 1,200 square foot apartment for *six months* after the baby's birth. No, Aaron's concern was for his beloved Cuddles. What if his in-laws slipped something in the cat's food? The Chinese are known for their "special herbs," after all! Aaron had good reason for concern: Afghans have a similar superstition, and shortly after his cousin had her first child, her cat died under "mysterious circumstances." Everyone knew what had really happened: Her parents had whacked the cat. Finally, Aaron hit on a solution: He told Brenda that if anything happened to Cuddles, he would replace her with two cats. It worked. The baby arrived, the in-laws invaded, but Cuddles remained in perfect health.

Shortly after the baby was born, Brenda and Aaron had the whole family over for a visit. It was a diverse group—Brenda's parents, who speak *only* Cantonese; Aaron's parents, who speak mostly Dari; and Aaron's brother, nephews, and nieces, who also speak English. The whole family was talking, laughing, and celebrating this new life. A mélange of languages swirled around them, people from three different countries brought together in this wonderful place that is New York City. As Aaron held his sweet baby in his arms he could not help but marvel over the promising future his child had ahead of him.

Finding Your Japanese Soul

When Ferrell married outside his race, no one was surprised. Ferrell's mom used to say he was color struck—an old-school term for black men like Ferrell who prefer lighter women. Ferrell, who grew up in Brooklyn's East Flatbush neighborhood—a neighborhood that is now predominately black but then was very white—always dated Puerto Rican, Asian, and white girls, but never really dated black girls. As you can imagine, growing up in the Black Power '70s, his tastes were not exactly popular. But by the time he'd brought home several Puerto Rican girls, a Haitian girl, a Burmese girl, a Colombian girl, a Chinese girl, a Korean girl, and finally a Japanese girl, his parents just had to get used to it. "Given the time in history, my family wasn't thrilled," says Ferrell. "But my tastes were pretty well formed, and they gave up on me early on." His friends from the neighborhood even gave him a nickname. "When they saw me, they would always say, 'What's up international lova lova?'" Ferrell says. "My friends started calling me that because, as they said, I was always dating some woman from West Bubble Fuck, on the other side of the planet. Places a lot of my friends had never heard of."

His mom may have called him color struck, but for Ferrell—as for many people who date interracially—it wasn't so much about color as it was about culture. "I was interested in other people's cultures, how other people lived," says Ferrell. "I learned early on that the way to really understand a culture is to date women from that culture."

Ferrell met his wife, Kimiko—then fresh off the boat from Japan—at a club in New York City. Kimiko and Ferrell were inseparable from the start. They got along well, and the sex was great—even if she had a few, er, idiosyncrasies. "When Japanese women get done having sex, they quickly get up and get some tissues, wiping themselves down first, and then the man," explains Ferrell, flashing a cocky smile. "But the funniest thing wasn't even the cleaning; it was the fact that they also thank you for the dick when you are done. To which I say, 'You are so welcome.'" Now I understand why so many men get the Yellow Fever!

After a couple years together, Ferrell and Kimiko were ready to take the next logical step: getting married. Beforehand, however, Ferrell would need to travel to Japan to meet Kimiko's family. Ferrell was wary. "I wasn't sure how her parents were going to take me," he says. Japanese society is very patriarchal; once a woman gets married, she is no longer considered part of her family, but rather part of her husband's. Ferrell wasn't sure how Kimiko's family would feel about "giving her away" to a black man. In fact, Ferrell had once dated another Asian woman who was disowned by her family for dating him, solely because he was black. Adding to his anxiety was the fact that Kimiko's family held a prominent place in Japanese society; her father had even received awards from the Emperor. To Ferrell, that meant they would have very high expectations for Kimiko's potential husband as it concerned his finances and occupation. Also, they would likely be concerned about keeping up appearances, or saving face, which might also kill his chances. "The fact that I was financially successful was the key to my acceptance," says Ferrell. "My father-in-law knew I could take care of his daughter." He adds, "It didn't hurt that I was working in the New York branch of a large Japanese investment bank so I understood a lot about the culture too."

But even working at a Japanese bank couldn't adequately prepare Ferrell for his first visit to Japan. "When we arrived," he says, "we were greeted by the whole extended family. There were all these little Japanese kids—Kimiko's cousins, nieces, and nephews—they all wanted to touch my dreadlocks." He scratches his now nearly bald head. "All the kids were sort of swarming around me touching me. At first I thought, 'This is racist!' And then I realized that it was just that they were curious because I was different. In fact," he adds, "I never felt any racism from her family. They treated me like their own right from the beginning."

Not that there wasn't some culture clash. First, there were the gifts. When Ferrell and Kimiko arrived, they were showered with gifts. Ferrell thought that was great—until he found out that in Japan, for every gift you receive, you must reciprocate with another gift. To Ferrell, all this gift giving and receiving seemed like a cycle that would never end. He found himself spending lots of time and money buying gifts purely for the sake of more gifts.

And then there was the tea. A few days after they arrived, an authentic Japanese tea ceremony was held in Ferrell's honor. The ceremony is a big deal in Japan, so he was excited to participate even if he didn't exactly know what he was doing. As you can imagine, participating in such an event can be a bit stressful in a place like Japan, where there is a "right way" to do everything. "Kimiko's 80-year-old grandma performed the tea ceremony for me," recalls Ferrell. "It was a big production. Everybody got served in a hierarchy—it's roughly oldest to youngest, but it's more complicated than that. And you have to bow a lot and drink a certain number of sips of tea." Ferrell demonstrates with his glass of merlot. "It is important that the family elders are respected at all times and that everything is done just right. I think I did okay, but I'm not sure they would tell me if I didn't." (Yeah, they wouldn't.)

Of course, there was the food. When Ferrell's future mother-in-law promised Ferrell a visit to a really good, classic, Japanese restaurant, Ferrell—a big fan of sushi back home in New York—was thrilled. But this place was more than Ferrell could handle. "I didn't know what most of that shit was," recalls Ferrell. "Even the vegetables were unrecognizable." He continues, "And it didn't taste good. I had to go old school, like when I was a kid. When they weren't looking, I would push the stuff onto Kimiko's plate." And all of it was raw—some way too raw. "They brought out this little snake-like eel fish," says Ferrell. "It was *still alive*. They eat it alive!" He adds, "It was hard for me to be polite with that one. There was no fucking way I was eating that."

And then there were the shoes. Ferrell had several Japanese colleagues, so he was prepared for the whole "no shoes in the house" thing. He would just wear special house slippers, no problem. But what he wasn't prepared for were the bathroom slippers. "I got in big trouble because of the bathroom slippers," says Ferrell. "You are supposed to take your house slippers off and leave them outside the bathroom. Then you are supposed to put on these nasty bathroom slippers that everyone in the house is supposed to wear. That can't be good for hygiene, right?" Ferrell shakes his head. "Well, I didn't know that. So I got in trouble for wearing my house slippers in the bathroom."

Oh, and don't forget the bath. The Japanese take pride in being a *very* clean society, so it is totally normal to do "clean things" together. So as part of Ferrell's visit, it was completely natural for his future father-in-law, Mr. Yamaguchi, to ask Ferrell to take a bath with him. At first, Ferrell tried to keep it cool, whispering to his wife in English that "In America, no matter who you are, no matter what the situation, one man does not ask another man to go in the tub with him." But he wasn't in America; he was in Japan. And in Japan, being asked to bathe with someone is considered a great honor as the Japanese believe that when you bathe with someone, you gain a closeness with them. To Ferrell's credit, he put away his provincial American attitudes and did it. He took a bath with his prospective father-in-law at a totally nude—not to mention co-ed—hot-spring spa. "Everywhere else, the Japanese seemed to be so shy," says Ferrell. "But the bathing was done totally out in the open." Mr. Yamaguchi's strategy worked; he and Ferrell did become quite close on that trip. "He doesn't speak much English and I don't speak much Japanese," says Ferrell. "But when we drink, he speaks a little more English and I speak a whole lot more Japanese."

Apart from the family nudity and the still-living food, there was a lot about Japanese culture that Ferrell found to be positive. "There are no moral absolutes," says Ferrell. "For example, there is no pressure to be a virgin before you're married. They could give a crap about that." Ferrell leans forward and lowers his voice. "They don't have any problems with masturbation; they don't tell kids it will make their palms hairy or anything. And they are very open about sexuality." That's an understatement; on that first trip to Japan, Ferrell was shocked when Mrs. Yamaguchi pointed out the local porn theater as a point of interest during his tour of their town. "Well Ferrell, there's the bakery, up the street is town hall, and on your left, there is our local porno theater." Ferrell sat stiff, too stunned to formulate an answer. What was he supposed to say to that anyway? "Great! Let's all take in a movie later!" "Yeah, it was so cute," Mrs. Yamaguchi continued. "I was taking little Hiroshi, my four-year-old nephew, shopping and we walked by here last week. He looked up at me and then at the movie poster—you see the one, with the woman with the big breasts?" Ferrell nodded mutely. "Well, he turned to me and he said, 'I used to suck on those when I was little.' It was so adorable," she chortled. Ferrell squeezed out an uncomfortable laugh. He was totally floored by Mrs. Yamaguchi's frankness and ease when discussing that subject.

When Ferrell and Kimiko got married, they had two ceremonies —one in Japan and one in the U.S. In Japan, Ferrell surprised Kimiko's family by making his wedding speech in Japanese. They were more than pleased; they were amazed, noting that Ferrell's speech sounded like it came straight from the mouth of a Japanese-born man. Kimiko's uncle shed some light as to why. He said that Ferrell had a Japanese soul, and that he was most likely a samurai in a previous life. As for this life, Ferrell was simply a happy man.

Jungle Fever

"Once you go Black, you never go back."

—African-American Proverb

I was born a poor black child—no, wait, that was Navin Johnson in *The Jerk*. Actually, I was born a poor *white* child. My father hates it when I say we were poor white trash, but as my mother now admits, we spent way too much time in trailers and homes with outhouses or no electricity to be called anything else. When I was three years old, my family lived in Jordan Valley, Idaho, a frozen, Siberia-like territory located in the middle of nowhere (or, as my father who was still living with us at the time—called it, Bum-Fuck Egypt). As you might imagine, I was very isolated in my early years. I saw very few strangers in Jordan Valley—and of course, *no* black men.

I know this will be painful for the millennium generation to comprehend, but we had no television. Instead, for entertainment, my mother played the banjo (Just kidding. We were country, but not *that* country.) Actually, when we had electricity, we listened to records. My mom liked the Beatles; my father preferred the Rolling Stones. But they both liked Bill Cosby. Back then, a decade before *The Cosby Show*, Bill Cosby was bigger than Jesus —a comic star of epic proportions.

That summer, my mother took me to visit my grandmother. Grandma lived in the "big city"—Martinez, California. Martinez boasted one strip mall, a movie theater, and a grocery store; compared to Jordan Valley, it was a veritable metropolis. One morning, my mother, grandmother, and I took a day trip to nearby San Francisco to visit a few museums and grab a bite.

Important to note here is that I was not born with an inside voice. Unlike most people, my voice has only one setting, outside-at-a-fireworks-display loud. My mother has tried through the years to help me to establish that elusive inside voice, but alas, it has been for naught. This well-known characteristic of mine was particularly alarming to my mother on this day.

As we were walking around San Francisco, I spotted a black man. "Mom!" I said. "There goes Bill Cosby!" Then, a few minutes later, I spotted *another* black man. "Mom! Look! It's Bill Cosby!" And then another, and another. ("Wow! I saw Bill Cosby *again*!") To my mother's chagrin, "Bill Cosby" was spotted all over the greater San Francisco Bay area that day.

Since then, of course, I have learned that not all black men are Bill Cosby. In fact, the population we refer to as "black" or "African American" is as diverse within itself as our nation is as a whole. Still, many members of that group share certain cultural similarities. From my own experience and that of many others, I have collected tips to help you navigate obstacles that may arise when you date a black man, as well as share with you the many perks.

Things to Know

When people think about interracial dating, they usually think about black/white dating—especially the *ultimate* taboo, a black man with a white women. Ooooh! Given that this is such a common topic of conversation, you'd think we'd know a lot about how these relationships work, but in reality, most people don't seem to have a clue. People still talk about black men dating white women purely for status, but that couldn't be further from the truth. And as for those hordes of angry black women? I have yet to see them heading my way. As for the sell-out drama, it's out there, but no one really pays it any mind. So let's downgrade the fear factor and find out what you really need to·know.

If He's with You, He's a Sell-Out

Historically, dating outside his race made a black man an automatic sell-out in the black community—and the lighter or whiter the woman, the more of a sell-out he was. This may have been true in the past, but based on my interviews, this attitude has clearly changed.

Most of the black women I spoke with did not support this notion. "That sell-out stuff is a cop out," says Ranisha, 35, black, PhD candidate. "The old mentality. It may have applied in the '60s, '70s, or even '80s, but now it's just a cop out."

"I don't think that sell-out stuff is true, but I have been around people who do—even if she is just light skinned, but still in our race," says Corrina, 48, black, call-center supervisor. "We have issues with color." She continues, "I thought that way when I was younger, but not anymore. People need to be with someone that makes them happy. Black women are just getting tired. We are starting to look beyond that too and date who we want to date. Do our own thing."

Black men don't support this stereotype either. "I know some people still think that way, but I came to the realization when I was a lot younger that I couldn't just put myself in that box," says Lawrence, 35, black, technology expert. "Life is too short. I am not going to weed out mates on the basis of race."

"I have never felt pressure that I am a sell-out," says Calvin, 30, black, actor. "I've gotten a dirty look maybe, but no one ever said anything to me. Society tells you to do a lot of things. At the end of the day, it's a personal decision about your own happiness."

"I was very conscious of that sell-out stuff when I first started dating my Italian girlfriend," says Mike, 37, black, personal trainer. "My brother was already dating a white woman, and I didn't want my cousins to see all the men in our family dating white women." He continues, "But I loved her, so after a while, I just had to get over it."

I can only find one word to describe this sell-out business: tiresome. Your background, race, and culture are part of you, regardless of who you date—and dating outside your culture does not make you any less faithful to or supportive of your culture. While things have changed for the better, this attitude has not completely disappeared. There isn't much you can do about it except be aware that it could come up and be supportive of your man if his friends or family give him the sell-out bullshit.

Debunking the White Woman Status Myth

The stereotype is that black men date white women not for love, but for status. In most cases, that is simply not true. The black men I dated were with me because they thought I was pretty, smart, fun, interesting, sexy, and they wanted to get into my pants—the same reasons a man dates *any* woman.

"I don't think it's really status," says Ranisha. "I think it's more because they find other races exotic." She adds, "Men are always interested in something different."

Lawrence has a different take. "I think that's much more generational. In my parents' generation, the Baby Boomers, if you had a white woman on your arm, it *was* a demonstration of your success." He adds, "For our generation, that's more of a load of crap."

And Mike, he just needs a vacation. "Dating white women was never for status for me," says Mike. "It was for a vacation—to get away from the neighborhood drama." He explains: "Sisters call you on your shit. I want a vacation, so I date a white woman. A white woman from Utah, Wyoming, or someplace will giggle and say, 'Oh, you New York guys are *so* crazy!' While a sister will say, 'Why you acting crazy? Put that away!'"

If concern about being someone's trophy has put you off black guys, I say game on! In most cases, they are no more likely to see you that way than any other man.

The Angry Black Woman

People continue to perpetuate the idea that if you date a black man, you will suddenly find yourself being pursued by hordes of bitter, angry, black women carrying torches and pitchforks, screaming, "You are stealing all the good black men!"

Yes, it's true that some of the people I interviewed did tell stories of scathing looks from black women and even the occasional comment. "I am light skinned, and I have been told that I am not 'black enough' to date black guys," says Caitlin, 30, black, physical therapist. "In high school, this woman, Tamara, even called me out to the parking lot after school and told me she would beat me up if I dated any of the black guys in school."

So yes, you may find the occasional small-minded black woman out there, just as you'll likely find small-minded women of any race. But to me, this description of black women is a pathetic caricature of what I know to be a vibrant, tolerant, thoughtful group. Most black women I encountered had no objections to my relationships with black men; in fact, they were often the ones who made the introductions.

"I know it's still out there," says Zahara, 29, black, nurse. "They think the white girl has something they want. But they are looking in the wrong place, looking outside instead of inside. They are too consumed with what others are doing instead of trying to fix what is wrong with themselves."

"It is out there," says Ranisha. "But no one said you have to love one type of person. It's a big load of crap to me. No one has a lock on anyone, no matter their race."

If concerns about angry black women have kept you from dating that cute brother at the office, stop your fretting. You're more likely to slip and die in the bathtub than be mobbed and run out of town by this dying breed. It's completely worth the risk.

So You Don't Fuck Up!

Some of the stuff in this section might seem a bit obvious, like greeting family members with respect. Others rely more on nuance, like watching your Street (translation: Don't act like a gangster rapper hoodlum around your man's family) and not quoting your "black friends"—and please, no Al Sharpton (translation: Treat black people like you would anyone else). Once you have gained respect in the black community, jokes about anything, including black culture, are welcome. The best advice I can give is to sit back, relax, and take some time and try to really understand the vibe. If you do, you will find that black culture is not as different from the broader American culture as you think.

Expect Old-School Parental Respect

When you meet your black man's family, you need to address them with the highest level of respect—maybe more than you're used to. "I remember when I was in high school, I would go over to my white friends' houses, and they would be calling their parents by their first name or yelling at them. Sometimes they would swear right to their face!" says Lawrence. "I could have *never* done that with my parents."

Caitlin concurs. "I was raised to always address adults as Sir or Ma'am. And my dad always was impressed when a boy took off his hat."

If you want to make a good impression on his family, mind your Ps and Qs, and keep the greetings formal.

Watch Your Street

The number-one pet peeve for most black people is when you start trying to act or sound G-H-E-T-T-O. It's okay to say something now and then as a joke—but *if and only if* you really understand the vibe. This is not something you can learn quickly and easily; it has taken me many years to get it down. And even then, you're bound to step in it on occasion.

"I hate that shit," says Ferrell, 44, black, business executive. "If you have been around black culture for a while and you use expressions of that culture and do it naturally, then it really endears you. If you look uncomfortable and are clearly trying to overcompensate, then it's just annoying."

"People tend to bring that stuff out *way* too early," says Lawrence. "It's just like getting to know any other culture. If you're unfamiliar, be quiet and observe. Don't walk in saying 'Yo moms, yo pops, what up?'" He adds, "I remember one of my white friends saying, 'I don't understand why they didn't like me.' I told him, 'You can't walk into someone's house like you are walking on to the set of *What's Happening!!* and expect them to like you.'" Let me say here that I totally agree with Lawrence and also that I love myself some Rerun!

Don't Quote Your "Black Friends"—and Please, No Al Sharpton!

Even today, many people of other cultures believe they can't "relate" to blacks. This can result in them offering up what they think are "black topics of conversation" or bolstering their arguments by quoting their "black friend from the office."

Don't do this! Look, I'm sure your black friend from the office is a straight-up guy. He may even be a genius. But the fact that he is black doesn't make his comments any more valid than yours. He is no oracle of blackness. Referring to him just makes you look stupid.

"I never did anything like that, thank God. But when I was with my black boyfriend, I did feel like I needed to be cooler somehow—tougher," says Rachel, 29, Jew, fashion brand manager. "I definitely would second-guess myself, worried about everything that would come out of my mouth."

"Sometimes you can see there is a real discomfort there as they try to find ways to relate to you," says Lawrence. "You take them out of their comfort zone, and they don't know how to act. I just want to say, 'Wait and see, you will be fine.'"

The fact is, black culture is much more similar to the collective American culture than, say, Latino or Asian culture. So contrary to what you might think, if you are American, "relating" to black people shouldn't be that difficult. Oh, and when "relating," you need not choose discussion topics like what Al Sharpton said on the news last night or slyly mention that it's black history month.

"That 'black topics' thing is not a good idea," says Caitlin. "My cousin hates Obama. I remember, we were sitting in a restaurant in Harlem right after Obama won, and this news crew wanted to get his thoughts on the election. All I was thinking was, 'Trust me, you don't want to do that.'"

Zoe, 50, white girl, technology manager, hits the nail on the head: "That comes from people trying to relate to the race, not the person."

What the Hell Did I Get Myself Into?

If you have no experience with interracial dating, you might think the biggest problem you would face dating a black guy is the "Are you looking at me?" factor—that is, other people making your relationship their bid-ness. In reality, it's not. In fact, I'd argue that's just your own paranoia talking. The *real* problems are what I call "the wall"—i.e., the fact that it can take a lot of time to gain a black man's trust—and "the postcard," which refers to the black man's desire to project a perfect image within his community. As for that last one, all I can say is God help you with that!

Are You Looking at Me?

In over a decade of dating black men in New York City, I can remember only one occurrence of someone saying something to me about race: someone yelling, "He should have married a sister!" from the other side of Central Park. Maybe it was because I dated big guys—6'4" and 250lbs—and no one was stupid enough to say shit to them. But more likely, that kind of thing just isn't as prevalent as people think. More often than not, it comes from us; we perceive people as disapproving when in most cases they couldn't really give a shit about who we are dating. Of course, there are always exceptions....

"That happened to me, and I have never even dated a white guy," says Nia, 36, black, executive assistant. "I was on the train one time with my brother. He was wearing a nice suit, really professional." Nia's brother is half white, half Japanese; Nia is half white, half black. "This black guy on the train started saying all this shit under his breath, 'She has no business being with this fucking white dude, going outside her race!' My brother was cool, telling me to ignore him. But you know I was just waiting. As soon as my brother got off the train, I went off on that guy."

"I know he was sorry he started in on that crap," I say. Nia can throw down with the best of them.

"He was sorry alright. I told him, 'Who I date is none of your business. And you were so focused on skin color that you never once looked at our faces. If you had, you would have noticed that we look exactly alike. That man was my brother. And whomever I date—Puerto Rican, black, white, anyone—it won't be a classless brother like you.' Man, when I was finished with him he was all cowering in the corner. He couldn't even look at me. I was so loud, everybody was listening. And when I finished, they clapped for me on the train."

"It's not often, but if someone does stare at me and my black boyfriend, it's usually white guys," says Tatiana, 34, white girl, health-care administrator.

"It doesn't happen much, but I do remember one time when I was on the train with my wife and some black guy said something about us like, 'Why is that brother with a chink?'" says Ferrell. "My wife wasn't as upset about them harassing us for being an interracial couple as much as pissed off because they called her Chinese when she is really Japanese."

"My friend, a white girl, got a lot of stares when dating her black boyfriend. I said, 'Just ignore them. Better yet, hug him a little tighter so they can look more,'" says Dominique, 39, black, nurse.

I've heard stories about people asking a woman dating a brother, "Is it true?" (Translation: Do black men really all have huge dicks?) And I've heard a couple stories about black men being called sell-outs or feeling the stares. Don't let this be a deal breaker. It doesn't happen as often as you'd think. Besides, if you're with a man who loves you, who cares what anyone else thinks?

Another Brick in the Wall

The '80s saw the rise of the phrase, "It's a black thing; you wouldn't understand." Obviously, it's a divisive expression. But I also think it demonstrates what I call "the wall"—and if you're dating a black guy, you should expect to run into it more than once.

When I started dating black men, it seemed like I was trying to join a club where no one wanted me as a member. No matter what I did, I still felt like I was on the outside looking in. The fact is, many blacks have a significant level of distrust of others, especially "whitey"—and for good reason. Centuries of white people enslaving, unjustly imprisoning, and killing blacks are not easily forgotten. And each injustice becomes just another brick fortifying "the wall."

"I felt that very much with my black boyfriend's grandmother," says Mary, 33, white girl, nurse. "I felt I really had to prove that I was good for him, serious with him."

"Yes. It's because you get guys like that guy in Louisiana. Smiles to your face, lets you use his bathroom, and then won't give you a marriage license," says Calvin. "Sometimes, people are considered racist until proven innocent, sure. But once you earn that trust from black people, they will have your back forever." (This has been true in my experience.)

"100 percent yes," says Mike. "I think it's the history, sure. We have to trust that you understand what we are talking about for me to call you friend."

Not all black people see it that way. "I am frustrated with the number of blacks looking for something to argue about when it comes to race, always with their guard up," says Caitlin. "Fight the good fight, don't fight the old fight." She adds, "I get that there is still racism. It's sad and disgraceful. But you just need to get over it. If you don't, there is nowhere to go."

Building a solid foundation of trust with black people can take time and real effort on your part. Understand, though, that *you can* eventually gain the trust necessary for a successful relationship. But pack for a long trip, sister, because it ain't going to be easy.

The Postcard

"The postcard" is the term I have come to use for the black man's burden to be "perfect." The demonstration of this perfection is the postcard that he sends out every Christmas. The postcard shows him, of course—the black father, with two or more perfectly smiling children. But what makes it perfect is the black wife.

What does that mean for you? When it comes to marriage, no matter how much he says he loves you, no matter how much he says you are the moon and the stars, he's still likely to crumble under societal pressure—and that means he's less likely to marry you. The pull of the postcard is strong.

"They are very focused on the image of their family and concerned about how their parents or their friends look at them," says Corrina. "There are black men in marriages that are not happy, but they will keep it going to make it seem like they're happy and just do their thing on the side." She adds, "It will catch up with them anyway, so why don't they just get over it? Kids can see what is going on. They see that you are miserable. Isn't it better if they see dad happy with someone else? Just get it over with, get a divorce, and raise your kids."

If he already has children with a black woman, no matter how toxic the relationship is, a black man will try everything to preserve that "perfect" image—even if he and the mother were never married or never even seriously dated. "Where I was really blindsided was by the power of the birth mother in the black community," says Zoe.

It's critical that you understand the pull of the postcard and address it before moving forward into a serious relationship with a black man. How does he handle the pressure of not marrying black? How does he feel about interracial marriage? If anything seems even a bit fishy, bounce.

What's Hot?

When it comes to what's hot about brothers, it's hard to know where to start. There is so much to say! Being more interested in you than your weight (as Sir-Mix-a-Lot said, silicon parts are made for toys), having the sexiest walk out there, and exhibiting old-fashioned chivalry are just a few of the things that are hot about black guys.

Come As You Are

There is a stereotype out there that all black men like fat women. That is simply not true. Physically fit, good-looking black men usually like physically fit good-looking women. That said, they are definitely not as weight sensitive as some other men. My friend Cindy, a tall, thin, beautiful white woman—a perfect size two—dates mostly white guys. And these white guys have told Cindy more than once that her thighs are too big. I mean, how is it even *possible* to squeeze big thighs into size-two jeans? I'm willing to bet you would *never* hear that from a brother. Black men appreciate a woman's body. Women are supposed to have thighs, ass, and breasts, and black men love every inch of them. And they probably won't even notice an extra 10 or 15 pounds. Once, when I was dating this brother, I put on 10 pounds. I was miserable, but he just said, "Love the new you. So bootylicious."

"Yes, they embrace everyone," says Dominique. "They are all about the love. They are all about the embracing. You'll see a buff black guy with a chunky girl. That is one thing that is really good about them: When it comes to the weight, they don't discriminate."

"I don't like skinny women," says Mike. "I find it harder to trust their cooking."

"I think most brothers like their women healthy. Not skinny, not fat, healthy," says Zoe.

"That is absolutely true," says Lawrence. "My wife is white. She still has the baby weight and keeps saying she wants to lose it. But what is so great about being thin? It's weird to me."

"If you date quality black guys, they are going to be more into the person, less into weight," says Calvin. "I have been attracted to a lot of different sizes of women. I am not stuck on one body type. What makes a woman sexy has less to do with the physical and more to do with attitude."

There is also a faction of black men that do like bigger (a.k.a. "thick") women, with lots of T&A and maybe a little extra tummy as well.

"They like it *thick*. I am not talking about *fat*. I am talking about *thick*. Hips and ass," says Nia. "Not straight skinny like you are fucking a boy. Guys who like that are probably really gay anyway."

The bottom line? Black men take you as you are. Good going brothers. Now that's hot!

Can I Have Some Fries with That Shake?

Undeniably, hands down, the hottest thing about the brothers is their walk. The patented black-man swagger breaks hearts all across the USA. It exudes confidence. It's so smooth and unbelievably sexy.

"Yes, that is the first thing I notice, that swag," says Ranisha. "I don't know where it came from, but it's all good. All about attitude and confidence."

"We practice it at home from grammar school on," says Ferrell. "We check in the mirror and make sure we have a cool walk—your hips sticking to one side and your hands swinging. We brothas call it the 'pimp dip.'"

When you pass that cute brother from down the block, don't forget to do the look back; otherwise, you could be missing the best part.

Old-Fashioned Chivalry

The first brother I dated was forever changing sides as we walked on the sidewalk. I had no idea what to make of his behavior. Eventually, I had to ask, "What the hell are you doing?" As it turns out, many black men have been raised to always walk on the street side of the sidewalk—a tradition that dates back to the time when horse carriages would splash mud on ladies' dresses.

"Yeah, I always do that for my wife," says Lawrence. "Even more so for my mother."

"I do think it's cultural," says Mike. "If I do that to a white girlfriend, they're like, 'Mike, what the hell are you doing?'"

Although it can make crossing the street more complicated, I always thought it was very sweet. Good, old-fashioned chivalry. Score another one for the brothers!

A Real Sense of Family

One of the real attractions of black culture is the high importance placed on family. Contrary to what is often portrayed in the media, black people take family very seriously. Family comes first. And families are often very supportive. All levels of family—from parents and siblings to grandparents and distant cousins—are considered part of the family "team."

"Even though you don't have a lot, you always try to help," says Dominique. "That is how it is with us, a black family. Close knit."

"We hold family near and dear," says Corrina. "Your family is who you struggle with, who you make things happen with." She adds, "We really respect the importance of family."

"To me, disintegration of the black family is a myth that is overblown," says Lawrence. "The black family community is very tight."

But don't worry: There is plenty of room for you, too. "You don't even have to be related," says Ferrell. "If you're around long enough, you just become part of the family."

What's Not?

After reading about what's hot about black guys, you're probably raring to take the plunge. But before you run out and find yourself a sexy-walkin' chivalrous hunk of manhood, let's make sure you also know what to watch out for. Wide variations in generosity, game-running, potential flight risk, and—I save the worst for last—the polygamy are all things that women cited in the Not Hot category.

Picking Up the Tab Is Not a Given

My own experience, along with that of other women, is that generosity varies widely among black men. Unlike with men in some other cultures, picking up the tab is not a given when you're dating a brother.

"I can't disagree with that," says Lawrence. "I think that has a lot to do with individual personalities."

"You would think a brother that made decent money would pay all the time, but not always," says Dominique. "I dated this guy once. He would buy nice stuff for himself all the time, but never for me. He didn't even buy me flowers. These black guys can be cheap as shit."

"In my case, my boyfriend always paid," says Rachel.

"I always pick up the tab, with dates of course, but even just with a female friend," says Calvin.

"We are like, 'If you got it, pay for it,'" says Mike. "I will take care of you other ways. I will work overtime. But don't pay and then bring it up among my friends, exaggerating, saying I never pay for anything. When that happens, then it's time to date a white woman. Time to take a vacation."

"He pays most of the time," says Tatiana. "But then he makes snide comments that I owe him, like 'I will put you on payment plan.'"

Watch Out for the Game

No doubt about it, brothers can talk a good game. They can make you feel like you are the most beautiful, sexy, amazing woman in the world. Don't let that fog your mind! As with any man, it's more important what a brother *does* than what he *says*.

"You have to watch out for the game because it is *heavy*," says Ranisha. "They practice that when they are practicing the walk. They get proficient in that young—eight or nine years old."

"Yes, and there is a smoothness in the delivery that you just *can't not* believe," says Caitlin. "It seems too genuine. That is why you put up with so much crap."

"They are smooth talkers," says Tatiana. "At the beginning, all the speeches he was giving me—and then a couple months later, I'm not sure if he even wants commitment, if we will get married, anything."

I know it's hard, but ignore the game. When they say you are beautiful and sexy, you should only hear the teacher in those old Charlie Brown specials: "Wah wah, wah wah wah wah." Hang tough. You don't have time for fairy tales. Show me something or get nothing—that should be your motto!

Flight Risk

If brothers are having a problem with you, are worried about getting too close, want to break up, or just stop feelin' you, they may not say anything. Instead, they may just disappear—often without much warning. You'll think everything's going great, and then all of a sudden, *poof*. To be fair, brothers aren't the only ones who employ this strategy, but it is a favorite among them. And boy, does it get women steamed.

"Yes, yes, yes! They just shut down—don't call, don't say anything," says Dominique. "Don't you respect me enough to say 'I am dealing with issues' or 'I need me time?'" She continues, "The brothers are notorious for that shit. They can't communicate.

They disappear, and then call me two weeks later like nothing happened."

"Yeah, that has happened to me before," says Mary. "It sucks because you never even find out why."

"I am sure someone has accused me of disappearing on them; not returning their calls," says Calvin. "I would never do that with a close friend or girlfriend, but if it's early on, it's not working, and we keep having the same conversation, sometimes I will make the decision and say, 'That's it.'"

As with anyone, it's important for you to make sure your brother-man is good at handling conflict before you let things go too far. You don't want to fall in love and then, *poof*!

The Polygamy

When interviewing Mike, I asked him whether I had left anything out—anything that women who are dating black men should know. "Are you going to talk about the polygamy?" he said.

"What?" I said, feigning confusion.

"About that fact that black men can't seem to stick to one woman," he said.

"I was worried it would be too, uh, inflammatory...."

"I don't see why you shouldn't discuss it," said Mike. "It's out there. Why can't we just have a healthy dialogue about it?"

Mike has a good point. What's more, cheating came up often with the women I interviewed. They also mentioned that even if the brother wasn't cheating per se, he always seemed to have multiple women in the pipeline—a sort of black-man back-up plan.

Mary explains: "My ex-boyfriend cheated. Even when we were exclusive, he was constantly talking to other women, his 'friends' he would say. It was just so easy for him to cheat with all those irons in the fire."

Zahara has an interesting take: "They do that because they are afraid to be alone. That's why they like to keep lingering, keep these woman on the hook."

Nia has this to say: "Yes, they do cheat—and it's not always about looks. When you see the other bitch, she always looks so crazy. My piece-of-shit, scumbag ex-husband? His girlfriend is a dead ringer for Fantasia from *American Idol*. She even has the same fucking haircut. Who in the fuck leaves Mariah Carey for Fantasia?"

Lawrence makes a good point. "I don't buy that at all. I don't think it's black men." He explains, "Some men are good, some men think they'll have their cake and eat it too. It's not a black-ism. Japanese, Italians, Middle Eastern guys all do it. There are dogs in all cultures."

Let me be clear: Not all black men cheat. There are certainly loyal, faithful black men out there. This section is not meant to discourage you from dating a black man as much as to make you aware of the issue.

Between the Sheets

"We will fuck any white girl. As matter a fact, the bigger the better. It's just more white to love."

—CHRIS ROCK

Americans have long been curious about the sexuality of blacks. John Howard Griffin, author of *Black Like Me,* experienced this curiosity first hand when he went undercover as a black man in the Deep South in the late 1950s. In his book, he said that people "all showed a morbid curiosity about the sexual life of the Negro...as an inexhaustible sex-machine with oversized genitals and a vast store of experiences, immensely varied. They appeared to think that the Negro had done all of those 'special' things they themselves have never dared to do."

Inexhaustible sex-machines with oversized equipment? *And* special things? Sign me up! Sadly, however, it's hardly a given. Some black men are incredible, affectionate, passionate, and creative lovers—and yes, some may have large equipment. Others... not so much.

The Equipment Is Not All Supersized

This was the stereotype I had the most displeasure disproving. The women I interviewed overwhelmingly reported that, contrary to the stereotype, not all black men's dicks are huge. In fact, there is a wide and varied distribution, from the dreaded pinky to nine inches of solid steel pipe. On the whole, my ladies testified that black men are in line with the American average of five to six inches.

"My biggest and my smallest were black men," says Zoe. "For the most part, I have found them to be average."

"They are not all packin'. Most brothers I have been with have been pretty much average," says Ebony, 37, black, receptionist. "I was with this Jamaican guy once who was very large, but it wasn't good. It felt like I was getting a hysterectomy. And then there are the guys that are curved at the end like an umbrella. You think you might like it and then you are in pain. A fucking umbrella dick. No good." Ebony, clearly an aficionado, continues: "I have also had the pinky, small and skinny. That brother recently contacted me on Facebook and I thought, 'No way. We don't need to revisit that shit.' Then there is the average length, but skinny like a pencil. It's no good either, like fucking an ice pick."

The Pros

Our professionals agreed. "What they say about black men all having big dicks, it's not true. They are usually fairly average," says Monique, 50, Cuban, madam.

Black men tended to agree as well. "Yes, it's regular sized," says Mike.

Lawrence makes a good point: "That myth is still out there. My wife says I'm above average. But size doesn't always mean much. I have heard plenty about guys that are huge, but terrible in bed. They just think they can phone it in."

You ladies who are thinking about dating a black man in hopes of finding your own personal Mandingo, sorry to disappoint. The vote is in, and average it is.

When It Comes to Sex, Their Focus Is in the Right Place

With respect to carnal talents, brothers run the spectrum. But although not all brothers are great lovers, most are focused on the right thing: the woman. For black men, it's as important—if not more important—for the woman to have an orgasm as it is for them to have one.

"Yeah, they want to do it from behind, side, it don't matter," says Dominique. "Whatever it takes to get it done."

"My ex-husband was so good in bed, he would bring tears to my eyes," says Nia. "You know what I also noticed? If he is Street or doesn't have a job, he tends to be extra great in bed to make up for it."

"Black men feel that if we have not pleased a woman, then we haven't met our responsibility," says Ferrell.

"I have had some very good black lovers," says Zoe. "And there is something about that contrast between the skin tones—the black and the white—that is so hot. So sexy."

"It's a mixed bag," says Ranisha. "The majority of the time, I am satisfied. But there are some slackers up in there."

Zoe is right: That contrast in skin tones is hot. And I agree with Ranisha: You will certainly see the occasional slacker. But on the whole, I think the brothers have their focus in the right place. As such, they generally get pretty high marks in the sack.

Brothers Get Down Downtown

There's an old-school stereotype that black men don't lick pussy. It is absolutely, unequivocally *not true*! Although I have heard stories of some Jamaican men having issues with pleasuring women below the equator, they are very much in the minority. Most brothers not only get down downtown, they do it with zeal.

"Downtown, around town, and across town," says Ferrell. "And if he licks pussy and he says he doesn't lick ass, he is lying. It's only an inch away."

"They act like they don't sometimes, but they can eat some pussy," says Dominique.

"Yeah. Oh yeah. Loved to. Preferred it almost to sex," says Rachel.

"Yes, I think they like it," says Caitlin. "It's like a mission. And if they get 'the tap,' they get very insulted."

And they don't just do it to get it; it's done with gusto, not begrudgingly. They take real pleasure in giving pleasure. Now that's what I'm talking about!

Foot Fetish

Remember the scene in *Boomerang* when, after having just slept with this beautiful sister, Eddie Murphy lifts up the sheets and sees she has jacked-up hammer toes? I always assumed it wasn't the toes so much as he was a playah playah and just looking for an excuse to dump her ass. But no! I have since learned that for black men, good-looking feet are *very* important. In fact, for some brothers, the foot is almost another sexual organ.

"My boyfriend's roommate just grabbed my feet one time and was going on and on, 'Damn girl you have some nice toes!'" says Rachel. "My toes aren't even that great. That's why I always have a pedicure to keep them looking nice."

"I definitely think that how a woman keeps their feet says a lot about how she takes care of herself," says Calvin. "Open-toed shoes with awful hoofs, all torn up, not good." He adds, "Don't know about the foot fetish. Maybe some guys. But for me, it's more to do with the grooming level."

If you're interested in that cute brother from the neighborhood, you'd better get your toes straight. On the plus side, if you have nice feet, getting that brother in your life to rub, fondle, or otherwise pleasure them won't be difficult. In fact, he might even volunteer.

Our Stories

Now you've heard the good, the bad, and the no-ugly-feet policy, you're probably wondering: What is dating black really like? These stories about real interracial relationships show supportive and loving partners as well as some who hung on to the postcard at all costs, how black topics of conversation are never a good thing, and how old-fashioned chivalry can make walking even just a couple blocks a very complicated proposition.

Privileged

There was a knock on the door. "Oh shit," I thought. "It's him." Glancing at the Champagne chilling by the bed, I strode across my Manhattan hotel room to the door, fumbled with the safety latch, and after taking a deep breath, I opened the door wide. "Hi," I said with a too-serious tone but with a smile from ear to ear. Phillip leaned down to kiss me. "Hi," he said softly. He was quiet, looking at me adoringly. "You are so beautiful." I smiled shyly, glancing down at the floor to avoid his eyes. "I am serious," he said. "You are *so* attractive, I don't think anyone will even believe I am really with you—unless they think I'm a rich football player or something."

"Stop being ridiculous," I say, hitting him playfully and then looking back to the ground. I didn't really come into my looks until I was 30—just the year before I met Phillip—so I wasn't used to all this attention. But as Phillip was my first black boyfriend, I also wasn't used to the thick game that the brothers can put on you—and Phillip's was *thick*. He could make me feel like I was the most magnificent woman in the world. Cindy Crawford, Charlize Theron, Heidi Klum—compared to me, they were a trip to the dog pound.

"Really," said Phillip, taking me into his arms. "You are so incredibly gorgeous. And the best part about it, you don't even know it. You are so sweet and kind, not bitchy like other pretty girls."

Phillip and I had been dating for just under a month, but because of our busy schedules and the fact that we lived in different states—he in Arizona and me in New York—this was the first time we had seen each other since we first met. Even so, we were already very much in love—despite having come together under the least romantic of circumstances.

After attending a work seminar in some boring retirement community in Louisiana, some colleagues and I hit the hotel bar to cleanse our minds of PowerPoint presentations and corporate jargon. This was not out of character for me; in my early 30s, I still equated "good times" with copious amounts of adult beverages. I quickly spotted Phillip at the hotel bar. He was cute, charming, outgoing—a classic BBB, as I used to say (big, black, and bald). I had always found black men very attractive, but was too shy to approach them. Phillip and I struck up a conversation.

Fortified with a few adult beverages, my Bravado meter now set to High, I leaned in and uttered those now infamous words: "I can drink you under the table." Born and raised in California, I was raised with a healthy respect—or, more likely, love—for good wine, so my alcohol tolerance was fairly high. However, Phillip—at just under six feet tall and twice my weight, a real beast of a man—could only laugh at my David and Goliath proposition. Tolerance aside, given my size and my lack of good throwing stones, I was no match for Phillip. I quickly fell to Goliath—or, as it turned out, *on* Goliath.

I don't remember much of the ill-conceived drinking contest, but the next day I will never forget. As I opened my eyes, the light hit my cornea like daggers. During a scan of my hotel room, I detected a lawn chair. Not the collapsible kind you take to the beach, but a full-sized, lay-by-the-side-of-the pool chaise—the big, heavy, metal ones that they have at hotels. It probably weighed as much as I did. What the hell was *that* doing in here? Was management planning to install a sunroof? Was there a pool party in the bathtub? After untangling my legs from the sheets, I placed my feet on the floor; the magnitude of my hangover washed over me. It wasn't a headache so much as an all-over body ache. I rose shakily and staggered to the bathroom, where I cranked on the faucet, cupped the running water with my hands, and washed my face. When I reached back to get a towel, I discovered that the towel rack had been ripped from the wall. "Jesus!" I thought. "What the hell went on in here last night?"

I looked at my watch: I had 30 minutes until the start of day two of the seminar. I cleaned myself up as best I could, shimmied into one of my short skirts, and managed to make it to the meeting on time. (At least I was a high-functioning drunk.) Technically, it wasn't the walk of shame, but as I entered the meeting room it sure seemed like it. I tried to play it cool, but all I could think was, Who knows what happened last night? The bald guy on the left? I think I saw him at the bar. The short blonde? She was definitely there. I sat down at the table with my colleagues, expecting a Grade A razing, but what I got was almost worse: No one said a word. As for Phillip, he was teaching the class, so I would have to wait until lunch to get the details.

I waited for everyone to leave for lunch, and then sauntered over to Phillip (well, more like swayed, given I was still a little drunk). "First," I said, "I just want to say I am sorry. Whatever I did last night, I hope I didn't offend you." (On the day after any drunken debauchery, it's my policy to apologize first and ask questions later.)

"No," said Phillip, chortling. "Don't worry about it."

"Er," I said, my eyes moving down to the floor. "I'm sorry to bug you, but no one seems to be brave enough to tell me. What happened last night?"

"Well," said Phillip, "you fell asleep at the bar." Classy broad ain't I?

"I am so sorry," I said, horrified. "And, uh, the lawn chair?" I was afraid to ask.

"Well, we were pretty drunk too," said Phillip. "At the time, me and my friends thought that the best"—and no doubt the most incognito—"way to get you back to your room was to put you in the lawn chair outside the bar and carry you."

Needless to say, I was beyond embarrassed. Mortified is more like it. But Phillip didn't care. He didn't care if it was the seminar or the tequila that brought him to me, he was just so happy to have met me. Phillip and I clearly had an affinity for each other from the start, which only grew after we consummated our connection later that same week. Even a few days into our new relationship, it was hard for us to separate. At the end of the seminar, we shared a cab to the airport. Phillip deliberately missed his flight so we could keep talking. Then, fortuitously, my plane was delayed. We must have spent 10 hours together that day, talking and kissing in the airport. Because we both lived in different states, I assumed we would just go our separate ways, but not Phillip. "I don't sleep with just anyone," he said. "You know you are a part of me now. I *love* you." That seemed like way too much and *way* too soon, but after only a few weeks of talking with Phillip on the phone, I realized that I, too, was falling in love. (Told you that game was good.) Less than a month after that ill-fated tequila contest, Phillip decided he *had* to see me and booked this room at The Plaza for a romantic New York weekend.

For both of us, it was our first black/white interracial relationship, and we were still adjusting to it. After a few hours of "adjusting" in our hotel room, we decided to have a late dinner—something that's easy to do in the city that never sleeps. We set off for the Manhattan Ocean Club, just a block from our hotel. As we stepped out the back door and into the street, a homeless man stopped us. "Hey son, can you help a brother out?" he said, coming up close to us and thrusting a cup toward Phillip.

"No, I'm sorry man," Phillip smiled, veering away from the homeless man and pushing me behind him to shield me.

"Hey, I know you have the money man," the homeless guy said, looking at me and giving a wink. His mouth cracked open in what would have been a toothy grin if only he'd had teeth. "Who do you play for anyway?"

Phillip couldn't answer him because he was already laughing too hard. "I told you," Phillip said, smiling at me.

"Have a good night," the man called after us.

"Yeah, you too," Phillip said, still laughing.

Although we were almost to the restaurant, Phillip insisted on switching sides as we walked, situating himself between me and the street. (When we stopped to speak to the homeless man, I had gotten out of order.) It wasn't until I dated Phillip that I discovered it was considered proper for the man to walk on the street side of the sidewalk—something Phillip took very seriously.

The Manhattan Ocean Club entrance was at street level, but the dining room sat below a long spiral staircase. The tables, lit by the soft glow of flickering candles, were covered with crisp, off-white linens, and there were fresh flowers everywhere. As we took our seats, I felt self conscious, like everyone was staring at us—that interracial couple. "Winthrop dear," I imagined one patron saying to her husband, "do you see that white woman kissing that colored man over there? What a disgrace." "I know Mildred," I imagined her husband replying. "They will let *anyone* in here these days."

In truth, when Phillip and I were together, people really couldn't have treated us better. We were so in love—that crazy I-can't-live-without-you love—that everyone just knew we belonged together. And even though Phillip might have looked to some like a big scary black guy, his self-deprecating, gregarious nature always put people at ease. I will never forget the time we ordered dessert—a chocolate and vanilla cheesecake. When the waiter read back our order to confirm, he said with a smile. "Okay so that's one espresso, one cappuccino, and one interracial cheesecake." We laughed for hours about that one.

Then there was the day when, on the way to lunch in the West Village, we passed another interracial couple on the street, proudly holding hands. Like us, they were a black-and-white couple—but they were also gay. We held it in until they passed, and then we couldn't help but laugh. We had been so worried about whether people would accept us; when we saw that gay couple, we suddenly realized how silly we had been. "We are going to have to be a whole lot more interesting if we want to get any attention in this city," said Phillip. After that, we rarely worried about how people saw us.

I never wanted to be one of *those* white women: dating a black man, but knowing nothing about black culture. From the time Phillip and I met, I had submerged myself in books about black history. Phillip always encouraged me, giving me a list of must-read books like Lerone Bennett's *Before the Mayflower: A History of Black America* and Alex Haley's *The Autobiography of Malcolm X*. On this trip to the city, Phillip had brought me something special: an out-of-print book he hadn't read since college called *100 Years of Lynchings* by Ralph Ginzburg. "I was reading through it on the plane ride out here," he said. I sat on the bed, and Phillip leaned back until he was on my lap. "I read it before, in college, but I wasn't in a relationship with a white woman then. This time, it had a different meaning to me. Like this one—it's so sad." He started reading:

> "'Inter-racial Love Affair Ended by Lynching of Man.... The dead man is accused of having been intimate with a white woman... Letters from the white woman were found in the pocket of the dead man after the lynching. One of them read as follows:
>
> Dearest Ed...I want to leave and go some place where people are sensible, where I can at least walk with you on the streets in the daytime without danger and fear. You often impress upon me the fact that you are colored and can't take any chances. I know that, darling, but love is greater than color in my case... Yours DEVOTED....
>
> After learning of the lynching the woman spent Sunday night in the swamps, crossing over the county line to Kingstree on Monday to seek the protection of the sheriff there.'"

Phillip sat up in bed and looked at me with his deep brown eyes—eyes that I was sure could look right into my soul. "You see," he said, "not so long ago, we would not have had the right to love each other, to be together. It is my privilege to kiss you, to hold you, to love you." He continued, "It makes you think. It was just over 30 years ago—around the time we were born—that the laws against interracial marriage were overturned. In our lifetimes, we wouldn't have been allowed to be together. We are so lucky. So privileged."

Phillip didn't fit any of the stereotypes that the broader American public may have about black men. He was highly educated, well off, and—much to my dismay—a Republican, but he still had a strong sense of where he came from. And he knew more about black history than anyone I have known before or since. Even so, he never had the attitude "It's a black thing; you wouldn't understand." Instead, he always encouraged me to share my thoughts and opinions on any aspect of black culture.

We never looked at our racial differences as a burden. Instead, we had fun with them. I asked him once about his lotion obsession—he put lotion on his skin 24/7—to which he replied, "That's right, you've never dated a black guy before! You don't know anything about getting ashy." He was right; I didn't.

I also learned the importance of "good hair" versus "nappy hair." (I guess that's why Phillip always shaved his head.) I thought "an eggplant" was just a purple vegetable, but learned from Phillip that it is also a racial epithet. He called me his "redbone"—a word for light-skinned sister (in this case, really light). He was my own personal Mandingo, and I was his cracker-ass cracker.

Like any relationship that begins at light speed, we crashed and burned faster and harder than a teenager high on a full pack of NoDoz with a Red Bull chaser. Before me, he was one of those brothers who always dated black. In fact, he had always been critical of black men with white women, calling them sell-outs. But he was in love with me. Shit! What should he do now? There was a lot of back and forth between us, but ultimately the pull of his soulmate, as Phillip often called me, was no match to the pull of the postcard. For me, it was heart wrenching. But it was in this relationship that I gained the confidence to expand my horizons, to tiptoe into the most taboo dating pool: black men. Ultimately, I feel privileged—privileged that this relationship helped me begin my journey of interracial dating experiences that, over a decade later, culminated in the writing of this book.

Bittersweet

Zoe had been hearing about William for a couple years; ever since she moved into the same neighborhood as his mother, Mrs. Baker. Several times, Mrs. Baker had mentioned to Zoe how William was single, how William was cute, and what a great couple they would make. Zoe could smell a setup. But in the two years she'd known Mrs. Baker, Zoe and William had never met—until one day, Mrs. Baker and Zoe wanted to play Spades, but needed a third. "William is downstairs," said Mrs. Baker, giving Zoe a little nudge. "Why don't you go down there and see if he wants to play?"

As Zoe reached the bottom of the stairs, she glimpsed William's mocha-colored bicep peeking out from the sleeve of a green polo shirt. When she turned the corner, their eyes met. "It was like kismet," says Zoe over sushi on the Upper West Side. "An instant connection."

"Well," said William. "I finally meet *the* Zoe." It seemed William had been hearing just as much about Zoe as she had about him. After four hours of a rousing game of Spades, Zoe excused herself to go home and make dinner for her daughter. As Zoe left, Mrs. Baker whispered in her ear: "I think I have a new daughter-in-law."

Zoe's and William's feelings for each other were immediate and palpable. It was no surprise that they saw each other again soon after their first meeting. Zoe needed some help with her apartment's electrical; knowing William was handy around the house, she gave him a call. That night, Zoe—a very good cook—made him one of her family's Greek specialties as a thank you. "Oh, avgolemono!" said William with a big smile. "I love this soup!" Zoe was terribly impressed—not just with his knowledge of Greek food, but also with his Greek pronunciation.

Zoe found William to be the consummate gentleman, always opening doors, walking on the street side of the sidewalk, and picking up the tab. And they didn't rush to bed; they had a long, old-fashioned courtship. "We fit into each other's lives instead of turning them upside down, like a lot of people in new relationships," says Zoe. "Shortly after we first met, he went on vacation for three weeks with his two kids—and when he is with his kids, he is *with his kids*. That's one of the things I love about him: how he is with his children." Zoe shakes her blonde head and bats her eyelashes. "I did hear from him as soon as he got back, but we still took it really slow. It was three months before we even kissed." She adds, "It was six months before we first slept together." I admit, I'm floored by her comments. A brother waited six months to sleep with someone? He's rare, a real keeper—or else that mo fo is gay. Down low? I'm just sayin'.... "I know," says Zoe. "It seems kind of weird. But it was just always so right. Intense, almost telepathic." ("That is it!" I think. "Maybe he's the Brother from Another Planet.")

Zoe, who is Greek, and William, who is black, found that culturally, they had a lot in common. Case in point: Both cultures are known for being a bit, well, tardy to social events—Greeks on "G time" and blacks on "CP time." "Greeks don't race to anything, even a funeral," says Zoe. "We take our time, stroll or even dance through life." Then there is the sound level. "Greeks and blacks are both known for being very loud," notes Zoe. And in both cultures, food and family are given high importance. "Culturally, we really were a perfect match."

Unlike with a lot of blended families, there was never any issue with the children not getting along. Having worked for years at the neighborhood youth center, Zoe was very close with all the kids in the area, including William's son Darrell and his daughter Chelsea. In fact, William's kids were already regular playmates with Zoe's daughter, Penelope. Over time, Zoe's relationship with William's children became particularly meaningful because they had no relationship with their mother, Yonette.

"I don't know how he even ended up with Yonette in the first place," says Zoe. "Knowing him now, it seems so out of character. He being from a prominent, wealthy family; it seems strange that they even crossed paths." She giggles nervously, "I guess you have to chalk it up to those young and stupid years." She explains, "He had just gotten out of the Army, and he was running wild. She was tall and pretty at the time—looked like a model. That doesn't explain it all, though; he knew better—at least to wear a condom. But he didn't, and then he had Darrell."

William and Yonette weren't married, engaged, or even boyfriend/girlfriend. She was nothing more to William than an occasional booty call. But when Yonette finally told William she was pregnant, he remained in close contact, helping her through the pregnancy for the sake of the baby. After the baby was born, they tried to make a go of a real relationship, but it became clear after only a couple months that that was out of the question. Simply put, Yonette had a drug problem. She had always tried to keep it from William, but now she was hitting the rock so hard it was impossible to hide. When Yonette, deep into the drugs, lost interest in her child, William assumed the responsibility of raising his son alone. Six months later, he received an unexpected call from the hospital: "You have a daughter; come pick her up." William hadn't even known that Yonette was pregnant again; now he was raising two kids alone—albeit with tremendous support from his family. Fortunately, William had put all that drama behind him years ago. By the time he started seeing Zoe, his kids were already five and six years old.

William, Zoe, and their three children became inseparable. They went to the beach, museums, the park, and even spent holidays together. William's mother, sister, brother—they all loved Zoe. They were one big, happy family—a veritable mixed-race *Brady Bunch*. And on the occasions when William and Zoe could get away alone together, it was always magical. Often, they went to the beaches on Long Island. Zoe was responsible for packing a picnic basket with Greek delicacies like babaganoush, lamb souvlaki, and tarama spread; William's job was to bring the wine. They would watch the sunset and talk for hours, sometimes falling asleep in each others' arms.

Eventually, word got back to Yonette about William's relationship with Zoe. "The women in the community were teasing Yonette," says Zoe, spreading her hands on the table in front of her and tapping her newly manicured mauve nails on the glass. "It was that 'You going to let a white woman raise your kids?' stuff. I guess they were really letting into her for a while, so believe it or not she got clean." Ah, the power of bigotry. At least it ended in something positive. "That was the one good thing that came out of all this," says Zoe. "She pulled herself together, found a job, and got off the drugs. But that is also when the trouble started with us." Zoe takes a deep breath and frowns into her wasabi-laden soy sauce. "When Yonette finally got clean, William and I had been together for four years and the kids were already nine and ten years old. But for some reason, William still thought the best thing to do was to buy Yonette a house and move his children in with her."

Zoe explains, "He was worried they would take the kids away because they usually side with the mother," says Zoe. "He was terrified. He thought there was no way the courts would side with a black man in a custody battle." So an "educated man," instead of getting a lawyer, instead of reviewing all his options, buys a house and not only hands a stranger the keys, but hands over his children without a fight—to a *crack head*? Educated, my ass! This brother needs to go back to school. "They didn't want to go either, especially little Chelsea," says Zoe, biting her lip. "She was nine by this time and petrified when William moved them in with Yonette."

"He got it in his head that this was the best way to handle it," says Zoe with a matter-of-fact tone, but a face showing the wear of many years of pain. "He thought if she had a house, maybe she would be more likely to keep it together and not go back to the drugs." She continues, "It was the guilt, too. He wanted to show them that he wouldn't abandon their black mother."

"Even though *she* abandoned *them*!" I say. "It's admirable that he wants to help her get on her feet, but handing over his children? That's just *crazy*."

"I'm not saying it made sense," says Zoe.

I'd seen this before: a classic case of the postcard. Even if they are incredibly in love with a woman who is not black, black men will succumb to intense pressure to "do the right thing" and be with a black woman. "It's that brother guilt," I say. "If she was white, he would have just taken those kids and left her crack-head ass in the gutter. But because she's black, he feels the need to buy her a house?"

"But it gets worse," says Zoe, leaning forward, trying to breathe in the courage to say what came next. How could it possibly get worse? "After a few months of the kids living with Yonette, her body just quits. She has two strokes in a row. Then goes into liver failure and then kidney failure. And she is one of only two percent that survive an aortic embolism." She continues, "William felt bad for her so..." her voice breaks "...he moves in with her to take care of her full time. They have separate rooms." She emphasizes.

Here is when I snap. "You are fucking *kidding* me," I say. "He has no relationship with this woman except that he slept with her a couple of times 10 years ago." I reach instinctively toward my head as if to tear my hair out. "He buys her a house and then, when she gets sick, he moves in with her? How about hiring her a *nurse*? And those poor kids. They weren't confused enough already?" All I can say is, William had better still have money, because Daddy will need to pay for a lifetime of therapy to fix this mess.

"I think it came from a good place," says Zoe. "He wanted to show his kids that he wouldn't abandon their mother. But the kids didn't handle it well. For years, the little one didn't want to have anything to do with Yonette."

"I am still confused," I say. "Let me recap. They were not married, right? No relationship to speak of ever?" I am still struggling to understand his behavior. "And weren't you two still together?"

"You are right; they never were married. They never really dated. Yes, he was still with me at the time. We were coming up on our four-year anniversary. Well, that is until he decided he wanted to move in with her."

"Please tell me you broke up with him?" I say, begging her.

"Yes I did. I still loved him, but I can't be with a man who is living with another woman," says Zoe, "even though he said that they were not together and that they were not having sex. It was so sad for me. I finally had someone I loved, someone I really wanted to fight for." She continues, "Then I realized he should be fighting for me too. I am Greek, and my life was becoming a real-life Greek tragedy!"

"You guys had such a great relationship," I say. "A wonderful family. And he gives that all up because of skin color. *And* he doesn't even marry her. He is not with her. But he is not with you, either. So no one wins—least of all him!"

"He was just so worried about being *that* black man—the one that abandons his family," says Zoe.

"That's exactly what he did!" I say. "He abandoned his family for some fake relationship to look good to others?" (In case you haven't figured it out, I've had a few go-rounds with the old I-got-dumped-by-the-love-of-my-life-for-someone-racially-correct in my time.) "And he thinks he's setting a good example for his kids? That you should not be with the person you love, and instead be in some weird manufactured relationship and sleep in separate rooms?"

"I know," says Zoe. "We talked about that. We talked about how great things would have been for the kids if they had grown up in a functional, loving home."

When Zoe cut it off with William, it was really off. Zoe even decided she had to move. "You are like a daughter to me," said Mrs. Baker, choking back the tears. "You can't go. I can't lose you"—a sentiment echoed by the rest of his family.

About a year after their separation Zoe and William ran into each other in Central Park. "It was like no time had passed," says Zoe, smiling and giggling like a schoolgirl in love. "When he saw me, his face lit up. We were so comfortable together. It was so easy. And the passion was still there, no doubt about it." At first, Zoe stood firm: They could be friends, they could even be in love, but she wouldn't sleep with a man who lived with another woman. After a couple years, though, even that final boundary fell. It was a bizarre twist on "the polygamy." Even if William wasn't sleeping with Yonette, he was still going back and forth between the two women, giving neither one 100 percent of his time, love, or attention. "I go home to my own house at night," says Zoe. "I don't have to deal with another person." She adds, "This whole thing is harder on him than it is on me." (Isn't that what parents say before they beat up their kids?)

"I believe in a future with him," says Zoe. "We belong together." She continues, "He tells me he cares about Yonette, but he just doesn't love her. We're just waiting to move on." Zoe pauses, "Waiting for her to die." A sort of sleeping beauty with a twist—except you don't get to sleep through it. "Don't get me wrong," says Zoe. "As gruesome as this waiting game may be, we—or at least I—haven't stopped living. I miss having him next to me at social events, but I don't let it ruin things for me. I still have a good time." Ah, me thinks the lady doth protest too much.

"I hate that there is all this stuff between us," says Zoe. "Sometimes, all you can think about is the frustration of us not being able to be together. But the truth is, being with him has done so much for me. He inspired me to start writing poetry; I used to say he was my muse." She smiles and lets out a shy giggle. "Sundays in the summer we would take long drives along the beach and listen to jazz. The simple things just meant so much to us." She draws in a heavy breath and shakes her head. "It's been almost six years of back and forth now, 10 years since we first started dating. It's been arduous in so many ways. The journey has been rough, but the relationship smooth. It's...it's so bittersweet," she says, a thin veneer of a smile, unable to cover the pain that lies beneath.

Don't Sweat the Small Stuff

Having only dabbled with the Match before, Lawrence decided he was now ready to get serious about Internet dating. It was time, he concluded, to ante up by joining eHarmony.

As anyone will tell you there is no "dabbling" with eHarmony. To use eHarmony, you must answer a bazillion-page questionnaire that requires in-depth answers about everything from your favorite type of dog to what brings meaning to your life. Then you must build a profile. Finally, you have to endure weeks —if not months—of back-and-forth "guided" communication with potential matches. "I felt like I had invested so much time with eHarmony that when it finally came time to go out with someone, I may not even like them at that point, but I was going to see it through, damn it!" Lawrence says over brunch with me one afternoon in Hell's Kitchen.

It was after this intense screening process that Lawrence found himself on an actual, bona fide, in-the-flesh first date with the lovely and talented Rosie. And it was on that first date that Lawrence really started to appreciate the eHarmony process. He felt like he already knew so many things about Rosie, and he liked her, right from the beginning. What Lawrence appreciated most about Rosie was that conversation with her was so organic.

With other women he had dated, Lawrence felt like he had to carry the whole conversation like a 40-pound sack of potatoes. But with Rosie, things were smooth, comfortable, and actually fun. And when Lawrence, a New Yorker, discovered during the course of conversation that Rosie had just moved to the city, he recognized that he had been given a golden opportunity: first dibs on a New York newbie. Lawrence had long since known that it was critical to catch women like Rosie quick, before they become jaded by men who are afflicted with I-Can-Never-Be-Committed-to-Any-Woman-Even-for-Lunch-Because-Kate-Moss-Might-Walk-In-at-Any-Moment-and-Offer-to-Be-My-Sex-Slave-I-tis. (Trust me, it runs rampant in New York.) It wasn't long before Lawrence and Rosie went on their second date, and then their third, and then their fourth....

Although Rosie was white and Lawrence black, it wasn't much of a case of opposites attract. Lawrence is thin, smart, and funny. Ditto Rosie. Lawrence is educated and shows good common sense. As does Rosie. The only real differences between them, apart from their race, are that Lawrence wears fairly sizable Urkel-like glasses, while Rosie wears contacts. And the typical male-female stuff: Lawrence tends toward the analytical, while Rosie is more creative.

The fact that Lawrence was black didn't faze Rosie. In fact, although Lawrence was her first black boyfriend, she didn't give the interracial nature of their relationship any thought. She just thought Lawrence was funny and enjoyed spending time with him. But it didn't take long for Rosie to get her first lesson in racism—ironically, from her colleagues at the inner-city elementary school where she worked. Although Lawrence had been calling her at work for a couple months now, he didn't "sound black" (black-guy pet peeve #248), so it wasn't until Rosie mentioned Lawrence's race in passing that all hell broke loose. Comments ranged from "Oh, I would have never guessed," to "Oh neat-o," to my personal favorite, "Are you sure you still want to go out with him?" This being Rosie's first foray into interracial dating, she was surprised by the reaction. Lawrence, having *not* just fallen off the turnip truck, was not. But Lawrence lives by the motto "Don't sweat the small stuff," so he didn't pay them any mind.

Unlike Rosie, Lawrence had lots of interracial-dating experience. Lawrence's family put a high value on education; as a result he had gone to a very highly regarded—but also very *white*—prep school. He realized early on that if he bought into that sell-out drama, restricting himself to dating only black women, he would likely date very little if at all. Besides, many members of Lawrence's family—including some of his siblings, aunts, and cousins—had had interracial relationships. He felt confident that his family would accept Rosie—but he wasn't sure whether Rosie's old-school, I-talian family would accept him.

Lawrence got his answer when Rosie's father, Mr. Romano, came for a visit. Thanks in part to his old-fashioned manners—always calling Rosie's dad only Sir or Mr. Romano—Lawrence made a great first impression. Mr. Romano found Lawrence to be career oriented, funny, and interesting. It was also clear to Mr. Romano that Lawrence cared a great deal for his daughter—something that anyone standing in the room would be hard pressed to overlook. Plus, Lawrence was a real upgrade from Rosie's last boyfriend. "Rosie had been dating this horrible guy before me and it had her father so worried," explains Lawrence, running his hand over his low cut hair. "The relationship should have ended in college, but instead it dragged on for years afterward. Worse yet, he escalated from pot-smoking loser to abusive stalker. That was why Rosie had moved to the city—to start over." At the end of Mr. Romano's visit, both parties felt relieved. Lawrence because he knew he was not in for a good, old-fashioned, I-talian beat down, and Mr. Romano because his daughter had finally found a "nice guy."

Sadly, dealing with the rest of the Romano family would not be as effortless. Mr. Romano knew there were pockets of bigotry within his family, but he was not going to let anything hurt his Rosie's chances for love. About a year into their relationship, Lawrence and Rosie planned to meet the entire Romano family at Easter dinner. Before they arrived, Mr. Romano said a few words to the family in preparation. "Rosie is bringing her new boyfriend Lawrence to dinner tonight," he said. "He's very successful, nice, and great to her. He is also black. Rosie really likes this guy, and if any of you assholes say or do anything stupid to mess this up for her, I'm going to kill you." Not surprisingly, Mr. Romano's speech was very effective. When Lawrence finally met Rosie's family, he found them to be extremely pleasant. "I didn't know about any of it until after," he says. "I was just shocked at the amount of prep work that went into that first meeting."

That's not to say there haven't been times since then when the Romanos have really stepped in it. Case in point: When Lawrence is around, Rosie's grandmother makes it a point to introduce some "black topics" for discussion—you know, so Lawrence feels "included." Like the time Grandma, originally from England, argued that the English are less racist than Americans because they abolished race-based slavery first. (Okay Grandma, but they also started it.) Or the time she asked Lawrence to shed some light on why "those people" (black guy peeve #301) are moving into her neighborhood and reducing property values. And then there was the time Rosie's cousin said to Lawrence—and I quote—"I guess since you're black, you're probably the first in your family go to college?" (In fact, Lawrence's family is highly educated. Lawrence's father has a PhD from Harvard, his mother has a master's degree, and all the kids in his family went to college.) These comments annoyed Lawrence, but he never let the ignorance of others affect him or his relationship with Rosie (i.e., "Don't sweat the small stuff"). "It's really weird," says Lawrence. "Some of her family that I was the closest to at first, people that I was joking around with, they seemed so nice. Then I would find out later that they use the N-word on a regular basis and have a lot of unflattering things to say about black people." This a great example of why "the wall" exists for so many black people. Everything is going great, and then *pow*—there's the N-word! It's hard to know who to trust. "It was almost like they treated me like the exception, carved me out of it," says Lawrence. "I am not one of 'those people,' but 'those people' are 'those people,' clear as mud."

A year into their relationship, Lawrence and Rosie had what Lawrence terms The Talk, prompted by carefully disguised hints from Rosie that contained the words "settling" and "down." They discussed such things as, Where were they going? What did they want out of life? Kids? Career? Lifestyle? Credit scores? (Lawrence likes to be thorough.) "So why do you think you asked her to marry you?" I say.

"Oh, it was pretty much the standard reason," says Lawrence. "I couldn't imagine my life without her." (Standard? Yeah, maybe if we all lived on Fantasy Island. "De plane! De plane!" Ah, if only life were really filled with midgets and mai tais....)

Surprisingly, when Lawrence announced his engagement, *his* friends became the biggest critics. "When I told them about our engagement some of my friends were so negative. Not about Rosie; just about marriage in general," says Lawrence. "I have a friend, Bob, that's been dating a woman for nine years. Nine years!"

Lawrence shakes his head. "He even bought a house with her. And if you ask him why they are not married, *he* says 'I don't want to rush into anything.'" He continues, "I have other friends that have kids, but aren't married. That's such a cop out. To me, the only reason not to get married is because you want to leave yourself open for a Plan B." He adds, "Then again, I have never been a commitment phobe."

Rosie and Lawrence's wedding was pretty uneventful—a real vanilla American ceremony, albeit with a chocolate twist. "I think probably the funniest thing at the wedding was looking down the aisle," says Lawrence. "There was a defined white and black side. On my side, my family is all white collar, highly educated, conservative, sitting so properly. And her whole family was much more casual, laid back, and very blue collar." Lawrence removes his glasses, methodically breathes on each lens, and then cleans them with a special lens cloth from his pocket. "My family was reserved and quiet, hers—loud Italian. It was just such a reversal of what I think most people would expect." It took a little while, but after everyone let their guard down, the party was a huge hit.

After the wedding, the couple discussed having children at length; then they waited a reasonable year before working on a family. Lawrence was older than Rosie and calm in demeanor; this was important when it came to the baby-making process, as Rosie had just the teeniest tendency to go overboard. "After the first month of us trying to have a baby, she freaked out, saying things like 'I'll never get pregnant!'" Lawrence waves his arms in mock panic. "She even got an online 'fertility friend,' some woman who was trying to have a baby for 10 years." Lawrence lets out a deep breath. "Rosie would talk to her and get all worked up. I was like, 'Look, you need to dial it back.'" Soon, Rosie got pregnant—disaster averted. And Lawrence quickly discovered that dealing with a pregnant woman was much more difficult than he had imagined. "She was so miserable," says Lawrence. "I thought I was good before, but that was when I *really* learned patience." He explains, "Sometimes I would barely get in the door and she would just attack me—the hormones, I guess." He continues, "And pregnant during those hot New York summers. She says I am not allowed to even touch her in any month that might result in her being nine-months pregnant in the summer again."

Rosie planned for a completely natural, drug-free childbirth. Part way through her 26 hours of labor, however, she decided an epidural wouldn't be the worst thing in the world. Lawrence, on the other hand, had a real problem with it. "We were in a teaching hospital, so the anesthesiologist was just observing. The resident was doing the procedure," says Lawrence. "I was fine with the Lidocaine needle, but then the resident pulled out the mother of all needles." Lawrence puts down his fork, the memory giving him a sudden loss in appetite. "Ordinarily, blood and gore doesn't bother me. But the resident couldn't get the needle in right, and after four times of him trying, of seeing this huge needle in my wife's back—I just couldn't take it." Lawrence tried to think of his motto—"Don't sweat the small stuff"—but this needle was way too big to fit under the heading of "small stuff," and he was already sweating, uncontrollably. Afraid he might be sick, Lawrence announced, "I gotta go to the bathroom!"

"No!" yelled Rosie. "You are not going *anywhere*!"

When Lawrence finally fessed up, telling the doctors he might be sick, they freaked out. Worried that he might barf or, worse, fall on his wife, they made Lawrence lie down on the floor until the nausea passed and called in a nurse to hold Rosie's hand.

At hour 26, still with no substantial progress, the couple decided on a C-section. "I will never forget it," says Lawrence. "My wife was laid out on the table on her back, like she was being crucified. Rosie was awake, but there was this drape between her head and where they were operating so she couldn't see anything." Lawrence demonstrates using his cloth napkin. "And then the baby started crying, but Rosie still couldn't see him, so she shouted for me to take pictures. I said, 'Of you? Or the baby?'"

To which Rosie, Our Lady of Eternal Tolerance, replied "No, of our son you jackass!"

Jackass, indeed.

It was instantly clear who Baby Landon took after. "He has some of my facial features, like my cheeks, but for the most part he looks just like my wife." says Lawrence. "Even his coloration. When he was born, he was as white as a sheet and almost as pasty as Rosie."

"Yeah, but they darken up over time, right?" I say—a fact that I didn't learn until I dated my first black boyfriend.

"Usually," says Lawrence. "I did when I was a kid. But it's been a few weeks now and Landon still gets lost in the sheets. I think the mix is going to be good, though. I'm hoping he'll look Brazilian, like a bronze god."

It was when she had to deal with "baby weight" for the first time that Rosie discovered one of the main perks of being with a black guy. "Right away after having the baby, Rosie kept saying that she needed to lose the weight, how she had to start exercising," says Lawrence. "I don't understand why white women get so worked up about that. I was like, 'Don't worry about it! You look great the way you are.'"

And then Rosie discovered one of the other benefits of being in a relationship with a brother: a close family. Rosie had always felt welcome in Lawrence's family. She got along particularly well with her mother-in-law, right from the beginning. And with Landon in the picture, they became even closer. Most new mothers don't want their mother-in-law within a mile of them, well, *ever*—but especially after they have just given birth. But for Rosie—whose mother is bipolar, making any relationship difficult—Lawrence's mom is like the mother she never had. It is to her that Rosie looks for companionship and guidance as a new mom.

The couple doesn't agree on everything, of course. "If there are three dishes in the sink, she'll come unglued," says Lawrence. "For me, dishes have to reach a critical mass before I do anything about them." And for Lawrence, it's all about the toothpaste. "I like to squeeze the toothpaste neatly from the bottom," he explains. "And she likes to squeeze it haphazardly from the middle. It used to drive me crazy, but now I just deal with it." It's like what I always say: People like to blame race when a relationship doesn't work, but race is rarely the problem. Lawrence agrees. "Relationships always break up because of things that seem like no big deal in the beginning, but drive you crazy over time." He adds, "I guess that's why I don't sweat the small stuff."

Curry Fever

"In doing something, do it with love or never do it at all."

—Mahatma Gandhi

When my best friend from college, Vishal, got married, a mutual friend and I decided to surprise him by attending the wedding in saris. This might not seem like a big deal, but it's actually a major effort.

First, you have to procure a sari. I was lucky there: My friend Chandani's mother generously loaned me two. Chandani also loaned me a bindi—the red dot you place between your eyes—and a set of gold Indian jewelry to wear on Vishal's big day.

Next, you have to find an Indian tailor to sew the matching crop top. You can't go to any old tailor because all the parts of the sari—including the top—are spun together on one long piece of silk, and only an Indian tailor knows where to make the necessary cuts. And trust me: Indian women will laugh your ass out of the wedding if you cut the wrong end.

Finally, on the day of the wedding, you have to sneak into the bride's changing room to ask one of the bride's aunties to tie the sari. Tying saris is a dying art; many young Indian women in the U.S. don't know how to do it. Once an auntie gets her hands on you, she will feverishly wrap twisted silk all around you and tuck it into the so-tight-you-can't-breathe petticoat, the structure that holds the outfit into place. I swear, you have to have a PhD to tie that shit.

And of course, you have to do all of this without tipping your hand to your best friend lest you ruin the surprise.

When Vishal saw us at the wedding, he was indeed surprised—not to mention honored and possibly a little freaked out. For a second, he didn't even recognize us. He couldn't believe the two of us, both white chicks, looked so natural in our saris. "If anyone asks," Vishal told us, "just tell people you are from Kashmir," a region known for its citizens' light skin color.

Vishal's statement is so apropos because it reflects what every Indian will tell you: It's tough to characterize the people of India because they are so diverse. It's true that there could be an Indian as fair skinned as I am (and not just an Indian albino) or as dark as the darkest African. India, the world's largest democracy, boasts more than a billion people whose language, customs, religions, dress, and habits vary substantially by region.

Some of you might be asking, Why a separate section for Indians? Why not just include them with the other Asians? The truth is, although Indians and other Asians are similar in some areas, overall they are just too different. This section outlines some of the experiences that the Indophiles (i.e., people with the hots for Indians) I interviewed have had with this widely varied culture.

Things to Know

There are probably more things to know about Indian culture than any other culture in this book. Not only are Indian men very different from men in Western countries, but they're often very different from each other depending on what part of India they or their family comes from. Then there are the roles that religion and food play in Indian culture. Oh, and don't forget one of the most important things to know: how you can tell if your Indian man is planning to ask you to marry him.

Where in India Is He from?

Maybe because India is so large and diverse, Indians in the U.S. tend to identify themselves by what part of India their family hails from: first, whether they are from the north or the south, and second, their state or territory.

"As far as I knew, I was just Indian," says Chandani, 37, Indian, pharmaceutical executive. "But when I got to college, everyone made a big deal that I must be from the north because I am so light skinned. I found out later that I am actually from the south. I guess north Indians are known for being fair skinned and playing cards. And south Indians wash their faces all the time because they are so dark. Ridiculous, I know, but that's the stereotype."

The south is known for its peaceful vegetarians. In the north, people are often meat eaters, larger in stature, and fairer skinned. People in the north have experienced significantly more war and religious unrest than those in the south.

As mentioned, another way Indians often describe themselves is by their family's Indian home state or territory. Each of the 28 states and seven territories has its own customs, language, religious practices, clothing, temperament, and—according to one edition of the *Kama Sutra*—sexual practices. So you're not just Indian, but Gujarati. And you're not just from the north, but Punjabi.

A Lot of What Is Indian Is Hindu

The vast majority of Indians—more than 80 percent of them—are Hindus. So a lot of what we think of as "Indian" actually comes from the Hindu religion. The caste system; the sacred cow; the 300-million colorful, talented, multi-limbed Indian manifestations of God; and a lot of other Indian cultural traditions—all have their basis in the Hindu religion. Hindus believe that art is the food of the soul and music is life, stressing the importance of being a well-rounded human being.

Hindus also recognize that women play an essential role in living a good life. "A wife makes you a perfect man," says Punditji Gupta, a priest at a Hindu temple. "Without a woman, you can't do anything. With a woman, you can become anything you want to be." In fact, every manifestation of God in the Hindu religion has a female counterpart—a yin and a yang, of sorts.

Also important in Hindu religion is the idea of Karma—that what you do and say have repercussions that you have to deal with the rest of your life (or, if you are Hindu, the rest of your lives). It's clear to me that if we all lived our lives with Karma in mind, holding it in at least as high regard as the season finale of *Survivor*, the world would be one step closer to perfection!

Food Is Love

Food is very important in Indian culture; the old adage, "The way to a man's heart is through his stomach," could not be more true for Indian men. "They associate food with love and mother," says Sally, 45, white girl, consultant. "Someone who loves you will cook you food. My Indian husband puts a lot of value into it."

"My husband Vishal has always been thin, which was a problem for *my* relatives in India," says Sujata, 35, Indian, homemaker. "When we visit, they say, 'You are so skinny!' and then turn to me and say 'Sujata, don't you feed him at all?' Like, he doesn't have a belly, so I don't love him."

And for some Indian men, when it comes to picking a mate, your cooking skills could seal your fate. "I have a friend that is considering an arranged marriage with a woman from India," says Emily, 25, white girl, master's candidate. "But one of his stipulations is that she would have to take cooking lessons from his mother first." Okay, this guy is definitely extreme. But this example does drive home how important food is to an Indian man!

If He Brings You Home, He Is Going to Marry You

Obviously, in every society, bringing your girlfriend home to meet your parents has some importance—but with Indians, it's even more so. Indians—female and male—often tell their parents little or nothing about their dating lives. Instead, theirs is a don't-ask-don't-tell policy (a.k.a. ignorance is bliss). So when an Indian man brings you home, it's a huge deal—and often an indication that he is considering asking you to marry him.

"Yes, it's so true. I didn't know anything about that when it happened to me," says Lisa, 39, Jew, lawyer. "My parents met every boy I dated since high school, but it wasn't a big deal. They just looked at it like they were meeting a friend. So when Taj brought me home, I had no idea how important that one night was going to be."

"He is seriously thinking about asking you to marry him if he brings you home to meet his parents," says Vishal, 37, Indian, physician. "He is showing his cards to them, which is huge." He adds, "If she hugs his parents and calls them by their first names, she is in trouble. But if she is polite and deferential to the traditional family structure, she will do fine."

It's important for you to understand the significance of this event so you can plan appropriately. Indians say that the best advice they can give is to be formal with the parents. Refer to them as Mr. or Mrs., offer to help in the kitchen, focus on the family more than your boyfriend, and remember: *no* PDA around mom and dad. Also, the first time you meet your Indian man's family, you should wear pants or a long skirt and a top with sleeves. Bare arms and legs are a big no-no with conservative Indians.

Also, you shouldn't take offense if you have been dating a while and your Indian boyfriend has never brought you home. Introducing you to his parents is not just one small next step, but a giant leap in any Indian man's life.

So You Don't Fuck Up!

There are so many differences between Western and Indian cultures, it'll be almost impossible for you to avoid screwing up a little every now and then. Not using your left hand, abiding by the rhyme "If it moos, do not choose," and never wearing white even *before* Labor Day are just a few of the things you'll need to know about Indian etiquette.

It's Never a Nice Day for a White Wedding

In India, white is reserved for somber occasions only; it's worn to Hindu funerals. And when attending an Indian wedding, don't wear red. Like white in the U.S., red is reserved for the bride.

"Hindus have very strong feelings about white," says Jill, 31, white girl, teacher. "My husband and I had two wedding ceremonies, one American and one Indian. At first, my Indian mother-in-law didn't want me to wear white even for the American ceremony. She eventually calmed down about it and it was fine, but Indians *really* don't like white."

So to review: Wear white to a funeral, and no red or white to a wedding. Got that?

Sirloin as Sacrilege

Indians don't eat beef for two reasons. One, cows give milk, making them a renewable food source; to them it doesn't make sense to kill them. Two, among Hindus, they are considered sacred.

"Sacred cows are so giving and nurturing," says Sujata. "We treated them like our mom. It goes against our morals to eat a cow. You wouldn't eat your mom, right?" Sujata continues: "To be honest, I would stay away from meat altogether for that first meal with your Indian boyfriend's family. It's not like you are trying to impress; you are just being respectful."

I love a good steak frites any day, but when dining with your Indian boyfriend's parents for the first time, remember this rhyme: "If it moos, do not choose." Given that a lot of Indians, especially south Indians, are vegetarian, a meatless dish is probably your safest bet.

For the Love of Ganesha, Take a Bite!

Just as food is very important to an Indian man, it's also incredibly important to his family. When you enter an Indian home, food *will* be offered—a lot of food. And no matter how full you are—even if you just ate two Big Macs with special sauce, lettuce, cheese, pickles, onions, on a sesame-seed bun—you have to take at least one bite. It's considered an insult if you don't.

"When I was little, my Indian grandparents would always force-feed us," says Sujata. "I hated it. My mom would look at us with these pleading eyes and say, 'Just take one little bite.' Once we took a bite, it was fine; they left us alone." Sujata concludes, "If you go into an Indian house, even if you are not hungry, you gotta take a bite!"

Not with the Left Hand

In India, it's considered in poor taste to use your left hand, especially for eating. That's because it's an Indian convention—sorry, there's no way to sugarcoat this—to wipe your ass with the left hand.

"Sometimes there is a toilet," says Emily, "but sometimes they just hand you a bucket and a cup and you have to shake dry.

Believe me, in India, they don't touch *anything* with their left hand."

This is also important for greetings; Indians usually shake hands only with the right. This is less of an issue in the U.S., but if your man's family is traditional, you might want to watch your hands. Remember: samosas on the right, TP on the left.

Off with the Shoes

The first time I went to a Hindu temple, I noticed a sign as soon as I entered the door: "No shoes after this point." I had been warned that you were not allowed to wear shoes in the temple, but what concerned me was that this sign was located two feet *in front of* the entrance to the bathroom. I looked at the sign, and then at the bathroom, and again at the sign. "Surely they don't mean that I should go into the bathroom without my shoes?" I thought. But I believe that respecting other people's cultures is paramount, so I took off my shoes and tiptoed across the bathroom floor. I was not grinning—more like wincing—but I bared it.

In India, it's customary to remove your shoes before entering places of worship as well as Indian homes. "The 'no shoes' thing is definitely true," says Lisa. "My Indian husband and I have been together many years now, but sometimes I forget. I will be at his family's house and realize, like, an hour later I still have my shoes on. It's horrifying every time it happens because I know it's so important to them that I take them off."

If you have a fungus amongus, jacked-up hammer toes, corns, or some other form of foot embarrassment, you need to get it cured or get over it because unless you want to deeply offend your Indian man's parents, those shoes are coming off!

What the Hell Did I Get Myself Into?

What's not to love about dating Indians, right? Well, as it turns out, a lot. Events that start hours late, parental roomies, Indians being not so honest (okay, not at all honest) right to your face, and the anointed queen of difficult mother-in-laws are just a few things about dating an Indian that might leave you asking, What the hell did I get myself into?

Indian Standard Time (IST)

No, this is not an officially recognized time zone, like Eastern Standard Time or Greenwich Mean Time. It's an expression Indians use to describe the fact that they are so often late to social occasions. In the U.S., if the wedding invitation says the ceremony starts at 1 p.m., you had better be on time—because by 1:15 p.m., that bride will be walking down the aisle whether your ass is in the pew or not. For an Indian wedding, though, you *never* want to be on time—or, worse, early. If the invitation says 1 p.m., don't be surprised if it doesn't get started until 3 p.m.

"What you said about IST is totally true," says Vishal. "Especially with social events, things always start really late."

"IST is very real," says Lisa. "I have been to an Indian wedding that started three hours late." She continues, "I was so worried for our wedding. My family is Jewish, type A, and super punctual. I was so panicked Taj's relatives would be hours late. I sent out constant reminders to everyone, and believe it or not, they were on time. My husband's brother said that it was the most organized Indian wedding he had ever been to."

Hinjew ceremonies are still the minority, however. Assume that in most situations, IST will apply. Don't get frustrated; just learn to take your time and always be fashionably late.

Honesty Is Not the Best Policy

There is an old Indian proverb: "It is better to say something pleasant than something true." So if the first time you meet your Indian boyfriend's family, his mother acts like you are the best thing since sliced naan, tells you you are smarter than Indira Gandhi, as kind as Mother Teresa, and as pretty as Aishwarya Rai, you might not want to get too excited. It's possible she doesn't even like you at all. As with most people, what your Indian boyfriend's parents *do* will likely be a better indicator than what they *say*.

"That is so true! I know a lot of people don't want to tell someone something unpleasant. Fine. But there is no need to gush to someone's face if you don't like them," says Sujata. "It's like they are overcompensating, trying to cover their tracks or something." Sujata continues, "But they shouldn't do that, because it can backfire. It's like faking an orgasm. If you fake it, he's going to think you liked it when you didn't."

"Yes, I would agree with you," says Sasha, 35, Jew, accountant. "My Indian husband does that. It's not like he's lying to me; he is just keeping it quiet. He doesn't want to say anything that might hurt my feelings."

No deal breaker here; you just need to be aware that some Indians may not be giving you the straight scoop. And if you are like me—i.e., brutally honest—you might want to tone it down, at least the first time you meet the potential in-laws.

His Parents, Your Obligation

For any apple pie–eating American girl, probably the most difficult thing to deal with is the sense of entitlement that many Indian parents have about their children taking care of them in their old age. Nursing homes are a big no-no in Indian culture; especially if your man is the oldest or only son, it is very likely that his family will expect to move in with you and for you—yes, *you*—to take care of them when they become elderly.

"It seems like most Indian children are conditioned to be with their parents out of obligation. And it's the expectation that you take care of them when they get older," says Sally. "Deepak's parents are only 60 now and they recently mentioned that they wanted to move to be closer to us. Not to help out with the kids, but so that in case something happened, *we* could more easily take care of *them*!" Sally continues, "I have two kids and a stressful job. I don't have enough time to take a piss. And they are only 60—it's not like they're invalids or something."

"They are always putting a lot of guilt on their children," says Sujata. "If you don't do what they want you to do, they will start in on that speech about how they came here with $8 in their pocket—I don't know why, but they always say $8. Anyway, they suffered by coming here to give us a better life, so they feel entitled to have us take care of them."

"Yes, normally that would be the case in India," says Taj, 40, Indian, accountant. "In the States, it depends more on the individual's situation. Indians are less likely to put their parents in a nursing home because there is a strong family bond there. And family is very important."

The Indian Mother-in-Law Wins by a Landslide

In the U.S. the mother-in-law with the worst reputation is probably the Jewish mother-in-law. But if you ask me, the Jewish mother- in-law has nothin' on the Indian mother-in-law. In her book *Culture Shock India,* Gitanjali Kolanad notes that for the Indian mother-in-law "the list of abuses goes all the way from actually murdering the new bride..." (by setting her on fire, of course) "...to preventing the young couple from having any time together and poisoning the relationship with lies and innuendos...." She adds, "This is a stereotypical view which has grown out of a harsh reality."

Ouch. Freud would have had a field day with this one! But of course, it is rarely taken to this extreme in the U.S. Nonetheless, Indian culture is known to have a very strong mother-son relationship, which may be very difficult for a typical American woman to cope with.

"It all comes from the older generation," says Sujata. "They feel entitled to have their son take care of them in their old age, so that means that *they* need to be number one in their son's life, *not* his wife. They act like it's a competition." Sujata adds, "That is why they fear interracial dating. They worry if their son marries an American girl, he won't stick to Indian traditions and will just go do his own thing."

What's Hot?

When it comes to dating, Indian guys have a lot going for them. They practice a long courting process, with no pressure to jump into the sack right away. They're goal oriented and driven to succeed, but always put family first. And something that seems unique to Indians: They not only don't avoid but actually *want* a commitment!

No Sex on the First Date

More often than not, an Indian man will *not* push for sex on the first date; the women I interviewed found Indian men noticeably less aggressive than other men. "I think we are less likely to take risky action [i.e., try to get into your pants] early on," says Amit, 36, Indian, analyst.

In most cases, Indian men expect to take the time to really get to know a woman before getting busy with her. They feel that a significant level of trust must exist before things get to the bedroom. "Sex is a big deal for us for sure—the first time, the 85th time, every time," says Vishal. "It's not true for everyone, but it's true for most Indian guys. When we have sex, we are really giving a part of ourselves."

"Yeah, when it comes to sex, they don't push you. You have to push them," says Sasha.

While this old-fashioned courting style is something many women may not be used too, most find it refreshing—and smokin' hot!

In for the Long Haul

When it comes to relationships, Indian men are much more likely to stay committed for the long term. "It's rare if they get divorced." Lisa explains, "Being divorced is a big deal in the Indian community. My Indian brother-in-law is divorced, and my husband's family refers to it as The Situation."

Although relationships do break up in the Indian community, an Indian man is much less likely than most to cut and run at the first sign of trouble. "Indian men tend to be very loyal," says Vishal. "That U.S. 50-percent divorce rate is not okay. Divorce has to be for the real deal, like someone being abusive." He adds, "In general, Indians are more willing to work things out, to compromise."

"I am the one who is more likely to cut and run if things get bad," says Marisol, 33, Mexican, saleswoman. "But my Indian boyfriend always wants to continue the relationship, to stay and work things out."

"Yes, a little too much in my Indian husband's case," says Sasha. "He was willing to work on it, even after he found out his first wife was cheating. If she hadn't eventually left him for someone else, he would probably still be unhappily married to her."

For Indian men, their main concern about marrying an "American woman" (a.k.a., a non-Indian woman) is that the woman might be less committed than an Indian woman, and therefore more likely to want a divorce if times get tough. If you date Indian men, you may find there's a bit of a role reversal; when it comes to commitment, *you* may be the one who has to convince *him* that you are in for the long term.

"I think if I were a white woman, I would consider settling down with an Indian guy," says Balaji, 38, Indian, analyst. "Women often want to have kids, and Indians are very family oriented.

Plus, I think there's less risk that it won't work out; Indian men are committed to their relationships. I think it's worth putting up with some cross-cultural issues to have a stable home."

Blazing hot.

Goal Oriented but Family Is Number One

Indian culture stresses financial success. As such, Indian men are often very goal oriented. Obtaining an education, a career, a proper home, and adequate funds to take care of a wife and children is of great importance to Indian men.

But unlike their Asian counterparts, they are—for the most part—not label conscious. They focus on saving for the future, especially for their children's education. And although a solid career is imperative, they strive to make sure it is not at the expense of family. Indian men give children and family the highest priority.

"That is true. It's a generalization, but it's absolutely true," says Sally. "They will do anything to make sure their kids have a good education. They want their children to succeed."

"When I came out, my dad said, 'I don't care if you are gay, as long as you get good grades,'" says Devak, 28, Indian, health-care executive.

"They are such hard workers. My husband Taj's father had three jobs," says Lisa. "His father always stressed the importance of school with Taj and his brother. Taj is career oriented, but not type A about it, like me."

If a goal-oriented family man is what you seek, an Indian man might be not too cold, not too hot, but just right.

What's Not?

Indian guys sound so great! No doubt, you're fired up for your first full-on Bollywood experience. But before you snag that sexy-eyebrowed, curry-eating, pro-commitment hunk of Indian manhood, make sure you also know what to watch out for. Regional variations in generosity, a God-awful stink, and interference from meddling family matchmakers are just a few of the things that women said are not so hot about dating Indian guys.

Picking Up the Tab Can Vary by Region

For Indians, generosity is a very individual thing. Some Indians are generous to a fault; others pinch every penny. Most Indian men are taught to pick up the tab on a date, but the women I spoke with said that in reality, it's not always a given.

"If he doesn't pay on the first date, that is a *big* red flag," says Indira, 37, Indian, lawyer. "You might want to look elsewhere."

"I went out with this Indian guy once," says Hanna, 30, Chinese, hairdresser. "He took me to this cheap restaurant in Union Square. The check came, and he didn't move. Then I got out my wallet—he still didn't move. Then I pulled the bill toward me—he *still* didn't move. And then, when I started to take money out, he said something like, 'Well, I usually pay for my dates,' but his hand *still didn't move*! And the bill was, like, $20. I put down my half and left."

"I pick up the tab," says Vishal. "But I am always looking to see what a girl orders. If she gets the lobster, that is a problem." He explains, "We look for girls that are going for value. Value to us is hot. If you are going to be with a woman for the long term, you want to know she's good with money."

The region an Indian man hails from can give you a clue as to his generosity. Gujaratis have a reputation for being cheap. When I shared this with Vishal, a Gujarati, he replied, "Yes, and we are proud of it!" Punjabis, on the other hand, are known for being generous—not to mention fun loving and partaking in large quantities of the Johnny Walker Black. (Not a tough decision for me as to who I'd rather hang out with!) Indians from Delhi also have a generous reputation. "My husband is from Delhi," says Jill. "He's not cheap. If anything he's really generous with everyone."

Knowing the state or territory your Indian man is from might not only help you know more about him, but it could also tell you more about how he treats his women.

What Is That Funky Smell?

Indian men, especially the ones who eat a lot of traditional food, can be—I'm sorry, there is no nice way to say this—a bit smelly. Some people say it comes out of their pores; others say it sticks to exterior skin; and some say it just sticks to everything. As it was described by the people I interviewed, the curry smell seems similar to the Seinfeldian rampant mutant BO, a Godzilla of stench that flattens anyone it comes in contact with.

"What is with the body smell?" says Ciel, 27, Dominican, office assistant. "And worse, they don't seem to smell it. This one Indian guy I dated, I swear, after he ate, I could still smell him hours later."

"Not me, but I am very meticulous about that," says Taj. "I have a kitchen with a strong exhaust fan. I don't want my clothes smelling like curry."

"Indian men are definitely smelly, especially if they are a FOB [fresh off the boat]," says Vishal. "The greatest gift you can give an Indian guy when he comes here from India is deodorant and instructions on how to use it." He continues, "Even Indian guys that grew up here smell sometimes. They like strong flavors—garlic, chili, raw onion. When I cook, I have on a fan and every window open in the house. I don't want to have that Indian house smell, where the whole house smells like the grease trap in a restaurant."

"My husband never smells. He takes showers all the time," says Sally. "But my in-laws have been staying with us for the last week, and the kitchen reeks of Indian food. The pillows even smell like Indian food. They burn the spices so they are more potent." She adds, "I am telling you: Don't ever buy a house owned by Indians. If you did, you would have to paint it top to bottom to get rid of the smell. And I'm not even sure that would do it."

If you need your house and your man to smell like roses, an Indian man probably is not a good match—although good luck getting *any* man to smell like roses....

Beware The Circuit

In India, 95 percent of marriages are still arranged. These marriages are considered more of a merger of two families than a marriage of two people. In the U.S., the percentage of Indians in arranged marriages is much lower, but they do happen. In fact, Indian parents often pressure their children to be on what I call The Circuit—that is, an informal Indian matchmaking network that can stretch across the globe. Indian men and women on The Circuit often get photographed in traditional Indian clothing, and their parents hand out the resulting pictures like baseball cards to prospective suitors or their family members.

For a non-Indian woman dating an Indian man, it's good to be aware of The Circuit; it would not be out of character for your boyfriend's parents to continue to look for an Indian wife for their son even after he has told them he is serious with you. And to please his family, he might even be taking the dates.

"This happened to me, and I am even Indian," says Chandani. "I was dating this guy on The Circuit. I don't know if he was just doing it to please his parents or what, but he just seemed to be going through the motions. We had been dating each other for a while, and I always had this hinky feeling about him." She adds, "We broke up, and a few months later he turned up with this serious girlfriend. I don't know if his mom didn't like her or his mom didn't know, but I guess he was dating her, too, the whole time."

Just like any interracial relationship, it's your boyfriend's job to stand up to his parents, tell them he loves you regardless of your race, and inform them that he is officially off the market. Until that happens, you can expect your Indian man to remain on The Circuit.

Bitch, Make Me Some Curry

Given what we have discussed so far, it's no surprise that some Indian men prefer traditional gender roles. "I think Deepak would like it if I was softer," says Sally. "Indians are used to more traditional male-female roles. I'm sure he wouldn't mind it if I had dinner at the table every night when he got home, either. Like that's going to happen."

"I found Indian guys liked their women submissive," says Ciel. "That didn't work for me. You tell me to do something, and I am more likely to do the opposite."

"My Indian boyfriend definitely likes traditional gender roles," says Marisol. "But I am Mexican, so I am already like that. "

"Deep down inside, they do, even if they won't admit it," says Sujata. "Even my husband wishes that I would be like that. But he knows I'm never going to change." She adds, "They want to be the protector, make the money. Women having babies is an amazing thing. They can't do that, so I guess being the protector and making money for the family is *their* amazing thing—well, the closest thing to it, anyway."

"It's a mixed bag. Some of us grew up watching our moms do everything, and it made us mad. I was like, 'Dad, get up off your ass and help mom!'" says Vishal. "I am sure the FOBs expect that, but Indian guys that grew up here are more Renaissance men. We don't mind helping in the kitchen."

"I believe my wife and I are equals," says Taj. "I cook. I clean. I think a lot of it is the difference between growing up here versus India. Indian men might be used to servants doing everything."

Between the Sheets

"I believe that the size of your penis is in direct correlation with how much sex you will have in your life. The smaller your dick, the more you will fuck...If you don't believe me, look at the two largest populations in the world."

—RUSSELL PETERS

When I started my research on Indians, I assumed they must be very comfortable with sex and potentially extremely talented. They wrote the *Kama Sutra* for Christ's sake! I was surprised to find, however, that most Indians are very conservative in this regard. They often carry a lot of shame about sex—especially sex before marriage.

Amit sums it up: "Indians are just not in touch with their sexuality."

No doubt, 100 years of pint-drinking, snooty-talking, crooked-teeth-having, oppressive British rule set the Indians back as far as sexual repression goes. But even my closest friends had a hard time dishing the good stuff, saying things like, "Oh, there isn't anything really notable about Indians and sex," or "You're probably not going to get an Indian woman to do anal, but other than that, there are no real issues." So while I did get some great comments from Indians and the people who date them, for the good stuff I had to go to the pros—and boy, did the pros dish.

Gotta Keep the Numbers Low

Most modern Indians living in New York City have given up the no-sex-before-marriage tradition, diminishing their guilt by keeping the numbers low—the number of people they sleep with, that is. "I have even gone as far as to get naked in bed and then call it off at the last minute," says Indira. "I was doing the math, and he just wasn't worth it." Not sponge worthy, I guess.

"No one else knows your number, you know?" I say. "You could tell people anything."

"Yeah," says Indira, "but *I* know the number."

Wow, that is some Indian guilt.

"That guilt comes from our parents," says Sujata. "They tell us, 'Good girls don't have sex,' but then you are supposed to have babies. How is that supposed to work?"

There is a double standard, of course; it is more acceptable for men to sleep around. But because of the close-knit Indian community, numbers guilt is very real for Indian men, too. Like Indian women, they are likely to have only a few sexual partners before settling down. "My husband Deepak had slept with a few other women before we got married, but not a big number," says Sally. "He didn't even date Indian women, but he really wasn't much for sleeping around. He usually had girlfriends."

Of course, there is one exception. (No one is perfect, right?) Some Indian men date outside the Indian community to "keep it off the books." By dating outside the Indian community—a surprisingly small world—he makes sure that others are less aware of the number. "Indian parents have a saying: no BMW—black, Muslim, or white," says Amit. "There are some Indian guys dating white girls that think of it as a fun time, but don't take the relationship seriously."

What is important for you to know? Indian men are less likely to be belt-notching, babe-bagging, playah playahs. As long as you make sure he's not keeping if "off the books" he might have great boyfriend potential.

The Equipment May Come Up Short

In 2006, the BBC published a story titled "Condoms 'Too Big' for Indian Men." It detailed a 1,000-person study that found that 60 percent of Indian men have penises shorter than the international condom standard. Naturally, this led me to believe that their equipment may come up short.

Actually, many of the women I spoke with disagreed. "That has not been true in my experience, but don't tell Deepak that because I like to make him sweat," says Sally. She concedes, though, that it might be an issue for other Indian men. "I think it might have something to do with nutrition. When Deepak's relatives visit us from India, they are a good foot or more shorter than his relatives in America." But, she adds, "Haven't you heard the saying? White too small, black too big, brown is just right."

It's no surprise that some Indian men also disagree. "I know you are saying Indians have small dicks," says Balaji. "But I look down at it all day, and I am telling you, that's not true!"

But not everyone. "Yeah, that is probably true dude, but I don't know," says Vishal. "You don't see many Indian guys in porn." He adds, "I will be honest: I ain't the biggest guy in the world. But get this straight: I *do* fit in regular condoms."

The Pros

The professionals tend to agree with the BBC. "In general, Indians are smaller," says Monique, 50, Cuban, madam. "I'll never forget this one Indian client. It was a real problem because he couldn't fit any of the condoms." She continues, "He was so small, and we are always safe, no exceptions. So, you know those finger condoms? Well, he couldn't fit any of the regular condoms, so we had to use the finger condoms instead." Wow. That is small.

On average, Indians seem to run on the lower end of the five- to six-inch U.S. average. But with more than 1 billion Indians on this planet, it's hard to know what you will get.

Warm and Sensual Lovers

When it comes to making love, Indian men have a good reputation. "I had a love affair with a man from Bombay, back when it was still Bombay," says Cindy, 30, white girl, analyst. "I had never before or since had sex with a man that was so seductive, so passionate, so sensual. No American man would be able to compete."

The Pros

Our professionals agreed: "It may take them a while to get comfortable with you sexually, but they are very warm and enjoy women that are warm," says Monique.

It may also have a lot to do with their attitudes toward women and sex. "To me, affection is even more important than sex," says Baahir, 37, Indian, consultant.

"Indian guys are really into the romantic aspects of love. Bollywood-type romance is almost more important than sex for an Indian," says Vishal. "It's hot for us to make our woman happy sexually. It's more about the woman, really."

Makes me want to go out and get myself an Indian boyfriend right now! If warm and sensual is your thing, an Indian man might just hit the spot.

Even North Indians Have No Problem Going South

Indian men do not have any inhibitions when it comes to licking pussy. Unlike some of the other cultures I've discussed, there is nothing in the Indian culture that makes an Indian man less macho or less a man because he is pleasing his woman. For Indians, pleasing the woman is the goal, not just a means to an end. "My husband has no problems in that department," says Sujata. "He insists on it." She adds, "Of course, I couldn't ask, because 'good girls' don't ask."

"I don't think Indians have any problems going south," says Baahir. "Me? Oh, no, no, no. I have no trouble doing that!"

Bi the Way

As I mentioned before, when it came to sex, some Indians found it hard to tell me the good stuff, the scoop, the skinny, the 411, the lowdown. As a result, I had to rely on the pros to fill me in on the juicier stuff—one of the juiciest things being Indian men's interest in, well, er, other men. This was best demonstrated by the pro's Gandhi story. Not to be confused with the famous savior of India, Mohandas (Mahatma) Karamchand Gandhi, "Gandhi" here is merely Monique's nickname for one of her johns. (All the johns at Monique's place had great nicknames: Trench Coat Tony, Butt J, and Napoleon to name a few.)

The Pros

"I think the most notable thing about Indian men is that they are more bisexual than they want to admit," says Monique. "I remember this time when Gandhi heard a couple in another room having sex and asked if he could watch. The couple said it was okay, so we let Gandhi in. And then these two 'straight men' ended up having sex with each other. And that wasn't the first time that kind of thing happened."

"Indians just never talk about that subject," says Vishal. "I am not saying, 'Oh my God, there are no gay Indians.' I am sure there are —a normal population. There are probably just a whole lot more in the closet because as an Indian man, you are not supposed to be gay."

Most Indians, like Vishal, say they are unaware of this phenomenon, but I think it's interesting that of all the cultures discussed at the cat house, only Indians were noted as being heavily bi.

Although being gay was illegal in India until only recently, there has always been a lot of outward closeness shown between men in Indian society, including public handholding. Most Indians will argue vehemently that this outward closeness does not mean they are gay, but it seems reasonable to assume that this behavior might result in some slippage into the nether regions. I'm just sayin'.

Our Stories

Now you have all the spicy details about Curry Fever. The stories in this section reveal what it's like to date Indian in the real world. As you'll find, sex can be dangerous, it's important to wear flame-retardant clothing to Indian weddings, and you shouldn't plan your outfit around your shoes. Oh, and don't forget the Indian amoebas!

The Dangers of the Kama Sutra

When Balaji met Allison, he had no idea what he was in for. Balaji came to New York City from northern India—the territory of Delhi, to be specific—for grad school. He was a total FOB when he met Allison, a cute, unassuming, shy little Irish girl with jet-black hair and a pretty smile. The two hit it off right away.

For their first date, Allison suggested they go to an Indian restaurant, Indigo. Balaji, who assumed that all Americans ate only hot dogs and hamburgers, was surprised to discover that Allison was a vegetarian. And Allison, not realizing that people from the north often eat meat (not beef, of course), was surprised to find that Balaji was *not* a vegetarian.

Balaji spent most of the dinner fielding Allison's seemingly endless questions about India. "Is it true that Indians don't eat with the left hand?" "What do you do if you're left handed?" "Is it true that all Indians smell like curry?" Allison sniffed in Balaji's general direction. "You don't seem to." "What is that stuff about the sacred cow, anyway? You believe cows are, like, god or something?" Allison, Balaji quickly discovered, knew just enough about India to be dangerous. Given her Indophile leanings, Balaji couldn't help but wonder whether Allison was only interested in dating him because he was Indian.

It wasn't the most pleasant date Balaji had ever been on, but Allison seemed nice enough. And since she was the only girl he knew in the city, Balaji decided they might as well go on a second date. This time, Allison suggested they go to yet another Indian restaurant. Balaji was disappointed in her choice; he was much more interested in seeing what America had to offer. But given the Indian propensity to say something pleasant rather than something true, he remained quiet.

Afterward, Allison invited Balaji back to her apartment. Although Balaji hadn't learned much in his short time in the U.S., he knew enough to realize that being invited to a woman's apartment meant one thing: gettin' busy. And while he was a bit taken aback by her invitation given that it was so early in their relationship, he decided to stay open minded and experience a bit of real American culture.

The first thing Allison did after opening the door to her apartment was to remove her shoes. Balaji relaxed a bit; this was just like being at home in India! But as it turned out, that was the *only* thing about Allison's apartment that was like home. When Allison excused herself to use the bathroom, Balaji let his eyes wander around her small studio apartment. Perusing her bookshelf, he quickly detected a theme: sex. In fact, a large section of the bookcase was dedicated exclusively to sex—positions, preferences, and techniques—and included several books on the Kama Sutra. Balaji froze, not sure if he should stay and get the ride of his life or run screaming into the night.

When Allison emerged from the bathroom, she was instantly aggressive. Balaji was shocked. He had heard that American women were more liberated when it came to sex, but this was much more than he had expected, especially from a good Irish Catholic girl. And of course, it represented a major deviation from the long courting process he was used to in India. But Balaji decided to go with the flow. When in Rome, right? Anyway, Indian upbringing aside, Balaji was a man, after all—and most men don't pass up free sex.

Things quickly progressed from the couch to the bed—and that's when things went from freaky to freaky deaky. As she kissed and groped Balaji, Allison pulled back the bedspread—and there, smack in the middle of the bed, was an enormous drawing of an Indian guy getting a blow job. Allison had Kama Sutra sheets, with very large and very graphic illustrations of a variety of positions. Balaji tried to put the drawings out of his head, but as he and Allison began having sex, he kept seeing this dude's penis out of the corner of his eye. With every stroke, he felt like he was pounding the guy, not Allison! And then when he kissed her, all he could see was the guy in the drawing, complete with handlebar mustache, grinning ear to ear. Now Balaji felt like he was kissing the guy. He couldn't take it; eventually, he had to override his Indian propensity to be pleasant and say something true. "Allison, look, no man wants to look at another man when they are sexually pleasuring a woman. I cannot do this. You are going to have to change the sheets!"

Allison obliged, which helped. But the sex still seemed more like torture then pleasure. In fact, every time Balaji came to Allison's apartment, she was waiting at the door, diagram in hand of some new move she wanted to try. She also regularly woke him up in the middle of the night to try different positions. Balaji wondered if this was what all American women were like. If so, why weren't there more American men in traction? Why weren't back braces a multi-billion-dollar business in the U.S.? To make matters worse, Balaji threw out his back while performing one of the more complicated positions of the *Kama Sutra* with Allison.

Bedridden (alone) for more than a week, he was unable to attend school or work. Thanks to Allison, Balaji's health, his grades, and his bank account were taking a hit. But, it seems, that wasn't even the worst of it.

One nice, sunny, spring day, Balaji and Allison took a stroll through Battery Park. After sitting together on a green park bench to rest and watch the boats, Allison rose and sauntered toward the railing. Balaji assumed she was simply getting a closer look at the Lackawanna clock tower, but he soon realized that she was walking toward an older couple. "I didn't know what was happening," says Balaji. "She just walks up to the water for a minute, and then I see her talking to these strangers, this older couple. Then I see her *hugging* this older couple. And I'm thinking, 'What the hell is going on here?' And then they are walking toward me." Balaji's voice grows louder, recounting the events as if they happened yesterday. "And then she introduces them. It's her *parents*."

Allison, Balaji realized, had neglected to inform him that they would be attending a meet-the-parents brunch. Being the consummate polite Indian, Balaji didn't make a stink; he went along with the plan as if he had known about it all along. But the brunch was difficult. Although Balaji's FOB accent had never posed a problem for Allison (perhaps because she was more interested in the language of love), her parents struggled to understand him. When the check came, Balaji offered to pick up the tab, generosity being an essential component of his Delhi upbringing. "It was maybe $200, but to a college student, that was a lot of money," says Balaji. "I remember my hand almost shaking as I put my credit card down. And her father did not refuse it." He adds, "I don't know why, but I thought at the time, if I didn't end up marrying this girl, at least I paid for the sex."

Incredibly, Allison's sex drive seemed to escalate after that. "I was worried I would come over and there would be a dog there or something," says Balaji. After six months together, the continued *Kama Sutra* wake-up calls at all hours of the night, and the surprise family brunch, Balaji had had it with Allison. He told her it was over, but she wouldn't listen. "I had to change my cell-phone number and even pay a $100 fee," says Balaji. "But it was so worth it."

Rich in Family Currency

Although Charles was born in the U.K. to blood-pudding-eating, pint-drinking, not-so-straight-teeth-having Brits, he emigrated to the U.S. at age three. As a result, he has no detectable accent and looks and acts like a hot-dog eating, TV-watching, flag-waving, beer-drinking American frat boy.

That was pretty much the impression Hita got when she first saw Charles—the drunken frat boy part, at least. It was no surprise, then, that Hita, a close friend of Charles' twin brother Bob, didn't think much of Charles. But Charles was hooked on Hita from their first meeting. He found Hita's Indian features and dark complexion beautiful and exotic. Her personality, he thought, was as warm as a double-shot, no-foam latte, and her mind as rich and complex as a well-roasted coffee. (Charles, working 90-hour weeks, was spending a lot of time at Starbucks during this period.) Every time Charles saw Hita, he wanted to say, "Your eyes are like bottomless pools of the richest chocolate and your wit as sharp as a Ginsu knife." But all that ever came out was, "That top is super [belch]. It makes your boobs look fantastic. You wanna go make out?" Needless to say, it was pretty hard for Hita to find Charles tolerable, let alone attractive. Plus, Charles was an investment banker, and Hita, rightly believing that all investment bankers are assholes, had sworn she would never date one. "I think the best way I could say it was that she was generally unimpressed with my approach," says Charles; for the time being, he would have to admire Hita from afar.

One evening, during a friendly get-together at Bob's, Charles spotted Hita alone on the terrace. Although both were seeing other people at the time, he still took every opportunity to speak to Hita. "It's a beautiful evening," he said quietly, stepping outside to join her. It wasn't the most original line, but it represented a big leap for Charles as it did not contain the words "boob" or "make out." Even so, Hita wanted none of it. "Yes it is," she said, turning away to deflect any unwanted advances.

"You know," Charles said, "the Empire State Building always gets all the attention, but I think the Chrysler Building has such an elegance about it." He continued, "It reminds me there is so much beauty in the world. I just feel so lucky to be a very tiny part of it." Hita was quiet, shocked to find herself hanging on his every word. He seemed so genuine! Who knew that under all that beer, Brooks Brothers suits, Hermès ties, and Wall Street lingo was an enlightened *human being*? Almost a year later, they ran into each other at another of Bob's parties. This time, both were single. And this time, thanks to Charles's friends (who had spent the last 12 months telling Hita what a great guy he was when he wasn't three sheets to the wind) Hita decided to give Charles a chance.

Charles—worried about Hita, who lived in New Jersey, finding her way around the city—arranged to meet her at Moondance Diner on the edge of Chinatown. Built from a gleaming silver Airstream trailer, the Moondance would be easy for Hita to spot. From there, they would walk to a nice restaurant nearby for dinner. But despite all their planning, and although Charles himself stuck out like a sore thumb—a tall white guy standing in a sea of Chinese in front of a shiny silver trailer on a huge empty lot—Hita blew right by him in her car.

Although their first date got off to an inauspicious start, the pair hit it off just fine after a couple of bottles of wine and an exquisite dinner at a nearby restaurant in Nolita. Afterward, though, Charles still wasn't sure whether Hita liked him. After all, Hita had lots of male friends; Charles couldn't tell whether she thought of him as serious dating material or if he was going to be stuck in the dreaded Friend Zone. Either way, given their history, Charles knew he had to be careful to be gentlemanly and to take things slowly. So he was really taken aback on the second date when Hita asked, "So when are you going to kiss me?" Fortunately, Charles could think on his feet. "How about right now?" he answered.

Soon after that, Charles and Hita decided to date each other exclusively—at least, they *thought* they were exclusive. In reality, because Hita was almost 30, her family had placed her on The Circuit—albeit stealthily. Suddenly, she was being introduced by her parents to random guys at parties and experiencing "Fancy meeting you here!" mishaps while she was out. Of course, in Hita's parents' defense, they didn't know she was dating Charles; like many young Indians, Hita had a firm don't-ask-don't-tell policy. She'd never brought a man home to meet her parents. (Soon, Charles would be the first.) Fortunately, Charles understood the situation. "The Circuit stuff never bothered me," he says. "I understood where her family was coming from." He adds, "Her parents had had an arranged marriage, and I never saw two people get along better. Plus, they didn't really know about me until after we were engaged."

That engagement came sooner rather than later. In fact, Charles's and Hita's romance wasn't whirlwind so much as warp speed. Just a month and half after their first date, the two decided to tie the knot. There was just one problem: Charles was, like most Wall Streeters from time to time, out of work. Sure, he was keeping up appearances by running a "start-up." And yeah, he might potentially do a deal at some point that might or might not result in him actually getting paid something more than the value of a Snickers bar. But mostly, he'd just printed some business cards with his name on them so he could weasel his way into industry and banking conferences. There was no actual paycheck involved—meaning that the chances of him earning Hita's family's blessing were slim. But Charles didn't want to wait to make things official with Hita's family. "I was just so filled with enthusiasm about Hita," says Charles. "I had to call her father right away and ask for her hand in marriage" (although he wisely neglected to go into any detail about his work situation). Charles was thrilled when Hita's father granted his request. Soon thereafter, Charles was again gainfully employed, although regrettably still as an investment banker. "Something just snapped in me," says Charles. "I realized, I love this woman. I need to get a real job."

One year later, Charles and Hita were married in a traditional Hindu ceremony. "My family is Church of England, or as I call it, 'Catholicism without the guilt,'" says Charles, laughing at his own joke. "We are not especially religious." He continues, "I wanted an Indian ceremony. Indian weddings are just a lot more fun."

Charles wasn't thrilled with every aspect of an Indian wedding, however. "I probably bought the most expensive polyester suit *ever* for my wedding—$700," says Charles. "The cut looked great—Nehru collar and everything—but it was white. White!" He slaps his forehead. "I am really white, so I ordered *tan*. It was clearly *not* tan. Even funnier," he says, "the tailor kept arguing with me, trying to convince me it was really tan." Besides which, any good Indian tailor should know that white is for funerals! Charles was also less than thrilled about the shoes. "Yeah, I refused to wear those Aladdin-looking things," says Charles. "You know, like in *Aladdin*: gold with the toe curling up into a point."

Speaking of shoes, the groom must remove his shoes at the beginning of the Hindu wedding ceremony; then, once married, he must put them on again to take his bride home and start a life together. It is tradition that during the ceremony, the bride's sisters or other family members kidnap the shoes and hold them for ransom. The groom, who needs his shoes to complete the ceremony, has to pay any ransom to get the shoes back. I always thought this was such a fun tradition, but Charles was underwhelmed. "It was mostly just annoying," says Charles.

There's a lot to a Hindu wedding, but one of the most important elements is the part where the bride and groom walk around a fire. This fire symbolizes the spiritual witness to the ceremony—

essentially, God. Charles, understanding the importance of the ritual, took his role in it very seriously. As he walked around the edge of the fire, the end of the traditional long, flowing scarf he was wearing wafted over the flame, as if in slow motion. For a split second, Charles, ever aware of his 100-percent polyester suit, saw in his mind's eye an image of a cartoon mouse lighting a stick of dynamite. Fortunately, he was able to snatch the scarf from the flame before it caught fire (though it was a bit singed). Neither the polyester suit nor its unwilling occupant would go down in a blaze of glory that day.

Charles dodged another bullet during the exchanging of the garlands. "As the man," says Charles, "I had to stand perfectly straight when Hita placed the garland around my neck." He explains, "It basically establishes who is 'in charge' in the marriage. If I bowed while receiving the garland, that would mean, essentially, I was her bitch." My ears perk up; I'm always interested in finding ways to make a man my bitch. "I had a little fun with it," he continues. "I stood straight and dodged my head a bit as she gave me the garland, as if I was going to give her a fight for it, but then I bowed my head slightly to her at the end to demonstrate that she runs the show too."

Charles had long since learned that Hita's family's generosity—with both their money and their time—knew no bounds. Their wedding was no exception. "To give you a sense, I would say if they only had $10, they would have spent $11 on our wedding. That is just how they are." (That must have added up to a pretty penny, seeing as how Charles and Hita had more than 300 guests—although to be fair, that would be considered a little on the small side for a typical Indian wedding.) "And it has nothing to do with showing off, or one-upping someone," Charles adds. "It's just the difference between being inclusive instead of exclusive." Case in point: Hita's family is from south India—specifically, the state of Goa, which is heavily vegetarian. Even so, to ensure that all their guests felt welcome, Hita's parents offered every type of food at the wedding, including the most blasphemous of meats, *beef*. And even more important than the food for some was the booze. "Hita's elder uncles don't even care about the food," says Charles. "'Just make sure the Scotch is good,' they'll say. That's all that matters to them." That worked fine for Charles. "For me, all the better," he says. "I only had one goal with our wedding: for people to have fun."

During the reception, Charles's father—known for being as stubborn as a goat with lead hooves—stood to make a speech. "I understood it was important for him to feel included," says Charles. "*All* I asked was that he not mention the British occupation of India." Charles held his breath when his father took the stage. He'd done his best to prepare his father and was hopeful the speech would be at worst inert—hopeful, that is, until his father opened his mouth. "India," his father began with some pomposity, "was the jewel of the British Empire...." Even still, the memory makes Charles cringe. "I asked him to do *one thing*: Don't mention the history! But he just couldn't do it." He continues, readjusting himself in his chair: "I looked out at the faces of Hita's relatives; they all looked like they were witnessing some sort of car accident. It was so embarrassing." Charles adds, "They were nice, though. They didn't make a big deal about it." I guess there are some times when the whole it's-better-to-say-something-nice-than-something-true thing works to your benefit.

Even though Charles's family hails from a country that occupied India for almost 200 years (and raped and pillaged its resources for far longer), he never met any resistance from Hita's relatives. "Her family is just so amazing," Charles says. "I always felt cut off from my extended family, partly because they were across the pond. But that isn't even it. She is in contact with all of her aunts, uncles, and cousins, even the ones in India." Charles pulls out his iPhone to scroll through some family photos. "My family is also not very touchy feely, but Indians are more physically comfortable with themselves and others. And me, they treat me great, like a prince. They always have."

In the end, it turned out the British occupation of India served as a bit of a boon to the couple in some ways. For one thing, both families shared certain cultural customs like drinking tea twice a day and funny English expressions. (Brilliant! The dog's bollocks! Cheeky monkey!) As far as cultural differences go, Charles found himself somewhat disappointed. "I always figured Hita would be spending all weekend cooking up great Indian food in the kitchen," he says. "But she doesn't really cook much." He continues, "I don't either. It was fine when we were living in the city, but when we moved out to Jersey to be closer to Hita's family, we almost starved to death. We both eventually had to take cooking classes."

For the most part, their racial differences are synergistic. They are never problematic for the couple or their families. But for strangers, there is often confusion. "When we pass people on the street with our two daughters, you see them—they are trying to figure it out," says Charles. "They look at me and then my oldest Rajani, who is fair skinned with red hair, and then at my wife, who is dark skinned, and then back to me again. You can tell they are mulling it over in their mind." He continues, "I swear, you can almost see the wheels turning. 'Is she the nanny? Or maybe he left his wife for the nanny?' They are not sure." When I ask if they ever say anything, Charles answers, "Sometimes. We all went to the Caribbean for vacation last week —Hita and the kids and her parents. They all went to the pool to relax and I came down later. 'Oh,' this woman said from across the pool. 'You explain so much.'" People are so fuckin' nosy.

Of course, how other people regard the couple is of little consequence to them. It's funny sometimes, but never material to their relationship. What *is* important is that Charles's being part of an Indian family has been so positive—or, better said, *enlightening*. "We went shopping just after our first born began walking," remembers Charles. "Hita and her family were swarming around Rajani like an amoeba. They weren't talking to each other, all going different directions, but at the same time knowing exactly where everyone was." He pauses for a moment, still trying to wrap his brain around the concept. "They were all supremely focused on Rajani. They were so in touch with each other, communicating without communicating, almost one being, this amoeba."

The most important thing Charles has learned from Hita is the importance of family. For Hita's parents, their children are the center of the universe—something that took a little time for an English American like Charles to appreciate. "After we got married, I was still in my investment-banker mode," says Charles. "Focused on making money and traveling a ton." He continues, "Now, I realize how stupid that was. Hita always tells me just to get a nine-to-five job. She doesn't care about the money. 'Your wealth is your children,' she tells me."

This idea of family currency—that our main charge in life is not meeting goals, developing a career, making money, or acquiring possessions, but making our homes a happy, supportive place for our children to thrive—was new to Charles. "With my oldest, Rajani, I was a real absentee dad in her first few years," recalls Charles. It sounds like guilt, but something about it rings more like sincere worry. That parent-child relationship is paramount; any hour, any minute, any *second* missed is an indisputable tragedy. "I really hope my daughters take after Hita," says Charles. "I think I have my focus in the right place most of the time now. I am not yet able to become part of the amoeba, but I'll never stop trying to learn."

The Laid-Back Indian and the Type-A Jew

Shortly after Lisa Lipschitz, a good Jewish girl, started her new job as legal counsel for an international technology company, she spotted a cute Indian guy, Taj. As far as Lisa was concerned, Taj was the hottest Indian guy in the place—which was really saying something, seeing as the majority of her company's employees were either Indian or Pakistani. She was instantly attracted to Taj, but it was more than that: Lisa was overwhelmed by a feeling she had never felt before. Without warning, it popped into Lisa's mind the very first day she saw Taj: "I am going to marry that man." For a few weeks Taj and Lisa said their hellos as they passed in the halls. But they had never been formally introduced, and Lisa wasn't sure how to facilitate an introduction.

One day, the usually proper Lisa was futzing around with Excel. All her colleague, Bob, could hear from her office were expletives. "What the hell is a REF? Is that English?" Lisa hissed. "And why can't I get rid of this circular reference? Pivot table, what the fuck is that?"

"Hey," Bob called out. "Problems with Excel? Why don't you just call that guy, what's his name again? Raj? No. Taj? That's right. Taj Mehta. Like Taj Mahal. Why don't you ask Taj from Finance to help you?" Perfect! And so it began over an Excel spreadsheet —the ultimate geek romance.

During one of their meetings, Lisa casually mentioned that she was training for a triathlon. It wasn't exactly a lie, but she knew nothing of triathlons. But she had heard that Taj was really into the gym. "It's my first one," Lisa said. "And well, uh, you know, I have never trained for anything like it." She paused for a moment, shifting her eyes to Taj's biceps. "You work out a lot don't you?"

"Oh yeah, all the time," Taj said, quickly getting back to work. "So, what you need to do is click in cell A1 and then put in an equal sign and...."

Lisa was undeterred by Taj's Indian work ethic. "Well, maybe you could help me with my training," she said. "It's just, I'm not sure what I'm doing, and a triathlon—well, there's a lot to it." And of course, our poor, unwitting, polite Taj obliged.

"All of our 'dates' were around this triathlon," Lisa says. There were workout sessions, during which Lisa did a lot of half-assed weight lifting with at least one almost-bionic eye glued to Taj at all times. Then there was the one bike ride they did. Although it was technically part of Lisa's "training," it was more of a joy ride than a prep ride, as Lisa spent most of it basking in the perfect weather or gazing at Taj's cute butt. Obviously, these were not your traditional dinner-and-a-movie dates; in fact, to Taj, they weren't even dates at all. Lisa had been so stealthy stalking her prey, Taj didn't even realize he was in a relationship—until jealousy reared its head. "You know Bob in Sales?" Lisa asked Taj one day in the office kitchen.

"Yeah, Bob, sure," Taj said, only partially paying attention as he poured his coffee.

"Well," Lisa paused for effect, looking down into her dark coffee specked with swirls of half and half. "It's the strangest thing. He said he has a single friend he wants to set me up with."

Her statement hung in the air, growing heavier as each second seemed to pass more and more slowly. "You dating other people?" Taj finally looked up from his coffee and into Lisa's eyes. "I don't think I like that." Hook. Line. Sinker. Taj was caught. Even today, Taj claims he was an innocent bystander, not realizing what was happening until he was finally and irreparably caught in Lisa's web. (Makes me think maybe Lisa should be writing her own relationship book....) They had been dating for more than several months without Taj even knowing it. But now they were official; that's when the real fun began.

Just six months into their relationship, Taj invited Lisa to meet the Mehta family. Because Taj was Lisa's first Indian boyfriend, she had no idea of the importance of this meeting. Even so, she took special care in choosing her outfit—particularly her shoes. (To call Lisa a shoe enthusiast would be an understatement; Lisa has a closet filled with hundreds of pairs of shoes, all individually categorized and labeled in clear shoe boxes. For Lisa, the shoes make the outfit, and the outfit makes the w-o-man.) For this first gathering with Taj's family, she selected a pair of tall boots that coordinated beautifully with her skirt and top. Although her only clean pair of tights had a hole in the toe, she wasn't worried; no one would see it under her boots.

Wrong.

As the couple pulled up to the Mehta home, Taj turned to Lisa and said, like it was nothing at all, "By the way you can't wear shoes in the house."

"I can't tell you the panic that fell over me," says Lisa. "And he waits until right before we are going in. I could have worn anything else, but I picked this outfit *specifically to go with the boots*. It just didn't work without the boots!" She adds, "And then, on top of it, I had this big hole in my tights. I remember taking my boots off in the hallway and then trying to move the hole to the bottom of my foot without anyone noticing. It was *horrifying*."

Apart from her footwear crisis, Lisa thought her first time meeting Taj's parents went pretty well. "What was most noticeable about Taj's family was that they are so calm," says Lisa. "No one raises their voice. Ever. And everyone is warm and welcoming." She adds, "Did I mention how calm they are? I had never seen anything like it." What she didn't know was how important that first meeting really was—until her office colleague, Lakshmi, clued her in. "Taj took you to meet his parents?" asked Lakshmi. "Oh, you know what that means. He is going to marry you. Indian men do not introduce a woman to their parents unless they are going to marry her."

Next was meeting *her* parents. "I think I was so impressed with how even-keeled Taj's family is because mine is so opposite," says Lisa. "My mom has regular freak-outs, and you never know what might cause them." She adds, "I warned Taj on the way to her house, but he was like 'Whatever. I am sure she's fine.'" Sure enough, later that night, Taj witnessed a real, honest-to-goodness, threat-level-red, Mrs. Ethel Beth Lipschitz meltdown. "My mom was bustling around in the kitchen and accidentally broke a pumpkin pie. She started screaming and crying. 'Oh my God! Oh my God! We have to get another pumpkin pie! Thanksgiving is ruined!'" Lisa waves her hands in the air, indicating the sort of the-sky-is-falling-because-I-broke-a-nail panic I'm used to seeing in my own family. "No kidding, she was sobbing on the floor." Lisa continues, "I went to the living room to check on Taj—I will never forget that look on his face. My dark Indian boyfriend was almost white, his eyes bugging out of their sockets. He had never seen anything like the freak-out of a Jewish American woman."

"I know this may be a crazy idea," I say. "But can't you guys go buy a pie?"

"No," explains Lisa. "My mom loves to play the martyr, and she makes everything from scratch. We went to the store to get one can of pumpkin, and Taj said, 'Why don't we get two cans, just in case?' I was like, 'No. You have to follow her instructions *to the letter*. If you don't, she will just freak out again.'"

"And he kept dating you?" I say. "What a saint." Or rather, a six-armed manifestation of the god of forgiveness and understanding.

Soon, Lakshmi's prediction came true: After they had been dating for around a year, Taj proposed to Lisa. Taj didn't really care what kind of wedding they had, but Lisa wanted to make sure both cultures were equally represented. So they planned—and when I say "they," I mean Lisa and her mother—to have an Indian ceremony on a Friday and a Jewish ceremony on the following evening. "I wanted the wedding to be perfect," says Lisa. "I will be the first to admit I am like my Jewish mother: overbearing and a control freak. Although Taj says I am a muted version." Naturally, Lisa was particularly nervous about keeping things on schedule, given her newfound understanding of Indian Standard Time. "Yes, IST," says Lisa. "I was so freaked out." Like mother like daughter. "I had been to one of his cousin's weddings that ran so late. They were so disorganized, they got all the way to the wedding hall before they figured out they had forgotten the bride's sari. Can you believe that? They forgot the wedding dress!" Lisa waves her hands around in the air. "And one time, I went to an anniversary party—and as the guests walked in, they were still setting up the tables. Nothing was ready. They don't have the same concept of time."

Their first ceremony, the Indian wedding, was pretty predictable—Lisa wore a red sari. There was a chanting of the Vedas, or vows, an exchange of garlands, and the fire—but with two key exceptions. First, there were only 110 people in attendance, versus the normal 300 to 500 at most Indian weddings. Second, the ceremony started on time. Taj's family, cognizant of Lisa's serious case of anal-itis, made an extra effort to arrive in a timely fashion. It didn't hurt that Lisa sent incessant letters and blast e-mails and made calls to most of the East Coast and half of India to remind everyone to be punctual. Unbelievably, the Indian ceremony ran like a Swiss watch. I guess it doesn't take a village after all—just one type-A Jew.

"The first ceremony went well, but it was Indian—something they were used to, except for the IST of course," says Lisa. "I wasn't sure how they would handle the Jewish ceremony. And my family is very punctual...." She continues, "But it turned out his family was actually the first to arrive—an hour and a half before the ceremony was supposed to start. I guess they were really worried about being late." Luckily, the chairs for the ceremony had already been set up, so the early birds—I mean early Indians—took their seats. But as most of them had never been to an American wedding, Taj's family sat as they always did: women on one side and men on the other. Luckily Taj's cousin Usha, who had also arrived early, handled the situation. "This is not an Indian wedding!" cried Usha. "You have to sit with your wives!" she said, pointing to the men. Long before the ceremony started, Usha had reorganized all the Indian men alongside their wives.

Lisa was also worried that Taj's family might unwittingly disrupt the Jewish ceremony. "Indian weddings are really long, so in the middle of the ceremony, they will just get up and go grab a samosa," she says, forming a triangle with her thumbs and forefingers to represent the fried triangles of goodness whose lure could surely disturb any sacred ritual. "I was really worried that would happen at our wedding." She explains, "A Jewish ceremony is short. So if you get up or you are not paying attention, you could miss the whole thing." And another thing: "Everyone is always talking during Indian ceremonies, and sometimes really loud." She continues, "Can you imagine a silent moment under the chuppah, and then a bunch of spectators from the crowd start talking amongst themselves?" But again, Lisa had nothing to worry about. The wedding started promptly at 6:30 p.m. on Saturday. (This was actually a couple of hours before sundown, so still technically the Sabbath, but since the Lipschitzes are Reform, they could fudge a little.) And everyone in attendance, including the Indians, displayed perfect Jewish wedding decorum. There was complete and total silence until the breaking of the glass.

One short year after the wedding, Lisa found herself pregnant with their first child. Shortly after, a great sadness came to the Mehta family. Taj's father, still relatively young, passed away. Lisa quickly discovered that many Hindu funeral traditions are similar to those of the Jews. In both cultures, women in the immediate family of the deceased are not supposed to cook. Jews sit shiva (not to be confused with Lord Shiva, a major Hindu deity) for seven days after the funeral; Hindus mourn for seven days before the funeral. But as much as is similar, there is even more that is different. Hindus wear all white, head to toe, when in mourning; Jews wear black. And then there's the sobbing. "This is going to sound terrible," says Lisa, "but a Jewish funeral is more, I don't know the word. Sophisticated? Composed? Classy? People cry during a Jewish funeral or when sitting shiva, sure. But after the first couple days, you are kind of cried out. Not at an Indian funeral. Every time anyone walks in the door, you are supposed to wail, scream, and cry at the top of your lungs. Every time. It was exhausting. I am surrounded by people screaming, crying and only speaking Gujarati, and no one would let me do anything to help. It was so hard." The whole thing left Lisa feeling like a fish—or, at eight months pregnant, a whale—out of water.

And then there was the food. The fact that the traditional half of the Mehta family doesn't use utensils was no big deal for Lisa. After all, she, too, frequently ate using bread in lieu of silverware: tortillas with Mexican food, naan with Indian food, and injera with Ethiopian food. But Taj's older relatives ate with their hands even if no bread was available. The sight, day after day, of Taj's relatives eating Indian food with rice and yogurt all swirled together and running down their arms was too much for a woman eight months pregnant to bear.

Then, Taj's family informed Lisa that she would not be allowed at the funeral ceremony. At first, she was offended. How could she miss her new husband's father's funeral? It was unthinkable. She was adamant about attending. But the Mehta family pleaded with her. "It's an Indian tradition," they said. "It's bad luck for the baby." After a week of wailing, swirling yogurt rice, and her ears ringing from the Gujarati, she acquiesced, staying home to get some much-needed rest.

Now, more than five years later, the couple is still going strong. Both families have been very accepting of their interracial marriage. (Lisa does admit she will never really know what Taj's mother thinks, given she doesn't speak English. But when it comes to Indian mother-in-laws, ignorance is bliss.) Both families are supportive of Taj and Lisa and love their two children to pieces, but there are some things about their relationship that confounds Taj's relatives. "We have never had traditional gender roles," says Lisa. "Taj does all of the cooking. And I love cutting the lawn. It gets me outside, a little exercise." Even after all this time, Taj's uncles are confused by this cooking Indian man and his lawn-mowing wife. "Every time his one uncle sees me, he says, 'You guys are p-thty p-thty right?'" says Lisa. She explains: "He means 50/50."

Taj jokes that he should have married an Indian woman because Lisa is not always the most easy-going. And Lisa teases Taj that she should have married a good Jewish boy—one who wouldn't show up three hours late for family functions because he was caught in a poker tournament. (Ah, north Indians and their card playing....) But both agree on the glue that holds them together: a mutual respect, focus on education, the highest regard for family...oh, and "Gujaratis are known for being cheap," says Taj. "But that's why my culture is so complementary to my wife's Jewish heritage: They really know the value of a dollar."

Shiksa Fever

"Oh, sure. They are Jewish and you are a shiksa... You've got shiksappeal. Jewish men love the idea of meeting a woman that is not like their mother."

—SEINFELD

My dear friend Saul has always joked that since I have attended a Jewish wedding, a Bar Mitzvah, a bris, and a Purim celebration, I am just one event away from becoming a full-fledged Jew: Passover.

"What about Rosh Hashanah or Yom Kippur?" I asked Saul, "Those are really important too, right? The High Holy Days?"

"Those are no fun," said Saul. "All that fasting and stuff. You don't need that. I think you should stick to the fun ones. After Passover, you've got it covered."

Not long after, I happened to eat lunch with my good friend Michelle (also a Jew) on Passover, and she invited me to stay for dinner. Turns out, it's a tradition to leave an open place setting on Passover anyway, just in case someone shows up unexpectedly. "It's kind of like Thanksgiving in that way," Michelle says. "You should always try to take someone in, regardless of their family relationship or religion. I think it's a great tradition." So that night, I ate Passover dinner with Michelle, her husband Ethan, and their four children. We lit candles, read from the *Haggadah*, discussed the 10 plagues, and of course, ate matzoh ball soup. Even as a shiksa, thanks to my affinity for the movie *The Ten Commandments* and for Yul Brynner ("So let it be written, so let it be done!"), I was already well versed on the 10 plagues. I am now officially an honorary Jew. Michelle says my certificate is in the mail. To help you, too, become an honorary Jew, this next part reviews cultural issues discussed by Jews I interviewed and those who date them.

Things to Know

When it comes to Jews, there is a lot to know, some of which is complicated. Like, are Jews even a race? Well, sort of—but they for sure have a distinct culture, the basics of which you really need to understand if you are going to date Jewish. Other things are easier to comprehend. Like, what's a shiksa? That one's easy: you. And erase from your mind any stereotypes you have of Jews looking and acting as they do in *Fiddler on the Roof*, *Yentl*, or *The Jazz Singer*—the majority of Jews don't fit that mold. All that and so much more is what you need to know about dating a Jew.

What Is a Shiksa?

The always-accurate Wikipedia says shiksa, a pejorative term for a non-Jewish woman, is from the Hebrew word *sheketz*, which means "abomination, impure, or object of loathing...." *Nice!*

Thanks for that. As a shiksa, I say we make this word ours, like gay men did with "queer." Long live the Shiksa Nation!

Fortunately, this term has started to get a more positive spin thanks to the episode of *Seinfeld* in which all the Jewish men got the hots for Elaine—what Seinfeld called the Shiksa Fever. Jewish men I spoke with also attributed a positive meaning to shiksa. "To me, shiksa just means non-Jewish woman," says Ozzie, 44, Jew, fitness-center manager. "It doesn't have a negative connotation." He adds, "If anything, it makes me think of women like you [i.e., me] that are shiksalicious. Women usually named Mary or Christine that are blond with a cute button nose and the world's greatest ass. To me, shiksa literally means 'adorable non-Jewish girl.' It's a good thing." So what better title could there be than "Shiksa Fever" for the section dealing with us gentiles who date Jewish men?

Jews a Race?

I can hear Rabbi Horowitz now: "How can you have Jews in your book? Jews are not a race!" Jews are often adamant about this distinction. Due to their long history of being kicked out of country after country, Jews come in all shapes and skin colors. There are blond, blue-eyed Jews; black Jews; Asian Jews; Middle Eastern Jews. They run the gamut. But my response to Rabbi Horowitz would be as follows: In the 1980s, the U.S. Supreme Court found that Jews were considered a race with regard to antidiscrimination laws. Plus, the religion is passed down through birth. If your mother is Jewish, you are Jewish—no ifs, ands, or oys. In my opinion, the fact that Jews inherit their religion through birth rather than adopting it through an initiation process (like a baptism) makes Jews more like a race. Yes, I know, Rabbi Horowitz, there is a Bar or Bat Mitzvah—a rite of passage of sorts. But if your mother is Jewish, and you *don't* have a Bar or Bat Mitzvah, guess what? You're still a Jew.

Not All Jews Are Created Equal

Judaism is one of the most misunderstood religions in the world, partly because it is one of the smallest. No doubt, much of the prejudice against Jews comes from lack of exposure to Judaism.

When people think of Jews, many think of the yarmulke-wearing (the little hats), no-milk-with-the-meat eating (keeping Kosher), home-before-sundown-on-Friday (keeping Shabbos) Jews. But this only accurately describes around 10 percent of Jews: the Orthodox Jews. The remaining Jews—mostly Reform and Conservative Jews—may or may not choose to observe any of the aforementioned traditions. "It's hard with the pace of modern life to keep up a lot of the old traditions," says Josh, 45, Jew, accountant. "So Jews end up practicing in many different ways." Important to mention is that there are also Jews who consider themselves non-practicing—that is, not religious at all.

What does this all mean for you, the shiksa? First, don't make any assumptions when dating a man who is Jewish. Judaism involves a lot of personal choice; you can't know how he practices or how you fit into the picture until you talk it over with him. Second, Reform Jews and non-practicing Jews are your sweet spot—the ones who are most likely to have a serious relationship with a shiksa.

Ashkenazi Versus Sephardic

Something that New York Jews like to throw around in conversation are the differences between Ashkenazi Jews and Sephardic Jews. While this concept can be complicated, a basic explanation of these groups is found in the book *What Is a Jew?* by Rabbi Morris N. Kertzer. Essentially, Sephardic Jews for the most part were forced out of Spain during the late 15th century and settled in North Africa and the Middle East. In contrast, Ashkenazi Jews are mainly those who were driven out of England and France in the 13th and 14th centuries and tended to settle in Poland, Germany, and Russia. Some Jews still care about this distinction, but for most, it's nothing more than a healthy rivalry.

"The Sephardics think they are better than us," says Saul, 40, Ashkenazi Jew, portfolio manager. "I think historically, we are supposed to wash their feet or something."

"You mean about how the Ashkenazis think they are better than us?" says Josh, Sephardic Jew. "Losers."

"Forget your shiksa issues with your Sephardic boyfriend," says Lizbeth, 47, Ashkenazi Jew, saleswoman. "If *I* was to date him, that would be interracial dating."

As an educated shiksa, all you really need to know is that these distinctions exist and maybe a bit about them. The differences come down to two main things:

- **Food.** Hands down, Sephardic food is better. There isn't much real debate on that one. Ashkenazis can keep their dreadful gefilte fish and their bland matzoh ball soup. I will take Sephardic kebabs, hummus, and saffron rice any day.

- **Language.** The Ashkenazis, like all the chosen people, have their own special gifts, the most important being the gift of gab. Yiddish is an Ashkenazi language, created from a blending of Hebrew and Old German, and it is truly magical. If not for Ashkenazi Jews, we would not be able to have a little *nosh* with a *schmeer* of cream cheese, *kibbitz* with our friends, complain about our *meshugana* boss, or even adequately communicate how miserable that *schlep* across town was. And don't forget Laverne and Shirley and their famous "Shlemiel!" (a dolt who is a habitual bungler) "Shlemazel!" (a person who suffers the screw-ups of a schlemiel) "Hasenpfeffer Incorporated!" Yiddish is such a great language, I get *verklempt* just thinking about it.

So You Don't Fuck Up!

There's a lot of personal choice in Judaism. There aren't a lot of hard and fast rules. That means it's relatively easy for you to screw up. While your Jewish boyfriend is the *only* one who knows exactly what traditions (tra-DI-tions!) he and his family practice, there are a few general guidelines you should observe (at least initially) to keep the offense level to a minimum.

Food Restrictions May Vary

With regard to Jews and food, there are a lot of important nuances for you, the shiksa, to understand. Savvy gentiles among you might think I'm referring to keeping kosher—only eating animals killed in a certain way, separating milk products from meat products, and abstaining from eating pork and shellfish—but I'm not. The fact is, fewer than 20 percent of Jews in the U.S. keep kosher—and the Jews who do keep kosher are probably devout, old school, and unlikely to be dating your shiksa ass anyway. That being said, some Reform and even non-practicing Jews do choose to adhere to certain dietary restrictions. This can be very confusing for a shiksa, as each Jew decides for himself which of these restrictions he will observe.

I like to share meals when I eat out. If I want to share a meal with my Jewish boyfriend, Josh, I can select from a wide range of delicacies, including chicken, chicken, and more chicken. I understand the whole pork and shellfish thing, but Josh doesn't eat beef, either. That's not even a Jewish thing, for Christ's sake! Although I was never a big fan of pork before I started dating Josh, I often find myself doing crazy things like hiding pork rinds under the bed or stashing bacon behind the peas in the freezer. And if I do eat pork while we are together, Josh jokes that he can't kiss me because I'm all "porky."

"I used to do that when I was younger: not eat pork or seafood. But I grew out of it," says Seth, 47, Jew, business-development executive.

"My Jewish boyfriend's family was conservative. They even kept kosher at home," says Maria, 25, Argentinean, real-estate agent. "But when he was out with me, he would eat a bacon cheeseburger, no problem."

Food restrictions can even vary day by day. "My Jewish fiancé absolutely loves my shrimp toast. Eats it all the time," says Rachel, 29, Jew, fashion brand manager. "But this year, we were hosting Rosh Hashanah at our house, and he threw a fit. 'There will be no shrimp toast at Rosh Hashanah!'" She adds, "He regularly eats scallops wrapped in bacon, and now he's making a big deal about the shrimp toast?"

"Most days, I eat whatever I want," says Isaac, 32, Jew, retail expert. "I do fast for Yom Kippur. I observe Passover, but I don't eat matzoh. That stuff is terrible. I just try to stay away from wheat that week."

While food issues may vary day to day or Jew to Jew, there is one thing that *all* the Jews I spoke with agree on: Goyim, you gotta cool it with the mayo. Yes, I am speaking of the condiment — the greasy, gooey, slimy, high-calorie may-o-nnaise.

"I dated this shiksa in college," says Ozzie. "She put mayonnaise on *everything*." He continues, "Pastrami on rye and *mayo*? What is wrong with you gentiles? Don't you know Pastrami goes with spicy mustard? Mayo on pastrami is an abomination!"

To recap: Do all Jews have elaborate dietary restrictions? No. Will most Jews you date care what you eat? No. But should you dial back the shellfish and give the pork a rest the first time you have dinner with your Jewish boyfriend's parents? Yes.

Santa as Sacrilege

Some might argue that Christmas has become a secular holiday —such as Thanksgiving. After all, Hindus, Buddhists, Agnostics, Indians, Chinese, Japanese, and even some Jews celebrate Christmas. But a lot of the Jews I talked to harbor just the teeniest bit of resentment about the holiday.

"The hardest thing I had to get used to when I married a shiksa was the Christmas tree," says Seth. "It just feels like a dilution of your identity."

"I don't believe it's a secular holiday," says Josh. "Christmas has 'Christ' in it, the Pope celebrates it. It is a Christian holiday!" He adds, "They hold Jews responsible for killing Christ. Do you think I want this tree in my house to remind me of that?"

"I don't mind going to my fiancée's family for Christmas," says Isaac. "I get great gifts from Santa." But, he says, "I wouldn't have a Christmas tree in my house. Even if my kids want one, we are not having a tree. We are Jewish."

Not all Jews are anti-Santa, however. "I do agree that Christmas is basically a secular holiday," says Ozzie. "It matters to me zero. The kids are going to be raised Jewish—that is important to me—but if my wife or the kids want a tree, I would have a tree. Who cares?"

"When it came to Christmas," says Maria, "I get the sense that it's more that Jews feel they don't belong. An insecurity thing, feeling left out." She adds, "My Jewish boyfriend was actually really excited to come for Christmas dinner, like he was finally included in all the fun."

In any case, if you don't want to mess up with your new Jewish boyfriend, you might want to keep your love of Christmas carols and decorations—at least the life-size Santa Claus (with eight not-so-tiny reindeer) lawn ornament on the down low. That's not to say there won't be room for both Chanukah *and* Christmas in your house; just be sensitive to what it means to your man. Eventually, he may even say "Happy Christmas to all, and to all a good night!" (Okay, that's unlikely, but at least he may learn to tolerate it.)

What the Hell Did I Get Myself Into?

Yeah, I could say something witty here. I could go into a cute little bit. But the fact is, this section is no joking matter. When it comes to dating Jews and saying, "What the hell?" there are three very serious and important concepts to understand: It's always tougher for shiksas, beware the JAPs, and look out for the infamous Jewish mother. Proceed with caution.

When It Comes to a Serious Relationship, It's Always Tougher for Shiksas

This point is so important, it needs to be set apart in the text in underlined bold font, with two asterisks and an exclamation point:

<u>****The most important thing for a shiksa to know about dating a Jew is that no matter how your man practices his religion—or if he even practices it at all—to most Jews, having Jewish children is paramount!**</u>

In fact, it is actually written in Jewish law that every Jewish man must have at least two Jewish children. "No big deal!" you're thinking. "I want kids someday, too, and I don't care what religion they are." Sorry, still not good enough. There's a catch. In Judaism, the religion is *only* passed through the woman's bloodline. Why? Most rabbis think it's due to the constant diaspora of the Jews throughout history. That is, proving a child's bloodline through the father could prove difficult; the identity and heritage of the mother, on the other hand, was never in question. Of course, these days, it's easy to establish paternity. (Just ask Maury Povich.) Even so, many Jews still believe that if the mother (that's you, the shiksa) was not born Jewish, then the children are not *really* Jewish—regardless of whether their father is. This explains why it's much easier for a non-Jewish man to marry a Jewish woman than for a shiksa to marry a Jew.

"He didn't even go to temple, so I thought it couldn't be that big a deal," says Sunshine, 42, white girl, graphic designer. "But he told me before we got married the kids had to be raised Jewish. It was like he was willing to choose the Jewish religion over me, and he didn't really even participate in it."

"That was a big issue with my Jewish boyfriend's family," says Maria. "I read Alan Dershowitz's *The Vanishing American Jew* and it helped me realize how important it was to them to maintain the faith." She continues, "I have faith in higher power, and there is a lot about Judaism that I like. So if I end up marrying a Jew, I would just convert."

"If you are a Jewish woman marrying a non-Jewish guy, it's not the end of the world because the kids are still Jewish," says Josh. "But for a man, suddenly, if you marry a shiksa, then that connection to Judaism could be gone if she doesn't convert or if you don't believe in conversion." He adds, "It may be an issue for some Jewish guys. It's like you traded down or something."

"My parents would be okay with me marrying a shiksa, but they would want her to convert," says Isaac. "Some people say that even if you convert, you are still not really Jewish, but I think that is a close-minded, foolish, old-world belief. I also have friends that are Jewish and they really don't give a shit if the woman they marry is Jewish."

This is by far the biggest problem for the shiksa-Jew pairing. Yes, there are Jewish men who genuinely don't care what religion you are. But it's important to stress this because at some point this issue will come up regardless of how devout he is—even if he is non-practicing or not religious. Be prepared.

Beware the JAPs

Sadly, the Jewish American Princess (JAP) is not an urban legend, like alligators in the sewers or people being kidnapped for their organs. Nor is it a myth like Sasquatch or the chupacabra.

No, the JAP is alive and well—at least, in New York City. In case you're not familiar with it, JAP is a pejorative term for Jewish women who are high maintenance, materialistic, selfish, spoiled, pampered, status conscious, greedy, bitchy, gold-digging, overbearing, frigid...well, you get the idea.

Get this straight: *Most* Jewish women are not JAPs. But JAPs are out there—and as a shiksa, it behooves you to spot and avoid them whenever possible. Why? Two reasons. One, as mentioned, they are materialistic and self centered. Two, they likely consider *your* boyfriend their fall-back plan if they are not married by 40. See, JAPs—even the ones who are short, fat, and ugly—believe that they deserve to marry an investment banker or brain surgeon who is six feet tall, looks like Pierce Brosnan (or a young Tony Curtis), and pulls down at least seven figures a year. (A girl has to maintain a certain lifestyle, you know.) But when Mr. Tall Dark and Loaded never appears, and the big 4-0 is lurking around the corner, even the most discerning JAP may be forced to give up on the shallow tall, dark, handsome, Jewish doctor pool in favor of the much deeper short, bald, geeky, Jewish accountant pool for a viable husband (before her eggs go south). At that point, to the JAP, any Jewish man is up for grabs.

What any shiksa must know:

- **First, spot.** "I went to a Jewish college; I was the only Jew on scholarship. So I have a lot of experience with JAPs," says Rachel Judith Goldstein. (The *ultimate* Jewish name!) "There is a science to finding a JAPpy Jew. First is the finger flare." Rachel Judith Goldstein demonstrates, flaring out all five fingers on her right hand. "Of course, the nails are manicured. French tips. Also, a JAP always puts her purse in the bend of her elbow so she can walk, carry her purse, and maintain the finger flare at all times." She adds, "When I was in college, Juicy Couture was big, so they all wore Juicy sweat suits. We used to call them Juicy JAPpy Jews."

- **Then, avoid.** "One time, I was out with my Jewish boyfriend, Les," says Alexis, 40, white girl, author. "We met up with some of his friends at a bar. There was this woman—typical JAP. Gucci this, Prada that, and those ridiculous long Jersey acrylic nails." She continues, "Right in front of me, she says, 'Well, if I don't find the man of my dreams soon, I am going to have to marry Les here.' Like I'm not Jewish, so he can't *really* be serious about me." She adds, "She was just so rude."

Jewish men were even more vehemently anti-JAP. "I dated a JAPpy JAP JAP," says Isaac. "Thought her shit didn't stink. It wasn't about us being together; it wasn't even about me putting a ring on her finger; it was about the *size* of the ring."

"It's possible that there are more Jewish women who are that way," says Josh. "But really, you don't have to be Jewish to be a JAP." He explains, "For me, a JAP is any woman looking for a man to marry her and take care of her the rest of her life." He adds, "And by the way the JAPs don't believe *all* Jewish men belong to them, they believe all *rich* Jewish men belong to them. The bald, fatty, nerdy, Jewish guy that works his ass off? They don't care about him. They think he is below them."

"When it comes to JAPs, you are never good enough," says Ozzie. "Judging me by the size of my wallet, not the size of my brain. I don't make $2 million a year and I can't afford to buy her a 3-carat diamond ring." He continues, "These materialistic women have whittled good Jewish men into little nubs. 'Beware the JAPs' is absolutely right!" He adds, "I am the real deal, and I will love you with all my heart. If you can't see that, go fuck yourself." Gee, Ozzie, tell us how you *really* feel!

As I said, there are a lot of wonderful Jewish women out there, but JAPs do exist. Keep an eye out for that finger flare and maintain a tight grip on your man!

The Infamous Jewish Mother

"So," you may be thinking. "That's it. I just get past the JAPs, and I am home free!" Oh, no no no. The only thing more frightening, more terrifying, more horrifying than a JAP is the notorious Jewish mother. Trust me: When it comes to her son, she has certain expectations—most important of which is marrying a Jewish girl. And not just Jewish, but hopefully from the same continent, the same country, and the same *village* where she grew up. Needless to say, this is not you. So don't be surprised if you aren't welcomed with open arms.

"Do I have a Jewish mother story for you!" says Amy, 42, white girl, artist. "I met Jacob and his parents for lunch. His mother asked me something that seemed innocuous: 'I hear you are from California. Would you ever want to go back there?' I said, 'Sure, maybe.' And then, out of nowhere, came the shit storm of the century. Jacob's mom stood up at the table, all rigid, and screamed: 'WHY WOULD YOU EVEN COME HERE AND GET SERIOUS WITH SOMEONE IF YOU ARE JUST GOING TO TAKE HIM AWAY?' It was totally psycho bananas. We weren't even that serious yet."

"The Jewish guys I dated were never helpless like other mama's boys," says Maria. "But their mothers were very *involved* in their lives."

Don't misunderstand me: The Jewish mother is not all bad. Many mothers do everything for their sons as they are growing up, making them helpless mama's boys. Jewish mothers don't do that. Instead, they use their parenting skills not only to teach their boys to take care of themselves but to take care of their women, too. So take the good with the bad, but be aware that his mother is going to take a prominent role in his life (and if things get serious with your Jewish man, in yours as well).

What's Hot?

While Jewish men may not enjoy the hot hot hot reputation that some of the other guys in this book have, there is actually a lot about Jewish men that is *crazy* hot: an incredible, almost orgasmic sense of humor; extreme patience; and (surprise!) their considerable generosity are just a few things that are hot about Jewish men.

Funny as Fuck

What is that saying? "The way to a man's heart is through his stomach?" Actually, I think it's probably a little lower. But we can all agree that the way to a woman's heart is through her funny bone. A woman always wants a man who can make her laugh—and no doubt about it, Jewish men can be *really* funny. Yes, I'm sure there is the occasional somber Jew out there, but all in all, most Jewish men are very gifted in the humor department. In fact, being funny is even part of the Jewish faith. The *Talmud* says you must "always begin a lesson with a humorous illustration." Of course, this might be because the *Talmud* is such a dense and incredibly difficult scripture that when studying it, one is in desperate need of a humorous illustration. But it also demonstrates how important humor is in the Jewish community.

"I am funny, so it must be true," says Josh. "Sometimes you don't get my jokes, but that doesn't mean I'm not funny. If a tree falls in the forest, does it still make a sound?"

"They are very funny," says Maria. "And they really know how to talk to women. To me, that is the biggest contrast between Jewish men and Latin men. Latin men don't see you as a friend; they figure you have women friends for that. Jewish men are the reverse. They treat you with respect like any guy should when you are dating, but as a friend at the same time. And their great sense of humor is a big plus."

"My fiancé isn't amazing looking or anything, but he's hilarious," says Rachel. "That is what won me over."

Not Allergic to Paying the Tab

There is a long-standing stereotype that Jewish men are cheap. This actually dates back to the Middle Ages, when Jews were forced to lend money to earn a living because they were barred from other occupations. But this stereotype has lived long past its expiration date. Yes, because of their history, money does have important significance for many Jewish men. In fact, most Jewish men I know can account for every dollar they have ever earned, going back to when their *bubbe* opened a savings account for them in grammar school. But that doesn't mean they won't spend it on the people they care about. And yes, most everyone agrees: They definitely pick up the tab.

"I know that's the stereotype—that Jewish men are cheap," says Alicia, 42, Filipina, hospital administrator. "It really pisses me off. My husband is Jewish and incredibly generous with everyone."

"I have dated Jews and have a lot of Jewish male friends," says Carolyn, 36, Filipina, hairdresser. "Jewish men are very giving. Not cheap at all. Very generous." She adds, "They give good gifts, like Hermès and Gucci." I need to find out who Carolyn is dating!

"Seth always paid the tab; that was never an issue," says Sunshine. "The more serious we got, the more generous he got. I got some serious presents—nice jewelry—and he even paid off my student loans."

"For myself, I always pick up the tab," says Isaac. "That is just part of the courting process. When I go out on a date, I am not going to say, 'Hey, you had the chicken parm and three glasses of wine, and that adds up to....'" He says, "My fiancée didn't pay for a single thing until we moved in together."

"I always pick up the tab. My mother brought me up to be a gentleman," says Aaron, 48, Jew, entrepreneur. "When I was dating my wife, I remember one time I stepped away, and before I could get it, Brenda had picked up the tab. I was really surprised. I really liked that she wasn't all JAPpy or gimme gimme. That's probably part of why I married her."

So don't let ancient stereotypes and malicious labels fool you. Picking up the tab is what's *hot* about Jewish men.

Patience Is Their Virtue

JAPs have a reputation of being critical and demanding; ditto Jewish mothers. So it's no surprise that Jewish men are known for their patience. In fact, some Jewish men have the patience of Job, Dr. Seuss's egg-incubating elephant Horton, and those two guys who waited for Godot combined.

"Jewish men are patient," says Rachel. But, she says, "Jewish women aren't. I am very impatient. Sometimes I don't know how he deals with me."

"Yes, very patient," says Maria. "I am always late for our dates, but my Jewish boyfriend never gets even remotely upset. He is very patient."

"Jewish men have a superior level of patience," says Ozzie. "We are well trained first by our mothers through their harping and relentless criticism and then from surviving the JAPs." He adds, "There are some assholes out there, but most Jews are great guys that just want to be loved. Is that so wrong?"

"Oh definitely. I am patient," says Josh. "It's been about eight months of patience since you moved in here, right?" He adds, "It's getting less and less as I get older, but I am still very patient." He is—and obviously very modest too.

"I am not impulsive, that is for sure," says Isaac. "My mother taught me that." He adds, "Also, I don't mind doing things like taking my fiancée shopping. I am more patient than she is. She can get to be what we call 'boiling'; when she gets close to the boiling point, watch out."

Jewish men seem to have no problem waiting patiently for hours in the department store as their wives shop, holding off until that new flat screen goes on sale, or taking time to get to know you before trying to jump your bones. If patience is what you are looking for, a Jew may be your best bet.

What's Not?

They don't call them "good Jewish boys" for nothin', right? But before you go stalking synagogues, Katz's Deli, or medical offices on the Upper West Side for that Jewish man of your dreams, let's not forget the bad that goes with the good. Heated discussions, extreme pessimism, hoarding tendencies, and incessant calls from Mommy are just a few of the things that had women who date Jewish men waking up in a cold sweat at night. (Okay, maybe that was just me. But other women definitely found some of these attributes disturbing.)

Family Closeness Can Lead to Asphyxiation

One of the real attractions of the Jewish culture is that family relationships are very important. But there's close—and then there's feels-like-an-elephant-is-sitting-on-top-of-my-chest-suffocating-me close. Be aware that it will not be uncommon for your Jewish boyfriend to talk to his family (i.e., his mother) daily and visit every week—probably on Friday night, a.k.a. date night. Be aware, too, that if your man's mother calls, he will answer, regardless of what other activities may be under way. My boyfriend Josh's mother has a sixth sense about when her son might be servicing his shiksa girlfriend and seems to call right when we are in, shall we say, a compromising position—and Josh *always* answers the phone.

"My mother-in-law calls my husband at least two times a day," says Nazan, 33, Turkish, banker. "If he doesn't answer, she'll call me. And if *I* don't answer, she'll switch from his office to my office, our home, his cell, my cell, until someone answers."

"I don't talk to my mom *every* day," says Isaac. "I can go four or five days without calling. But longer than that, she will start to get upset." He adds, "I think my fiancée is actually looking forward to marrying into my family because we are so close. She doesn't mind talking to my mother."

"I used to talk to my mother every night," says Ozzie. "I would call her at, like, 11 p.m., and then at 1 a.m. I would have to say, 'Ma, I gotta get off the phone, I got work tomorrow.'" He continues, "I loved to talk to her, though. We would laugh for hours." He adds, "I think we all secretly want to be mama's boys, always want our moms around. No one can understand you like your mom, but no one can drive you crazy like her either."

Of course, like most things, family closeness has its pluses and its minuses. It is up to you to try to manage it so it doesn't become too intrusive.

Not Born with an Inside Voice

As I've mentioned, I was not born with an inside voice. It can be a big negative for me; I regularly cause ruckuses in restaurants without meaning to, and my downstairs neighbors frequently pound on their ceiling in a vain attempt to get me to quiet down. But with Jews, I fit right in.

"I ask my Jewish mother-in-law, 'Why do you have to yell? How about starting the conversation at level 3, not level 12?'" says Amy. "Things just escalate so much farther and faster with her. Pretty soon, *everyone* is yelling."

"Yes, my Jewish boyfriend was always yelling!" says Alec, 25, white guy, art-gallery manager. "I don't like yelling. When I have a loud boyfriend, at some point, I always think to myself, 'Why am I dating this person again?'"

"My Jewish boyfriend's family is more intellectual than my family," says Maria. "I like that they talk about important topics. But it's more an argument than a discussion. A *loud* argument."

"I am probably the most guilty of that," says Isaac. "My father and I can really get into a loud debate. He is a lawyer, though, so that could be part of it too."

"Not so much yelling, but a very easy trigger," says Ozzie. "We're pretty sure of our opinions and we will let you know what we think. With my family, it usually comes from a good place—the fact that we care about each other. If I didn't care, I wouldn't yell."

I have the same issue with Josh. He'll say we're just having a spirited discussion, but I feel like I'm under attack. I'm no match for a Jew on the rampage. So if you are a low talker, quiet as a mouse, or just don't take to "spirited discussions," a Jew may not be for you.

Glass Half Empty

Granted, it's probably for a good reason, what with their whole history of great tragedy, but Jewish men can be a tad bit—okay, *very*—pessimistic. It's not that they can't also be supporting, loving, and even happy, but they often seem negative.

"When it comes to Stan's family, they automatically assume the worst," says Amy.

"I remember with my Jewish boyfriend from college, everything was very 'Woe is me.' 'This happened to me again.' Victimizing himself," says Maria. "It is a turnoff when men complain."

"For thousands of years, people have been trying to kill us, kick our ass out, or steal our money," says Josh. "I think we have every right to be pessimistic!" Josh does have a point on that one.

"I think it is an intelligent realism," says Ozzie. "Most likely, life is not a bowl of cherries—more likely, a bowl of pits. More times than not, the silver cloud has a grey lining. Life is hard, and then you die [point, set, and match]. Unless you meet a yummy shiksa that is into crazy wacky sex, and then that can lighten the mood a little. An ex-cheerleader with superior intellect, maybe? Did I mention I am a severely handsome bald Jewish man?"

When dating a Jew, don't be surprised if he is a bit defeatist, seems down in the mouth, or reminds you of Pooh's sad friend Eeyore. If you want someone who has a rosy-colored outlook at all times, a Jew may not be your man.

It's Still Good!

Jews have a hard time letting go. I'm not talking about relationships here, more like stuff—even stuff most of us would consider garbage. Take Josh, for example. He loves to save little travel soaps. Every so often, when the plastic container in which he stashes these precious items overflows, I stealthily put some in the trash. If he catches me, he inevitably retrieves the soaps from the garbage, saying something like, "I can't believe you threw these away; they're still good!" To Josh, just because the soaps have petrified from age and the lotions have solidified over time doesn't mean they go in the garbage. "You say it's hoarding," Josh says. "But it's not. It's like a museum, and they are things of interest. Everyone has a right to collect what they want. Just because someone lives in a small space and things might pile up a bit doesn't mean they are hoarding."

"I can't ever tell Seth we are giving things to Goodwill," says Sunshine. "If he sees the bags, he will start taking things out. 'What's wrong with this sweater?' It's ugly, purple, and he hasn't worn it since the '80s, but he still won't let it go. 'It's still good!' he'll say." She adds, "I get those Hefty bags now, the ones you can't see through, and hide them in the closet somewhere. Otherwise, we would never get rid of *anything*."

"I have this old towel that my fiancée wants to get rid of," says Isaac. "I told her, 'Okay, maybe it's a little gross, but it doesn't affect you.' She can't wait to throw it away! I finally told her, 'Look, after we get married, I will adapt to new towels, but I don't have to like it.'" He adds, "I also still have the T-shirt from my Bar Mitzvah."

"Yes, my boyfriend had a lot of old T-shirts—dated and immature clothes that he needed to throw out but wouldn't part with," says Maria. "Oh, and a huge comic-book collection."

Shiksa Secret #132: What he doesn't know won't hurt him. Just toss it.

Between the Sheets

"Be patient until her passion is aroused. Begin with love. And when her mood is ready, let her desire be satisfied first. Her delight is what matters."

—YENTL

This section can have a whole different meaning for some Jews. For one extremely small sect of Jews, Hasidics, the expression isn't "between the sheets," it's "through the sheet." Hasidics are said to have sex on their wedding night through a slit in a sheet. Right before this procedure, the wife must also shave her head. Fucking a bald woman through a sheet—now that's hot!

To clarify, this section is about the majority of Jews (98-plus percent) who fuck *between* the sheets—and have no particular inhibitions. In fact, they have a good reputation in the sack.

They Schtup with the Best of Them

In the woman-centric Jewish culture, women are treated with care and respect—something that translates to the bedroom. Eager to please, Jewish men focus on meeting their partner's needs first. Obviously, this is key to being a good lover in general. Overall, sex is one thing—apart from accounting—at which Jewish men really excel.

"It is clear that my Jewish husband has sex to make me happy," says Alicia. "He's always asking me if it was good, or is there something else he should do. He's totally focused on making me feel good."

"My Jewish boyfriend was a very attentive lover," says Alec. "At one point, we lived four hours apart. You know it had to be good to be worth all that driving!"

"There is no doubt that we want to please the woman," says Ozzie. "It's important that the experience is good for you." He explains, "I think it's partly a guilt thing. If you don't get there, I feel guilty that I didn't do what I was supposed to do." He adds, "I want you to have your toes curling in earth-shattering orgasm."

"I try to be an attentive lover. I don't want to get off unless she does," says Isaac. "I think part of it is the Jewish guilt. Fuhgeddaboudit."

Guilt as an aphrodisiac. Who knew?

Schmeckel, Shvantz, Putz, Schmuck, Pitseleh, Zayin—It's All Good

Why do Jews have so many words for penis? Maybe it's pride. Although there are rumors out there that Jewish men are small below the belt, this was well disputed among the women I spoke to. The Pros were even more complimentary, noting that they are average to large. In fact, this great nation's most legendary male porn star, Ron Jeremy, is a Jew. He almost followed in his father's footsteps by enrolling in rabbinical school. Can you see him as Rabbi Jeremy or Cantor Jeremy? No, didn't think so. His Elohim-given talents seem to be best used in his current occupation.

Fasting Is *Only* for Yom Kippur

Jews get high grades on their orals. Known for their hard work, they have no problem putting in the time here. Funny story: In his teens, my friend Alex—a New York Jew, born and bred on the Upper West Side—went out for dinner with his father, a sort of father-son night. The two sat down at the bar and Alex's dad ordered a dirty martini and a dozen oysters. (Not very kosher.) When the oysters arrived, Alex said the normal kid thing: "Ew, oysters. Yuck!"

Alex's dad grabbed Alex by the shoulders and looked hard into his eyes. "Son, if you can't eat oysters, you can't lick pussy. And if you can't lick pussy, you will never make a woman happy. So eat up," he said, pushing the oysters toward Alex. Today, Alex is happily married with four children.

"Ask the shiksa," says Josh. "I think I do okay. I never say no to good pussy."

"For me personally, that is probably my favorite thing in the world," says Ozzie. "I want to be up to my waist, roll up my sleeves, hold all my calls, put the waders on—I am headin' down south."

So if you want a man who knows how to muff dive *and* do your taxes, a Jew may be just what you're looking for.

The Stealth Orgasm

While this is not true in the majority of cases, it seemed worth mentioning, as several of the women and men I talked to indicated that Jewish men can be extremely quiet in the sack, even during orgasm. "You know, now that I think back on the Jewish men I dated, that was kinda true," says Carolyn. "They were all quiet. I wonder why that is?"

The Pros

For the professionals this was a frequent occurrence—and to them, a serious issue. It's not real sexy to turn around and ask, "Hey, I didn't hear anything. You done back there?"

Why are they silent? Shy? Worried The Pros charged by the moan? I don't know—and neither did our Jewish men.

"It's true we are very quiet in the sack," says Ozzie. "I don't know why, but it's true. Maybe it's because the last time I had sex, it was when the movies were silent. Plus, that was before electricity, so I couldn't see who I was with."

"It's not just me," says Josh. "There are a lot of Jews like that." He continues, "Why are men supposed to make noise anyway? It's like, some people scream at football games, some people don't.

I am just not a screamer."

I am not saying that shiksas need a warning per se—definitely not that "I'm coming! I'm coming!" crap. But a little something to tell us where we are in the process would be great—a little moaning, some shaking, smoke signals, something.

Our Stories

Now you've got the nuts and bolts—not to mention a little of the nitty gritty—on dating Jewish. But what is a Jew really like? Of course, there's no way to tell exactly what *your* relationship with a Jewish guy will be like. But the following stories will certainly help you see how some real relationships can play out. Dealing with crazy JAPs, hoarding to the 10th power, and what's a Jewpino already? These are just a few things you will learn from people's real-life Jewish dating experiences.

New York Jew Meets Peace, Love, and Tofu

One sunny Saturday morning, Seth emerged from the Equinox gym on 22nd and Broadway, then paused for a minute, trying to decide what to do next. "So," he heard a woman say. "Did you have a good workout?" Not realizing she was speaking to him, he didn't answer. "Did you have a good workout?" she asked again. Seth looked up and around; suddenly, he grasped that the woman was talking to him.

She was pretty—thin and shapely, wearing a bright-yellow sundress with white-daisy–patterned trim. He knew right away she was from out of town; New York women do not speak to strange men on the street. And she was altogether too bubbly and friendly, all smiling and light-hearted—definitely not a native.

"Hi," Seth said.

"Hi," the woman chirped. "I'm Sunshine."

"Of course you are," Seth mock-chirped back. "You're not from around here, are you?"

Seth was right: Sunshine was not a native New Yorker. Raised in the golden state of California, she was peace, love, and tofu personified. And because she hadn't lived in the city for long—only three months—she hadn't yet developed the neuroses that Seth had observed in typical New York women. "You see, most of them don't make good money," says Seth. "They live in these crappy little apartments with shitty views, like of a brick wall. They run around in these tiny apartments like rats in a hole and eventually it makes them nuts."

Seth and Sunshine exchanged pleasantries but not numbers, and both went their separate ways. But when Seth spotted Sunshine at Paragon Sporting Goods the very next day, it sure seemed like fate. He recognized her immediately, in part because (as she had just done the laundry) she was wearing the exact same yellow sundress with the daisy-pattern trim as the day before.

"Sunshine," Seth called out. Sunshine, thinking she must have misheard, shrugged it off; no one knew her here. But there it was again: "Sunshine!" That not being the most common of names, she looked up and saw Seth moving toward her from across the store. "Fancy meeting you here!" said Seth. After chatting for a while, they hit the Starbucks next door for some coffee. "So, what do you do?" asked Seth as they sat down—the first thing any five-Starbucks-a-day-drinking, 90-hours-a-week-working, money-hungry Wall Streeter asks any new person he meets.

"I'm a graphic artist," said Sunshine.

"Ah," thought Seth. It all made sense: the hippie-dippy California smile, wearing the same dress every day. She must be a starving artist, one of those rats in a hole. She just hadn't lived in the city long enough to develop a case of New York Studio Neurosis. He felt sorry for her. Maybe he could help her get some work! Then she might even be able to afford to buy a new dress. "My friend Melanie owns a graphic-arts company," said Seth. "She's having a party this weekend. Do you want to come?"

As it turned out, Sunshine and Melanie hit it off; they were instant old friends. And Melanie did throw some work Sunshine's way. But it turned out that Sunshine, despite the impression given by her recycled yellow-with-the-daisy-trim sundress, had quite a booming business of her own. Seth was shocked—dare I say, a little dismayed—to discover that Sunshine's graphic-arts work had afforded her an even bigger apartment than his own job on Wall Street.

They started dating almost immediately. Sunshine wanted to see everything the city had to offer, making Seth an accidental tourist in his own hometown. They went to the Met, the Guggenheim, and the Whitney. Sunshine found modern art intriguing and thought provoking, while Seth reacted with the typical "I could do that" at the Pollock and Matisse exhibits. They went roller-blading in Central Park and biked along the Hudson River. Sunshine even dragged Seth all the way up north to see Grant's tomb. He learned to love New York even more through her eyes.

"We were really vibing on each other," says Sunshine. In fact, three months in, they were getting along swimmingly—that is, until The Talk. "Seth," said Sunshine, "we have been dating a while. We spend all our free time together, but we are not technically exclusive. Does that make sense to you?"

"I am fine with how things are," Seth said. "I don't think anything has to change."

Wrong answer. Seth and Sunshine broke up.

By now, Melanie and Sunshine had become good friends. When Melanie needed a last-minute babysitter, Sunshine—three weeks off her breakup with Seth and having no plans—was happy to volunteer. After putting the kids to bed, Sunshine was relaxing in Melanie's West Village apartment when she heard a knock on the door. She looked through the peephole: It was Seth. He was in the neighborhood and, not realizing that Sunshine was sitting for the kids, had decided to pop in on

Melanie. With some trepidation, Sunshine opened the door; they stood in the doorway, gaping at each other.

It took only a few minutes for Sunshine and Seth to realize that as weird as this coincidence was, it also kind of made sense. The gym, the sporting goods store, and now this—some greater force was clearly trying to put these two together. Standing there in the hall, looking at Sunshine, Seth realized he had made a huge mistake; he would have to get Sunshine back. After that, their exclusivity was never in question. In fact, Seth and Sunshine just got closer and closer. When Seth required a minor but very uncomfortable surgery, his mom flew in from her home in Florida to take care of him only to find that Sunshine was already tending to the patient like a regular Florence Nightingale.

With a name like Seth Hirschfeld, Sunshine had surmised that he was Jewish, but that had never been an issue for the couple. She didn't sense that Seth's heritage would be a factor until their relationship got more serious and she began interacting with his family. That was when she made two important observations about the Hirschfelds. First, they communicate by yelling, which to a gentle and laid-back Californian like Sunshine sounded like a hard stab to the ear. "His whole family does that," says Sunshine. "I think it's a Jewish thing. They start out shouting, and as their pace begins to quicken, it becomes more feverish. They start to talk over each other and that makes them talk even louder." Second, there seemed to be a lot of tension when Sunshine visited Seth's family. It was nothing she could put her finger on, but something was always lurking below the surface.

The root of the problem became clear when the couple went out for dinner with Seth's brother, Samuel, and Ester, his Orthodox fiancée. Seth and Sunshine had been going out for a year and were clearly serious about each other. Ester started in, flaring out all five French-manicured fingers as she spoke: "Seth, I have a friend, a good Jewish girl. I told her all about you. How you were cute, *single*, had a great head of hair, a Wall Street job....

She said she would love to meet you. Oh, Sunshine," Ester paused abruptly. Sunshine was sure that Ester had caught herself and realized how insensitive she was being, but alas, no. Instead, she turned to Sunshine and asked, "Would you pass the mashed potatoes?" Sunshine stared at Ester with a look of one part shock, one part angry Khrushchev, barely resisting the urge to remove her shoe and pound it on the table. Ester just prattled on as if Sunshine didn't exist.

In fact, Ester and Samuel tried this on several occasions, but Seth never paid them any mind. Sunshine had really been there for him in his time of need. The care and attention she gave him following his surgery was the clincher; just over a year after Seth was greeted by the smiley Californian on the steps of the Equinox, he and Sunshine were engaged.

Incredibly, they had still never discussed religion. Sunshine was agnostic and open to exploring many faiths. Seth was a non-practicing Jew. He didn't wear a yarmulke, keep kosher, go to temple, fast at Yom Kippur, keep Shabbos, or practice the faith in any way. So naturally, Sunshine didn't think religion was important to him. She soon learned, however—as all of us shiksas eventually do—that even if your man isn't a practicing Jew, his being Jewish—and, more importantly, any potential children being Jewish—is usually a sticking point. This became undeniably apparent when Sunshine attended a Hirschfeld family baby shower shortly after becoming engaged. When Sunshine rang the bell to announce her arrival, the door opened, revealing an older woman wearing full make-up, a beige pants suit, glasses hanging loosely around her neck, and a well-etched frown. Sunshine recognized her right away; it was Seth's mother, Mrs. Hirschfeld. Although the two hadn't seen each other for some time, there were no pleasantries exchanged. There was no "Hi, how are you?" There was no warm hug. Seth's mother uttered only these words. "So, are you going to raise the kids Jewish?"

As an agnostic, Sunshine did not have any fixed ideas about religion—especially the religion of her nonexistent children. But she found out soon enough that Seth did. "They must be raised Jewish!" Seth said. That, he insisted, was not negotiable. Seth explains his position to me over pulled pork and barbecue ribs at Rub on 23rd, *his* favorite lunch spot: "There is an unspoken commitment to propagate the faith, which is related to a) the fact that Jews are a visible minority and that we don't want to shrink any more, b) you have an ethical duty to reverse the effects of the Holocaust, and c) family pressure" (a.k.a., good, old-fashioned Jewish guilt). The irony is not lost on me: Seth, the stubborn Jew, insisting on raising his kids Jewish, while eating pulled-pork ribs in a barbeque joint. Also not lost me is the warmth between Seth and Sunshine as they kibbitz about their lives together—what event happened when, who said what, and of course which were the better ribs.

"It just really upset me," says Sunshine. "It was like he was willing to chose the Jewish religion over me, and he didn't even really participate in it." In the end, they bargained. "If you get to raise the kids Jewish," said Sunshine, "what do I get?"

"You can decorate the house any way you want," Seth said.

Deal.

They got married on the glass bridge between the world financial towers, overlooking the boats in the harbor. The ceremony, attended by 20 or so guests and the rabbi, was brief. In keeping with Sunshine's hippie-dippy roots, they wrote their own vows; and in keeping with Seth's New York Jew roots, he broke a glass at the ceremony's close. The reception was a wild party with 40 or so guests on the roof of Seth's apartment building.

The Hirschfelds are members of a Reform temple, which recognizes patrilineal descent—meaning Sunshine was not required to convert. But per Seth's wishes, and the wishes of his family, the couple's two boys are being raised Jewish. That doesn't mean Seth hasn't also made compromises. The Christmas tree took some getting used to, and there is still a bit of rivalry around the holidays. "We do Chanukah and Christmas presents," says Seth.

"But I don't want them to get all the good stuff for Christmas."

"Aren't Chanukah presents just, like, socks?" I ask.

"Sometimes," says Seth. "So I have to make sure the kids get some good presents for Chanukah, too."

After 10 years of a strong marriage, Seth's family has warmed to Sunshine—although there is the occasional reminder that no matter what concessions she makes, she is still not part of the tribe. Like when they got a bill in the mail recently. "His mom has a family plot that *I* can't be buried in, and yet *we* still have to pay for it. Do you believe that?" laments Sunshine, her voice growing louder with each word.

"It's, like, $10 a year. Big deal," says Seth. "And my mom is fine with you being buried there. It's the cemetery that has a problem with it."

"It's the principle of it," retorts Sunshine, almost yelling. "I am not allowed to lie next to you for eternity? Your own *wife*?" The way she sounds, I can't help but wonder if the Jewishness has rubbed off on her after all these years.

"Look, who cares?" Seth yells loudly enough for the whole restaurant to hear. "I don't care. We will be buried somewhere else *together*. You know that stuff is not important to me! Just get the cheapest pine box and drop me off somewhere!"

It seems to me, as Sunshine continues arguing, waving her hands and peppering her speech with the occasional *feh* and *oy veh* and Seth digs into his ribs, that what Seth and Sunshine have achieved is just the right combination of sticking to your guns and negotiating a peaceful compromise. I picture them at 80, sitting around the table, their grandkids wearing their Chanukah socks and their Christmas designer watches. Sunshine will say to the littlest of them, "And can you believe we had to pay for a plot *I can't even be buried in*?" Little Shlomo will shake his head. "No way Bubbe!" At which point Seth will be heard screaming from a distance, "It was only *$10*!"

Beauty and the Mensch

Alicia was at a really good point in her life. She had just bought her first home, and she had boatloads of friends. For Alicia—a beautiful Filipina with a small frame and gorgeous, long, black hair—meeting men was never hard; her dance card was usually full. Even so, she was fiercely independent. She felt no pressure to get married, even from her Catholic family. And she had never experienced any of that crazy biological clock stuff. Her life could not have been more complete—or so she thought.

Alicia, a hospital administrator, met Ira at work. At first she didn't pay him much mind; Ira was an old man after all. But Ira, a Jewish doctor, noticed her. For almost two years, Ira took every opportunity to walk by her desk and strike up a conversation, even if the topics were sometimes a bit of a stretch. Like, "Hey Alicia! Did you see the cafeteria took lime Jell-O off the menu and replaced it with strawberry?" Or, "Did you notice they repainted all the lines on the hospital floor? Really makes it easier to find your way around, huh?"

While Ira was clearly flirting with Alicia, she never returned his advances. "It wasn't the fact that he was Jewish," says Alicia. "I had dated a few Jewish guys before. Like Ira, they were all doctors." She giggles. "I was starting to think it was some club or something. I mean, can't Jews have other jobs?" (Of course they can. They can also be lawyers or accountants.) Alicia continues, "I was baptized Catholic, but the differences in our religion didn't bother me. It was just that he was *so old*—like 20 years older than me. I mean *really* old."

We got it, he's *old*. Damn! But in Alicia's defense, a woman of almost 40 long since over any daddy issues usually doesn't find herself attracted to a man whose high-school prom coincided with her kindergarten graduation. A man who is more likely to watch *Lawrence Welk* than to yell "I want my MTV," more likely to quote *The Graduate* than *The Breakfast Club*. What would a young girl need with an old man like that?

While Alicia tried to ignore him, Ira's attentions did not go unnoticed by others in the hospital. "I don't know why you just don't go out with him already and put this to rest," sighed Alicia's office mate. "He's such a nice guy. Give him a chance!" No offense to the old man, but Alicia didn't really want to date anyone. Things were going so well in her life; she just didn't want anything to disrupt the delicate balance. But with a lot of help from Alicia's co-workers, Ira finally wore her down; she begrudgingly agreed to go on a date.

Ira picked her up in his vintage Corvette. Cool car, to be sure, but Alicia couldn't think about that. All she could think about was that the car was probably older than she was. "Yeah, it's a 1969," said Ira, trying to make conversation. (Okay, she was older than the car, but only by three years.) "Isn't it a beauty? I got it when I graduated from med school." Oh! Not helping!

Ira chose a great restaurant in Manhattan's chi-chi SoHo neighborhood, but its appeal was lost on Alicia. Her head was spinning with thoughts of her toddler self climbing into Ira's Corvette, of changing his adult diapers, or how their next meal might be in the nursing home. She decided to skip the small talk; instead, she launched an onslaught of questions, one after the other, so quickly Ira couldn't get in even one answer: "So, you have been married before? I hear your kids are older, in their 20s? Does that mean you are not willing to have other children? How *Jewish* are you?" And the grand finale (drum roll please), "So exactly how much *older* are you anyway?"

Ira, ever patient, just sat there and listened, not the least bit unnerved or annoyed by her questioning. When she finally stopped to take a breath, he smiled at her. "Well, I see you have given this a lot of thought," he said. "Let me make sure I address all your questions. And please, stop me if I missed anything." He answered her questions even faster then she had asked them: "Yes, I was married before. We have been divorced for over 20 years now. I have two wonderful children: a son, age 27, and a daughter, age 22. As for other children, I am open. How Jewish am I? Well, I go to temple about once a month. As far as whether any future wife of mine has to be Jewish," Ira paused, taking a big breath for effect, "I did that. My last wife was Jewish. And it didn't work out. A woman's religion is not a big deal for me. I'm 59, by the way. I think that puts me exactly 20 years older than you. But that's okay, because I still fuck like I am still 29. Does that answer all your questions?"

Alicia laughed. She felt silly—embarrassed, even. "After that first date, that was it. We were together," she says. What turned her around? "I didn't realize until that night how *funny* he was. It was his great sense of humor that really won me over." She continues, "I was just so focused on his age, but that has never been an issue. He is so young at heart. And luckily for me, he was also so very patient." Alicia raises a carefully plucked brow. "But most of all, I just never felt so pampered as when I was with Ira, so well taken care of. He wasn't romantic like in a sappy movie, but he was fun and so generous."

Ira was also the opposite of the Asian guys Alicia usually dated. "I had dated a lot of Japanese, Chinese, and Filipino guys. With Asian guys, when it comes to sex, it is all about them." Alicia frowns. "But with Ira, he was always concerned that I was pleased. It took me a while to learn that I could be a little selfish, want something for myself. I don't understand why more men don't get that; when they are giving, it makes you want to give back so much more."

Something else was new for Alicia: For the first time in her life, she found herself jealous. "I didn't know why it was happening at first, but I was so insecure when I would get around his ex-girlfriends. Most of his ex-girlfriends were closer to his age." She brushes the lint off of the sleeve of her Gucci dress. "I always felt like these older, more-experienced women were looking down on me. You know, where did this young thing come from?" She continues, "Sometimes, we would run into his ex-girlfriend, Monica. After she'd leave I would say things like, 'I hope she remembered to take her Geritol today,' or, 'Is it just me, or did you just get a whiff of mothballs and Gold Bond Powder?'" Alicia grins. "I knew I was really starting to fall for him because I had never felt like that before." And the old ladies were tough! It appeared they were not ready to give up on Ira without a fight. "Months into our relationship, they would still be calling him—sometimes at, like, midnight!" says Alicia. "He brushed it off, saying they were just friends. But I said, 'Look, I don't care if she's 60. If she's calling you at midnight, that's a booty call.'"

At first, Alicia's family was accepting of her relationship with Ira. But when things started to get serious between them, her parents began raising concerns. Not about his race or religion; in fact, that never came up. His age was the problem. "My parents were so concerned about his age, they didn't even have time to worry about the Jewish thing," says Alicia. "My mother was obsessed with the fact that he might not be able to have kids. And my father just kept telling me, over and over again, 'He's going to die!'"

Because Ira's parents were deceased, Alicia didn't have to contend with any Jewish mother drama. Whew! But his kids were a concern. She had never dated a guy with children, let alone grown-up kids. "Once things really began to get serious, I had to meet the kids," says Alicia. "It was just so weird. Not that they weren't nice; they were great. Neither of them were living at home. Their parents had been divorced for 20 years, and their mother was remarried. They had no real problems with it." She continues, "I was just 'Dad's girlfriend.' But it was bizarre meeting these adult people and knowing they were my boyfriend's children."

Two years into the relationship, Alicia and Ira decided to get married. "You know, I always thought I would be married in a Catholic church," says Alicia. Instead, they were married outdoors under a chuppah in a dual-faith ceremony, with a priest and a rabbi. "As far as religion goes, I had to compromise," Alicia notes. "But then, that is how I got to have Ira in my life. I don't think religion is ever a problem if you are truly open minded."

Although they were not married in a Catholic church, Alicia and Ira did include several Filipino Catholic traditions, including the unity candle, coins, and the cord ceremony. And in keeping with Jewish tradition, Ira crushed a glass at the ceremony's finale. "Some of the pictures were, uh, different," says Alicia. "Typically, at a Filipino wedding, there might be a picture of the bride and groom's hands and sometimes the priest's hand connecting them." Alicia fights back a fond giggle. "But our picture has all four hands: mine, Ira's, the priest's, and the rabbi's."

Although Alicia's family had known Ira for two years, they still knew very little about his faith. Alicia was shocked when, during the reception, her mother asked, "Why is Ira wearing that little hat?" Incredibly, Alicia's mother had never even seen a yarmulke. "My mom knew he was Jewish," says Alicia. "But she didn't really understand anything about what that meant."

Ira's and Alicia's wedding was a true merger of both religions and cultures, with one exception: the food. Guests at a typical Filipino wedding might be served morcon, paella, callos, embutido, and caldereta, and most importantly, one or more large pigs on a spit. But given Ira's faith the couple chose to pass on the pigs on a spit and offered a more generic continental cuisine at the reception.

Their marriage was solid—easy—from the beginning. Any issues they had were minor at best. "Sometimes it was hard for me to let him do things for me, even after we got married," says Alicia. "I was so used to doing everything myself, so independent." Despite Alicia's father's dire predictions, Ira didn't die. In fact, he remains very active, playing tennis at least three times a week. And Alicia sees to it that tennis is not the only exercise he gets several times a week—which also explains the arrival of their beautiful baby boy three years into their relationship. Looks like Alicia's mom struck out on her prediction too. Little Nathan—The "Jewpino," as Alicia's best friend calls him—attends both church and temple. And the family honors all the Jewish and Catholic holidays—which, of course, means double the presents for Nathan. (Cha-ching!) "I even eat matzoh for a week on Passover," says Alicia, puckering her face in distaste. She explains, "It tastes like cardboard, but I have to eat it. I want Nathan to know that I respect his father's religion." She adds, "And it took me a little while, but I also make a damn good matzoh ball soup."

A Mitzvah My Dear

Although Josh and I had worked at the same small, shitty Wall Street firm for five years, we had rarely talked except the occasional polite hello. Then, my boss laid me off in the worst market in 100 years.

When everything goes to shit, you never know who is going to be there for you. People you've known for years (people who claim to be a loyal business partner or your best friend), can simply vanish—or worse, make things more difficult. But then, people you hardly know seem to be there right when you need them. That's what it was like for me. My closest friends had all but disappeared. It was Josh—who I barely knew—who made an effort to check in on me.

I was beyond stressed. I wasn't sleeping. I was losing weight, eating nothing except the occasional Ben & Jerry's—okay, and sometimes Häagen-Dazs. I rarely left my apartment. Some days, I didn't get up at all. I'd lie in bed all day, lacking the will even to put on pants.

Mostly, I was terrified of losing my home, a gorgeous apartment on the 24th floor of a beautiful doorman building, complete with a terrace and a full view of the Chrysler building. It was my baby. I had bought it four years prior, hoping that finally owning a home would give me the stability I had always craved growing up with a single mother who was constantly on the move. Now, with no job, minimal savings, an interest-only ARM coming up in less than a year, and the Manhattan housing market in freefall, I was faced with losing my home and possibly everything I had put into it.

But there was Josh, calling me every week to see how I was, and taking me out to dinners I had grown accustomed to but could no longer afford. "If I take you out once a week," Josh joked, "I know at least you're eating something." The Jews call it a *mitzvah*. An act of human kindness. A good deed. I'm not sure why Josh, a Persian Jew, chose me for a *mitzvah*. Maybe he had a crush on me. But when we went out, he was never sleazy. Never once did he hit on me. I was used to men trying to get into my pants; I was less sure how to handle a man who showed me the compassion that Josh did without wanting anything in return.

We were friends, I realized, and that was that. Besides, Josh was hardly my type. He was Middle Eastern, but not dark. Just a typical short, stocky, bald, Jewish guy—a far cry from the tall black guys I usually dated. His Sean Connery chest hair, visible at the neckline of his shirts, wasn't much of a draw either. Plus, Josh was a bit fashion challenged. Whereas I, like any New York fashionista, made it a point to dress to the nines, Josh insisted on dressing comfortably—standard American Man-ese for a mish-mash of pants, T-shirt, and funky bargain-bin shoes. "People must think if I'm with you, I'm either rich or have a big dick," Josh said once. "Since I don't dress that nice, they must think I have a big dick—which is okay with me."

When I was finally able to get out of bed and put on some pants, I listed my home for sale. With the job market looking worse than bleak, I didn't have any other choice. I also resolved to do something about my income (or lack thereof). I consulted my friend John, a banker. I was hoping he would give me a job, but instead, he asked me, "What is your passion?" I didn't know, so he tried offering suggestions. "What about this? What about that?" But I couldn't answer. I felt nothing. I was just tired. Numb. Then he called me about a short story I had sent him featuring one of my old boyfriends. "Why don't you write about dating black guys?" he said. Still a curmudgeon, I pooh-poohed his suggestion. But a few weeks later, it came to me. How about I do a book—a very different, funny, great book, not about dating black guys, but about interracial dating, with many racial groups? The idea was born.

But two months into my unemployment and just a couple weeks into my new project, things went from horrible to nightmarish when my brother, at age 32, died suddenly in a car crash. (My sister and I were raised by my mother, but when my dad got married to his third wife, I had the good fortune to pick up two wonderful brothers.) Devastated by the news, I called Josh at work; he rushed to be by my side. I left the next day for California, where I spent two hellish weeks with my family. It was horrible. I was crying all the time. I missed my brother. I missed the city. And I missed Josh.

My flight back to New York was miserable—there was a five-hour delay. Thank God, I had asked Josh to feed my cat. By the time I staggered into my apartment, I was exhausted and starving. I dropped my suitcase in the hall and lurched into the kitchen, hoping to find a scrap of sustenance. I turned on the light and there was food *everywhere*—spread all over the counter were cookies, tortilla chips, salsa, and fruit. My fridge, which had never been more than 10-percent full, was brimming with Greek yogurt, cottage cheese, and other goodies. My heart leapt. *What if there's ice cream in the freezer?* Cautiously optimistic, I opened the freezer door. There was! Three different kinds! But that wasn't all. On the dining-room table were two dozen roses, with a card from Josh: "I hope these cheer you up." And next to the flowers was a photocopy of a book I had asked Josh to take back to the library for me. He had Xeroxed all 300 pages, just in case I still wanted to finish it. *What man does that?*

That Sunday, Josh came over for dinner. We sat on the couch, and I caught him up on my depressing family reunion. Then the strangest thing happened: As I was talking to him, I felt this urge to kiss him. And as the night progressed, my attraction to him only grew. When Josh finally got up to leave, he turned to say goodbye, and our typical peck became a real kiss. Shit! I was hardly in the right place in my life to start a relationship. I had no job, no money, and would no doubt soon be homeless, either selling my apartment or due to foreclosure. How could I start something with him given my situation? I talked to my friends, my sister, my therapist—anyone who would listen. They all agreed: I should wait.

Naturally, we started sleeping together shortly after that.

At first, it didn't seem like we were compatible in the bedroom. It didn't help that it wasn't just Josh's chest that was hairy; like a lot of Middle Eastern men, he was furry head to toe—hence my christening Josh with several nicknames, including Monkey, The Missing Link, and Teddy Bear. But hair or no hair, within a couple weeks, things started to get hot. I think the fact that Josh was Persian accounted for his sometimes brutish and very passionate fucking style. When we had sex, his expression often became serious—almost angry. I called it his "terrorist face." And Josh was funny. Once, in the middle of sex, he asked, "Why are you smiling so much?"

Come on, that's easy: Sex is my happy place. But I decided to give him a hard time anyway. "What," I said. "Women you usually sleep with don't smile when you are having sex?"

"I guess I just never noticed, given that they always have a sheet over their head," Josh quipped, alluding to the fact that Hasidic Jews and some other people from the Middle East have sex on their wedding night through a sheet.

But our relationship quickly hit a wall—a wall of JAPs, that is.

Josh's closest friends were three 40- to 50-something Jewish American Princesses—Abigail, Deborah, and Ruby—all of whom were incredibly threatened by his relationship with me. But then, who can blame them? Before I came along, Josh's JAPs had it great. Josh did everything a boyfriend did—but without them having to put out. He was a JAP's dream! He showed the patience of a saint, shopping with them for long hours, fixing things around their apartments, and going on trips with them.

He even got in the habit of calling them his "wives," like in *Big Love*. Mind you, he never slept with any of these women. There was no romantic connection whatsoever. But when I came into the picture, all hell broke loose. Josh—who, despite being 45, had never been in a significant romantic relationship—suddenly had this smart, sexy, funny woman who he really liked, but the JAPs couldn't say a single nice thing about me. I could hardly take it personally; except for Abigail, who I'd met once years ago at a bris, they'd never laid eyes on me.

Of the three, Abigail was the worst. Abigail, who was accustomed to having Josh at her beck and call, quickly spiraled into eighth-grade antics like avoiding his calls, leaving messages on his home phone when she knew he was out with me, and then claiming he was never available to her. I should have known she would take the news about us badly. I think she thought of him as her fall-back guy, the guy she'd marry if Mr. Tall Dark and Circumcised never arrived. Abigail was known to say things to Josh like, "When I get married I want a three-carat ring" or "Why would any girl want to marry a hairy bald guy?" And she'd follow that up with "You probably have a small dick anyway."

They had always liked to travel together, so as a peace offering, Josh invited Abigail on a trip to Barcelona—something I encouraged. After all, I thought, they had been traveling together for 10 years. Why shouldn't he take a trip with a friend? It was Abigail who didn't approve. "I don't think that's appropriate," Abigail said—because of me. But it all worked out; Josh decided to take *me* to Barcelona instead. We had a blast—lots of eating, drinking, and wild Spanish sex. Aside from my occasional grumpiness from low blood sugar and Josh's obsessive picture taking, we found we traveled well together.

Shortly after we got back from Barcelona—and only a little over a month into our relationship—Abigail called Josh and told him their friendship was, and I quote, "irreparably damaged." Why? Because of his relationship with me, of course. She was willing to throw away a 10-year friendship with a man in whom she had no romantic interest because he had been dating someone for a couple months. What kind of bizarro JAP universe was I living in?

Unfortunately, Josh's friends weren't the only ones who opposed our relationship. His family had plenty to say about it as well. What the hell was he doing with this shiksa? This made little sense, given that Josh's brothers were all married to Asian women. In any case, on Passover, I had hoped for an invitation to dinner, but Josh's family said no. They claimed it was because of his dad's illness—Josh's father, pushing 90, was constantly in and out of the hospital. I understood; I had nothing but sympathy for his condition. But I still felt that if I had been a Jew, there would have been room for me at the table.

So, fine. I could deal with a gang of unfriendly JAPs, and even with Josh's family's seeming disapproval. What I *couldn't* deal with was what Josh said to me one Sunday night, soon after Passover. I could tell something had been bothering him; he had been lashing out at me. Sure, it was always under the guise of a joke—he'd mention sleeping with other women or my lack of employment. But none of it was the least bit funny; cruel, was more like it. Finally, that Sunday night, he exploded. He carped about all the grief he was getting from his friends and family about me. Then there were his long hours at work, his clients on the side, and his father's illness. And then he said it—those words you can't take back: "I know I may not be very religious, but you don't understand. If you ask any Jew, they will say you have to marry someone Jewish." That was it, then. Because I was a shiksa, I would never make the grade.

After he left that night, I didn't care to speak to him for a while. I didn't call him, and when he called me, I kept it short. By then, I'd met with The Pros while researching this book and what they said kept ringing in my ears: how Orthodox Jews say that sex with a shiksa doesn't count. I couldn't help but wonder whether that was what our relationship had been all about.

When I finally did see Josh again, he said I was making too big of a deal of it, that I shouldn't worry my pretty little head. He was fine with things the way they were. Under better circumstances, I would have put on some pointy boots and kicked his Jew ass out, but as I barely had the strength to put on pants, let alone boots, I would just let things stand. I was just too tired to put up a fight.

A few weeks later, things took a turn for the better. I showed my apartment to this nice couple. Unlike so many of the clowns I'd dealt with, they weren't buying it for their spoiled 25-year-old son or as a *pied à terre* for their shopping trips. No, they were hard-working people—about my age—who were actually going to live in the apartment. I could tell they really liked it, as they made no attempt to talk the price down by knocking the space. The minute they left, I called Josh. "You won't believe it, baby! Full asking price!" I had done it: I had finally sold my place.

Things were better with Josh, too. We seemed to have put our problems behind us. Even the situation with his JAPs improved. Although Abigail, the Grand Poobah of the JAPs, continued her boycott, Deborah invited me to brunch. Incredibly, we had a lovely time. A few months later, Ruby turned 50 and hosted a birthday party. At first, Josh didn't want to invite me. "You won't have a good time," he said. A room full of JAPs in Bum-Fuck Jersey? Damn right, I wouldn't have a good time. But I was the girlfriend, goddamn it, and that's who you take to these things! I poured myself into a tight sweater dress and we headed for Jersey.

When we arrived, I didn't even need to introduce myself; Ruby knew who I was. "I am so glad you could come," she said, giving me a warm hug. It was not the greeting I had expected, given the last several months of drama. It dawned on me that maybe it was just Abigail—my nemesis, the ultimate JAP—who was causing all the trouble. My suspicions were confirmed when Josh introduced Abigail to me later that evening. "Nice to meet you," I said, mustering up my best smile for someone I already despised, forgetting for a moment that bris all those years ago.

"Well," Abigail said, nasty as can be. "We *already* met."

"Okay," I said, shocked. Did that bitch just *scold* me? Josh picked that moment to excuse himself to get his camera. So there I was, standing with my archenemy and some other random JAP. Obviously, I knew *no one* at this party. And what did Abigail do, aware I probably felt a little out of place, knowing I was her "best friend's" girlfriend? Make small talk? Excuse herself to go to the bathroom? No. The minute Josh left, she simply turned her back to me and began talking to the other JAP, as if I weren't even there. I stood frozen, figuring she would lasso me into the conversation at some point. But no. She didn't. After a few minutes, I just left and found someone else to talk to. I felt so sorry for Josh—sorry that this was supposed to be his best friend, and that this was how she treated someone he cares for. Instead of acting like a good friend, she was just jealous and petty.

We survived Abigail. Josh was still around. In fact, soon he would be even more around. After I'd struck out finding an apartment that a) didn't cost a fortune and b) wasn't the size of a dog kennel, Josh said I could stay with him. Incredibly, though, I had never seen his apartment. I never felt the need; he wasn't some stranger I'd met online. I knew he wasn't hiding a wife and kids in there. Given the state of his office, stuffed with teetering stacks of paper, and what with him being a single man and all, I figured his studio was probably messy—but when I finally saw it (the weekend before I was due to move in) it was worse than I could have even imagined. There were papers everywhere. You could barely push open the door because of the shopping bags piled up in every corner. The kitchen table was so covered with crap I could barely see the glass below. Josh assured me he would clean the place up, insisting that it was so messy—get this—because he had pulled out all the stuff he needed to throw away in anticipation of my moving in. I had to decide: an expensive apartment rental or Josh's abject shithole. I chose the shithole.

The scene was *so* New York: a 40-year-old woman and a 45-year-old man living in 550 square feet. With our stuff combined, just walking through the place was out of the question. I was constantly tripping, stubbing my toe, or bashing my knee on his fucking midget bed. (Platform beds suck.) Sleeping was also a challenge: Josh likes to stay up until two or three in the morning, and I like to go to sleep at 10 p.m. Plus, on the weekends, the phone would start ringing off the hook at 10 a.m.—mostly his friends. I dubbed it the JAP hotline. I wanted to clean things up, but Josh kept saying, "I'll get to it. I'll get to it." But he never got to it; he was too busy working or tending to his father, who was by then very sick. While I understood and sympathized—really, I did—I could not walk or sleep, let alone *write,* in that mess. This went on for a few weeks: me trying to get Josh to clean and Josh just moving all the bags around but no real progress was being made. I bounced from trying to convince myself that we could make this work to silently vowing to move out while Josh was at work, leaving only a note that read, "Fuck you and your antique piles of *The Wall Street Journal,* and by the way, I never want to see you again."

Finally, Josh and Abigail decided to take a trip together. I was glad they were working out their issues, but I was mad he was going away instead of taking a week off work to clean the apartment. Then I began to see his vacation as an opportunity: I would clean while he was gone. And it was then, gentle reader, as I embarked on this mission, that I realized this mess was not recent. This was not stuff he had pulled out to sift through, organize, and put away. No, this was the work of a hoarder—a person with serious issues. I felt like a modern archeologist, uncovering more about Josh's personality with each pile of crap.

There were the aforementioned bags—shopping bag after shopping bag stuffed with wet naps, free candies from restaurants, ketchup packets, papers, old trip itineraries, screws, bank receipts, credit cards, all mixed in among random pieces of paper yellowing with age. The bags were like those Russian matryoshka dolls—inside one bag was another bag, and another, and another.

And even though 95 percent of the stuff was garbage, every so often you'd find a diamond ring or an envelope with $400 in cash, so you couldn't just toss the whole bag. You had to go through it all. And of course, instead of displaying the beautiful pieces he'd bought on his trips—art, crafts, sculptures—he simply cast them on the floor. As far as I could determine, he never took the tags off of anything—even things he had obviously had for years. (Just in case he might want to take them back?) At first, I was careful to save everything. But over time, I became more ruthless. If it didn't have sentimental or monetary value, it went down the chute.

And what can I say about the refrigerator? The fridge, which was about one-tenth size of a suburban icebox, was packed to the gills with 1970s Tupperware containing food that was wholly unrecognizable—meals that in some cases his mother had prepared for him two years ago, maybe longer. Even worse were the dirty reused pickle jars that held a few ounces of something disgusting and a mush of vegetables, with black goo around the lid. Although my first impulse was to call in a Hazmat team for those (or at the very least don a pair of thick rubber gloves and walk them to the building's garbage chute), I saved them, worried they might be some weird Persian thing that he would miss. (Good move. I learned later the jars contained *toorshi,* a mixture of garlic, onions, carrots, peppers, and eggplant, all pickled in vinegar. It's a Persian delicacy that some people keep in their fridge for as many as 20 years!)

It took me five days—and when I say days, I mean getting up at 7 a.m. and going to bed at 2 a.m.—to sift through and scrub down every inch of Josh's apartment. But I wasn't sure how he was going to take it. A lot of my friends said my cleaning his place would be the end of us, but the way I saw it, *not* cleaning would have been the end of us, too. When Josh returned I tried to soften the blow by answering the door in a blue and yellow Agent Provocateur set, complete with high heels and a garter belt. He looked around, stunned. "Yes," I said. "It's your apartment."

"Where is all my stuff?" he said, finally. Not "Thank you." Not "Oh my God, how great it looks!" But, "Where is all my stuff?" I crossed my arms and frowned. Josh recovered: "Um, you look beautiful?"

"Nice rally, baby," I said. "But I was more looking for, 'The place looks great!' Or, 'Thank you for all your help!'" No matter. Since then, the mess has not returned—although we do still battle over it. He has even admitted he likes that it's clean. Who says you can't teach an old Jew new tricks?

I've learned from Josh too—specifically, some Farsi words and phrases. Like, *Halet che tore?* (How are you?), *Cosa ma belise!* (Lick my pussy!), and *Namak nashnas* (essentially, beggars can't be choosers). (I learned that last one when I moved into Josh's studio.) But my favorite—the word I had engraved on the money clip I gave Josh for his 45th birthday—is *azizam*. I will never forget the first time he said it to me. We were lying in bed, and I was pestering him: "Say something to me in Farsi!" I had had so many multicultural relationships, but none of them with men who spoke a foreign language—especially one as exotic as Persian.

Josh's face grew serious. "*Azizam*," he said.

"What does it mean?" I asked.

"My dear."

I don't know if Josh and I have it in us to last for the long haul. After all, it's hard to get a couple of stubborn 40-somethings to agree on where to eat dinner, let alone whether to spend their lives together. But I do know that I will always want to know him. To help him. To care about him. To me, he will always be *azizam*.

Further Fever

When I started dating interracially almost 20 years ago, there were few—if any—books on the topic. Now, there's a lot more available—books as well as some great movies. I listed materials I have found useful over the years that may help you understand more about your mate's culture. For additional information please visit my website: www.igotthefeverbook.com. Good luck in your relationship!

Salsa Fever Books

- *Bless Me, Ultima* by Rudolfo A. Anaya
- *One Day of Life* by Manlio Argueta
- *The House on Mango Street* by Sandra Cisneros
- *Dreaming in Cuban* by Cristina Garcia
- *Down These Mean Streets* by Piri Thomas

Salsa Fever Movies

- *Like Water for Chocolate*, 1992, directed by Alfonso Arau
- *Real Women Have Curves*, 2002, directed by Patricia Cardoso
- *City of God (Cidade de Deus)*, 2002, directed by Fernando Meirelles and Kátia Lund
- *Amores Perros*, 1998, directed by Alejandro González Iñárritu
- *Stand and Deliver*, 1998, directed by Ramón Menéndez
- *El Norte*, 1983, directed Gregory Nava
- *My Family*, 1995, directed by Gregory Nava
- *The Milagro Beanfield War*, 1988, directed by Robert Redford
- *Farmingville 2004*, directed by Carlos Sandoval and Catherine Tambini
- *La Bamba*, 1987, directed by Luis Valdez

Yellow Fever Books

- *The Chrysanthemum and the Sword: Patterns of Japanese Culture* by Ruth Benedict
- *A Gesture Life: A Novel* by Chang-Rae Lee
- *Native Speaker* by Chang-Rae Lee
- *China Boy* by Gus Lee
- *Pink Box: Inside Japan's Sex Clubs* by Joan Sinclair
- *The Joy Luck Club* by Amy Tan

Yellow Fever Movies

- *National Geographic: China's Lost Girls*, 2005
- *Japan's War in Colour*, 2005, directed by David Batty
- *Chinaman* (a.k.a. Kinamand), 2005, directed by Henrik Ruben Genz
- *Love My Life*, 2006, directed by Kôji Kawano
- *The Wedding Banquet*, 1993, directed by Ang Lee
- *Shall We Dance?*, 1996, directed by Masayuki Suo
- *The Joy Luck Club*, 1993, directed by Wayne Wang
- *Marriage Is a Crazy Thing*, 2002, directed by Ha Yu
- *Saving Face*, 2004, directed by Alice Wu

Jungle Fever Books

- *Before the Mayflower: A History of Black America* by Lerone Bennett, Jr.
- *Having Our Say* by the Delany Sisters
- *Narrative of the Life of Frederick Douglass: An American Slave, Written by Himself* by Frederick Douglass
- *The Souls of Black Folk* by W.E.B. Du Bois
- *Black Like Me* by John Howard Griffin
- *The Autobiography of Malcolm X* as told to Alex Haley
- *Roots* by Alex Haley

- *Selected Poems* by Langston Hughes
- *Bullwhip Days: The Slaves Remember* by James Mellon

Jungle Fever Movies

- *Something New*, 2006, directed by Sanaa Hamri
- *Guess Who's Coming to Dinner*, 1967, directed by Stanley Kramer
- *Chris Rock: Kill The Messenger*, 2008, directed by Marty Callner
- *Undercover Brother*, 2002, directed by Malcolm D. Lee
- *Jungle Fever*, 1991, directed by Spike Lee
- *Malcolm X*, 1992, directed by Spike Lee
- *The Original Kings of Comedy*, 2000, directed by Spike Lee
- *Mississippi Masala*, 1991, directed by Mira Nair
- *Rosewood*, 1997, directed by John Singleton
- *Soul Food*, 1997, directed by George Tillman, Jr.
- *Chris Rock: Bigger & Blacker*, 1999, directed by Keith Truesdell

Curry Fever Books

- *The Complete Illustrated Kama Sutra* by Lance Dane
- *Arranged Marriage: Stories* by Chitra Banerjee Divakaruni
- *Culture Shock! India: A Survival Guide to Customs and Etiquette* by Gitanjali Kolanad

- *Interpreter of Maladies* by Jhumpa Lahiri
- *The Namesake* by Jhumpa Lahiri
- *Unaccustomed Earth* by Jhumpa Lahiri
- *Maximum City: Bombay Lost and Found* by Suketu Mehta
- *Shantaram* by Gregory David Roberts

Curry Fever Movies

- *Slumdog Millionaire*, 2008, directed by Danny Boyle and Loveleen Tandan
- *Bend It Like Beckham*, 2002, directed by Gurinder Chadha
- *Earth*, 1998, directed by Deepa Mehta
- *Fire*, 1996, directed by Deepa Mehta
- *Water*, 2005, directed by Deepa Mehta
- *The Namesake*, 2006, directed by Mira Nair
- *Mississippi Masala*, 1991, directed by Mira Nair
- *Monsoon Wedding*, 2001, directed by Mira Nair
- *Salaam Bombay!*, 1998, directed by Mira Nair
- *Russell Peters: Red, White and Brown*, 2008, directed by Jigar Talati

Shiksa Fever Books

- *The Vanishing American Jew: In Search of Jewish Identity for the Next Century* by Alan M. Dershowitz

- *Living a Jewish Life: Jewish Traditions, Customs, and Values for Today's Families* by Anita Diamant
- *Anne Frank: Diary of a Young Girl* by Anne Frank
- *What Is a Jew?* by Rabbi Morris N. Kertzer and Rabbi Lawrence A. Hoffman
- *A Guide to Jewish Religious Practice* by Isaac Klein
- *The Complete Idiot's Guide to the Talmud* by Rabbi Aaron Parry
- *Essential Judaism: A Complete Guide to Beliefs, Customs, and Rituals* by George Robinson

Shiksa Fever Movies

- *Jackie Mason Comedy Trilogy*, 2002
- *The Frisco Kid*, 1979, directed by Robert Aldrich
- *Jackie Mason: The Ultimate Jew*, 2008, directed by Barry Avrich
- *A Serious Man*, 2009, directed by Ethan Coen and Joel Coen
- *You Don't Mess with the Zohan*, 2008, directed by Dennis Dugan
- *The Jewish Americans*, 2007, directed by David Grubin
- *Fiddler on the Roof*, 1971, directed by Norman Jewison
- *White Palace*, 1990, directed by Luis Mandoki
- *Schindler's List*, 1993, directed by Steven Spielberg
- *Yentl*, 1983, directed by Barbra Streisand
- *The Diary of Anne Frank*, 1959, directed by George Stevens

Acknowledgments

I'd like to acknowledge the following people, whose comments, contacts, support, and hard work allowed for the completion of this book:

Alyshia Comedy Davies (a.k.a. Alygator). To say that I couldn't do this without you doesn't cut it. You were my editor, writing coach, cheerleader, and unlicensed book therapist. I am so sorry we missed 20 years, but so glad that writing brought us back together. I love you, sister.

Sweet Monkey. Although you mentioned frequently I should just get a "regular job," you also took me in, listened to my bitching, and supported me in every way possible so I could get this book published. Your kindness will never be forgotten.

Toi Pritchett-Jones (a.k.a. my main b-hach). Not only did you give me great stories, super commentary, and expert feedback, you also supported me every step of the way in everything I have done. I love you babe.

My remaining support system. Darren: Thanks for always believing in me, encouraging me, and being available at a moment's notice to talk me down from any of my freak-outs. Ken Siri: Even though you couldn't help me with the book (as "making out with a Dominican girl once" does not count as interracial dating), you were still a great friend, daily supporter, and long-time unemployment buddy. Stacey Gibson: Thank you for sharing your stories, being one of my experts, and reading every word of my book before it went to print. Michele Skupp: You always said I was "too good for Wall Street." Thanks for all your encouragement.

Those who went above and beyond, sharing experiences, harassing friends, reading endless drafts, and doing anything necessary to help me get this book done: Kim Schultheis, Paul Choi, Gaurisha, Trelisa Rochelle, Julie Lin, Liz Tsaoussis, Melissa Horowitz, Heidi Boo, and Steve.

Thank you to everyone who had the courage to share their experiences and their contacts to help me make this book all that it could be: Raisa, Jimmy, Michael Walker, Carlos Carrero, Gabe Sirota, Les, Lucia Vazquez, Kelvin Bullock, Jay Ringel, FERD, Sachin Roopani, Alison, Staci, Eli, Janelle, Ashish, Gloria, Greg, Kristen Walker, Maribel, Dave, T.N.C., Rich, Trisha Robinson, George Tsaoussis Carter, Felix, Kristin, Keelee, Bill, Ro Diddy, Roseann, Elizabeth, Anna, Sandra, Jennifer, Rita, Carmen, Jasmine, Lisa, Esmirna, Matt, Ricardo Roca, Wei, Jorge, Joe Tsokanos (a.k.a. Joe from Jersey), FAB, Jenny, David, Ellen, Suetlana Tsybulnik, Milan Zdravkovic, Tatjana Lukic, Anil Joseph, and Andrea Bici.

Special thanks to the literary industry professionals who made this book possible. Kate Shoup: Your editing helped me tell it like it is. Shawn Morningstar: You are an incredible woman, patient wife, excellent mother, and life-saving artist and graphic designer. Thanks for sharing your insightful comments and designing my book. Marian Hartsough: Brilliant Internet marketer and publisher. You did everything necessary to help me, including holding my hand. And thanks for all of your hard work: my great Web designer, Steve McClenning; David Wolf and Lisa Digernes, my crack literary law team; Katherine Stimson, excellent indexer; my spectacular marketing intern, Allyson James; Steven Bedney, super duper copywriter; Michael Tanamachi top notch book cover consultant, and Tonya Maddox Cupp, proofreader extraordinaire.

The talent that made my cover amazing: My cover designer Jeff Brandi, who managed to design my cover and logo somewhere in between having a new baby and raising three other children.

Bill Bernstein, world-famous photographer, who took a while to convince that naked beats tuxedos. (I am sure that you are happy with the result.) Rene Garza, fashion stylist to the stars (and me), who made me look great for the cover shoot. Zach Bako, crack photography assistant. My hair team—and yes, it did need a team—Julie Lin, who fixed a botched cut and color the night before the shoot, and Barbara Lhotan, who saved our asses doing some amazing last-minute hairstyling at lightning speed. Pauline Coutroulis, who does the best makeup that makes you look like you are not wearing any makeup. And last, but definitely not least, my gorgeous male models: Kyle Ely Goldstein, Rushi Kota, Travon McCall, Juan Carlos Ruiz, Nattavut Trivisvavet (a.k.a. Joe).

Finally, I'd like to thank Luna Piena, Public, Eatery, Cafeteria Restaurant, Klee Brasserie, Juan Valdez, and my grandparents, Warren and Mellie Carleton, for letting me set up camp for hours, sometimes days, while I interviewed people for the book.

Index

D

E

F

G

H

I

J

Q–R

S

T

U–V

W

Y

www.feverbook.com
The fun doesn't have to end!
Check out author J.C. Davies' daily blog, "Racy JC." She's the world's first interracial Dear Abby. Ask J.C. a relationship question, read her hilarious commentary about the love and lives of interracial daters, get the inside scoop on how the book was written, learn more about the author, and see when J.C. is coming to your area. And most importantly, discover what type of guy might be best for you!